Hate Crime

Hate Crime

Impact, Causes and Responses

Neil Chakraborti and Jon Garland

Los Angeles | London | New Delhi
Singapore | Washington DC

HV
6773.5
.C 53
2009

H

First published 2009

SAGE Publications Ltd
1 Oliver's Yard
55 City Road
London EC1Y 1SP

SAGE Publications Inc.
2455 Teller Road
Thousand Oaks, California 91320

SAGE Publications India Pvt Ltd
B1/I 1 Mohan Cooperative Industrial Area
Mathura Road
New Delhi 110 044

SAGE Publications Asia-Pacific Pte Ltd
33 Pekin Street #02-01
Far East Square
Singapore 048763

British Library Cataloguing in Publication data

A catalogue record for this book is available
from the British Library

ISBN 978-1-4129-4567-7
ISBN 978-1-4129-4568-4

Library of Congress Control Number: 2008940339

Typeset by C&M Digitals (P) Ltd, Chennai, India
Printed by CPI Antony Rowe, Chippenham, Wiltshire
Printed on paper from sustainable resources

Mixed Sources
Product group from well-managed
forests and other controlled sources
www.fsc.org   Cert no. SGS-COC-2953
FSC   © 1996 Forest Stewardship Council

Neil – For my father
Jon – To Rosa and Amber, with love

CONTENTS

LIST OF TABLES, FIGURE AND CASE STUDIES

FOREWORD

I am pleased to be able to include a foreword in this work and I do so in my capacity as the Hate Crime Lead for the Association of Chief Police Officers (ACPO). We are currently in a period of change so I am grateful of this opportunity to set out how ACPO will continue to improve our efforts to combat these insidious crimes. This work is particularly welcome because, despite the high importance given to hate crime by Criminal Justice Service (CJS) agencies, there is a scarcity of research material to help us understand the impact of such crimes, particularly on the psyche of the offenders and the impact on victims or those who live in fear of such crimes.

Hate crime is a term which is well used but has grown to mean many things to many people. What it means to most is a crime where the offender targets the victim because of who they are or what they believe. This targeting of a victim makes the crime more insidious and the limited available research would suggest that it takes a victim much longer to recover from a comparable crime. This is part of the reason why hate crime needs to have an enhanced response from the police, prosecutors and the judiciary. Such crimes adversely affect the confidence of the community and damage community cohesion. It is for this reason that hate crime is a priority for government and criminal justice agencies.

I represent ACPO on the cross-governmental hate crime programme called 'Race for Justice', which is led by the Attorney General. A key objective of this programme has been to enhance the service to victims of hate crime, to improve data collection and training for the police, Crown Prosecution Service and the judiciary.

One of the key tasks of 'Race for Justice' has been the agreement of a consistent definition of hate crime. While we all seem to accept the concept of targeted offending, there has been confusion about which 'strands' of target groups we should include. Most people would include racism within hate crime, but some could argue that attacks on people because of their job or even football violence could be included as targeted crimes. While we do not wish to deny the existence of such crimes as being motivated by hatred, there is a need to identify the most prevalent and damaging crimes, and this is the reason that we have sought to define 'monitored hate crime'. The final agreed document will be finalised during the autumn of 2008 but the CJS agencies have already agreed to monitor five strands of crimes, being those motivated by disability, race, religious belief, sexual orientation and transgender.

One of the most significant milestones in my police career has been the murder of Stephen Lawrence in a vile racist attack in 1993, and the subsequent Inquiry has brought about significant changes to the way we investigate such crimes. As we approach the tenth anniversary of the publication of the report it is timely to assess our progress.

Fundamental changes included the recognition of our role in combating 'non-crime' hate incidents, in order to prevent an escalation to more serious offending. I know of no case where an offender has committed a murder as their first such offence: there is inevitably an escalation of offending and it is for this reason that we all have a responsibility to tackle the 'lower-level' bigotry. This responsibility must be shared by all statutory agencies, whether they are education, health or local government.

Another key change has been the recording of hate crimes based on the perception of the 'victim or any other person'. This means that no official should challenge a victim's assertion that a crime is motivated by hate. Clearly, our colleagues in the Crown Prosecution Service need to have tangible evidence to put before a court if we are going to seek the enhanced sentences available under the criminal law, but we will still respond and record as a hate crime even where this evidence is not available. This approach, together with our determination to increase reporting, has meant that our recorded crime data is very high compared to other states, but we know from research such as the British Crime Survey that we still have a significant under-reporting of hate crimes. It is a challenge for us all to reduce this under-reporting.

In her speech to the European Hate Crime Conference in November 2008, the Attorney General Baroness Scotland set us a clear challenge: to provide the same high level of service to all victims of hate crimes, across the five 'monitored' strands. She highlighted how the service to victims had improved since 1993 when the family of Stephen Lawrence had been so poorly served by authorities, including the police. She drew on comments by the families of Anthony Walker and Jody Dobrowski, who had been murdered in similar bigoted crimes in 2005, and they felt the criminal justice process had helped them to deal with their tragedy, rather than adding to the distress they suffered.

Baroness Scotland correctly stated that we must not be complacent about our improvements as there are still occasions where we fall short of the standards we all seek. Her challenge to apply the same high standards to all victims is more significant where victims are isolated in our community. The Race for Justice Board have identified four areas where we have our greatest challenges, and they are:

- Asylum and refugee communities
- Gypsy and traveller communities
- Transgender victims
- Disabled victims

The last area presents a particular challenge for all agencies and third-sector bodies. The data from MIND in their 'Another Assault' report in 2007, and other similar research, has highlighted the extent of crimes targeted against disabled victims, particularly those with learning disability and mental health disability. The data is all the more chilling given the number of high-profile murders, such as the tragic killing of Brent Martin in 2007. The nature of these crimes is different from that of Stephen Lawrence, Jody Dobrowski and Anthony Walker, notably because the victims have often seen their killers as friends before being systematically abused and murdered. What is consistent is the disregard for the life of someone who is 'different' and, in these cases, extremely vulnerable.

ACPO is currently working on a refresh of its hate crime manual which will be published in 2009. It will reflect the challenge of the new broad definition but will also provide policy in the following areas:

- Minimum standards of investigation
- Crimes committed over the internet
- Hate crime committed to our staff by colleagues or the public
- 'Third party' reporting of crimes
- Relationships with other statutory agencies, particularly in relation to non-crime incidents
- Hate crimes under new and existing 'incitement' legislation.

We have made great strides since 1993 but we cannot afford to rest. APCO is determined to obtain greater understanding of hate crime and use that learning to improve the service we offer to victims and communities. I am grateful for the work of the authors and I am confident that this book will help to inform our efforts to combat hate crime.

J.A. Harris
ACPO Lead on Hate Crime
Assistant Chief Constable

ACKNOWLEDGEMENTS

There are a number of people to whom we owe a considerable debt of gratitude. First, we would like to offer thanks to students on our hate crime module whose lively contributions to seminars inspired us to start thinking about writing a book on the subject. Of all the modules we have taught over the years, the hate crime module has, without question, engendered the most animated response from students who appear to have been fascinated with, and at times quite perplexed by, the complex range of issues associated with the concept. Today's students are often criticised for being indifferent or apathetic, but teaching a hate crime module has enabled us to see just how passionate students can be about issues that have typically been marginalised from criminological discourse.

Special thanks too go to Caroline Porter at Sage, who has been a pleasure to work with throughout and whose advice and support has been invaluable. Colleagues at the Department of Criminology, University of Leicester, have also helped us along the way, as have Mike Rowe, Paul Iganski and fellow criminologists with whom we have debated hate crime issues at various conferences and seminars, so thanks to all of you. It would be remiss of us not to give due regard to the advice we have received from hate crime practitioners and policy-makers, whose important work in this field often goes unnoticed, and we would like to pay thanks to Rik Basra and Pete Bumpus at Leicestershire Constabulary and Paul Giannasi from the Race Confidence and Justice Unit at the Office for Criminal Justice Reform.

Neil is grateful to Mark Bell, Jonny Burnett and Zoe James for their ideas, and to Billy Davies and Paul Jewell for making the 2007/08 season an especially memorable one: when times were tough on the writing front DCFC, could always be relied upon to make things feel a whole lot worse. Jon would like to thank Finola for listening to him wittering about the book, Clare for listening to him stressing about the book, Keris, Reg and Adrian for the debates about the subject of the book, and Andy, Matt, Mark and Eliot for all the football-related fun – if only Norwich City were as good on the pitch as their fans are off it, eh?

Last, though certainly not least, our respective partners – Tara and Karen – deserve an enormous amount of credit for their love and patience during what has been a testing couple of years. You'll see more of us now, we promise, though whether that's a good or a bad thing is debatable.

1

UNDERSTANDING HATE CRIME

―――――――――――――― **Chapter summary** ――――――――――――――

Hate crime is a relatively well-established term within American scholarship but it
has a much shorter history within the UK. While hate crime encompasses numerous themes that have formed a central feature of contemporary social scientific
enquiry, including marginalisation, victimisation and difference, attempts to
examine these themes through the conceptual lens of hate have been in comparatively short supply. To some extent this is not altogether surprising as the 'mainstreaming' of hate crime within academic and political circles in the UK has
occurred only recently, but it would appear that the term has been widely adopted
without there being any definitive clarity on its actual meaning.

This chapter seeks to develop a clear conceptual understanding of hate crime
by examining a variety of influential academic and official definitions put forward in recent years. It also outlines the legal framework that underpins hate
crime and summarises what have been identified as the core characteristics of
hate offending and victimisation. Through the course of this discussion, we shall
see that understanding hate crime is a far from straightforward task due to the
ambiguity associated with the concept.

―――――――――――――― **Introduction** ――――――――――――――

Hate crime is a term that has assumed increasing salience within academic, political and social discourse in the UK over the past decade. Although the forms of
'othering' that we now collectively refer to as hate crime have been long-standing
problems in this country, it is only relatively recently that the expression 'hate
crime' has emerged within our vernacular. As a number of scholars have noted
(McLaughlin, 2002; Ray and Smith, 2002; Hall, 2005a), popular usage of the term
in the UK appears to have gained currency in the wake of much-publicised events

that took place towards the end of the last and the start of the current century. In particular, the racist murder of black teenager Stephen Lawrence in 1993 – and the ensuing publication of the Macpherson report in 1999 following the inquiry into the flawed police investigation of that murder – drew widespread attention to the problems posed by crimes committed against members of minority groups, as did the racist and homophobic nailbomb attacks of 1999 instigated by the neo-Nazi David Copeland in the diverse London communities of Brixton, Brick Lane and Soho. Similarly, the terrorist attacks in the USA of September 11 2001 and the July 7 bombings in London of 2005 have prompted a well-documented backlash against some minorities on the basis of their faith, and correspondingly there is now much greater recognition given to religiously, and not just racially motivated, offending. Although the rationale for choosing the word 'hate' to describe these varied types of offence is somewhat contested, the coining of 'hate crime' as a collective descriptor unquestionably has the capacity to inspire media headlines and to demand public attention. Accordingly, the various types of victimisation associated with this label are now widely accepted as significant social problems and are prioritised within research and policy agendas to a much greater extent than ever before.

While the term has emerged only recently in this country, hate crime has a considerably longer history within the USA. Arguably, its origins stem back to the post-Civil War period and the drafting of the US Constitution (Levin, 2002), although the impetus behind modern American anti-hate crime campaigns has its roots in the convergence of a series of progressive social movements during the 1960s, 1970s and 1980s, most notably those relating to black civil rights, women, gays and lesbians, those with disabilities and the markedly more conservative victims' rights lobby (Jenness and Broad, 1997; Grattet and Jenness, 2003b). With its capacity to unite disparate social pressure groups through the collective emphasis on rights and discrimination, the anti-hate crime movement drew attention to the violence directed towards, and political victimisation experienced by, ethnic, gendered, sexual and disabled minorities. Consequently, the stage was set for the emergence of hate crime as an issue of widespread significance, and since this time hate crime has duly been classed as a distinct category of criminal law in many American states, and at federal level, as a result of the continued pressure exerted through the mobilisation of campaign groups and sustained lobbying at county level. Indeed, the absence of explicit hate crime legislation in the UK when set against the relative proliferation of hate crime laws in the USA is an important distinction between the two countries and will be discussed at greater length in this chapter.

Given the comparatively recent adoption of the concept of hate crime in this country, it is perhaps not altogether surprising that the majority of literature on hate crime has been produced by academics from outside the UK. Clearly, that is not to say that the types of offence commonly associated with the hate crime label have not been researched and debated extensively within this country. Issues of 'race' and racism in particular have been explored at length, as have relationships between the police and minority ethnic communities, while a growing body of sociological and criminological literature has provided important insights into sexual and religious identities. Equally, we can turn to a substantial set of texts on victimology and victimisation in order to develop our understanding of the experiences, expectations and perceptions of hate crime victims. Hate crime cuts through numerous themes central to social scientific enquiry, whether this be 'race', ethnicity, gender, sexuality or simply 'otherness' *per se*, and the empirical and theoretical contributions from writers on these themes will naturally be relevant to our understanding of hate crime. At the same time, however, relatively few attempts have been made to examine these themes through the conceptual lens of hate, chiefly because it is only of late that the notion of hate crime has been mainstreamed within popular and political UK discourse. As such, specific texts on the subject have been in short supply. Within the past decade British scholars such as Paul Iganski and Nathan Hall have begun to critically assess the application of the hate crime label to the UK context (Iganski, 2002, 2008; Hall, 2005a) and it is to be hoped that their work can act as a catalyst for further academic enquiry within this nascent area of study.

There is a distinct need for further academic enquiry as it would appear that the term has been widely adopted and utilised without there being any definitive clarity on its meaning, applicability and justification. Put simply, hate crime is inherently more complex than the nomenclature suggests, or as Gerstenfeld (2004: xv) observes: 'hate crimes seem to be a topic of interest to nearly everybody, and yet few people really know much about them'. As we shall see, 'hate' is a slippery, emotive and conceptually ambiguous label that can mean different things to different people, and this has important implications for the way in which we conceive of the offences that fall under its umbrella framework and the actors involved in a hate crime, whether these be victims, perpetrators or agencies of control. Moreover, hate crime is an extremely contentious issue that has the capacity to evoke passionate responses from those who have supported its adoption and those opposed to the introduction of legislative intervention: for instance, while supporters of hate crime can quite rightly point to the increased recognition now afforded to traditionally marginalised and vulnerable minorities that has come with the maturation of hate crime policy, critics can justifiably point to the dangers of punishing offenders on the basis of thoughts and not merely actions in a liberal-democratic society. These arguments will be analysed more fully in due course, but before assessing the usefulness, or otherwise, of the term, it is important first to be clear on what we mean by hate crime, its core aspects and the extent to which the concept is enshrined within UK law.

Definitions of hate crime

Academic definitions

As Jacobs and Potter (1998: 27) point out in their influential text *Hate Crimes: Criminal Law and Identity Politics*, hate crime is a social construct with no self-evident definition. Therefore, efforts to measure the scale of the problem, or the appropriateness of policy responses to it, will depend upon how hate crime is defined. Establishing clear-cut, universal definitions of any form of crime is an inherently difficult task in the context of evolving social norms, constant changes to the law and the varying influence of political, cultural and environmental factors in different societies. Hate crime is no exception to this rule; indeed, it could be argued that defining this particular category of crime is especially problematic due to the subjectivity associated with conceptualising hate and the inconsistencies inherent to academic and practitioner definitions. Attempts to clarify the meaning of hate crime have, not surprisingly, been more forthcoming within the USA, and the suggestions of American scholars have strongly influenced our understanding of hate crime in a British context.

When asked to conceptualise hate crime, one's most immediate and obvious response might be to suggest that the term refers to crimes motivated by hatred. Curiously though, this is not actually the case: hate crimes are not crimes in which the offender simply *hates* the victim, and in reality crimes do not need to be motivated by hatred at all in order to be classified as a hate crime (Gerstenfeld, 2004: 9). Rather, for Gerstenfeld, the pivotal characteristic of a hate crime is the group affiliation of the victim, and not the presence of hate on the part of the perpetrator. She sees criminal acts motivated, at least in part, by the group affiliation of the victim as the defining feature of hate crime, though she is quick to acknowledge that this simple definition lacks precision in a number of respects, not least in terms of deciding which types of group affiliation should be included under the hate crime umbrella. Petrosino (2003: 10) offers a slightly more expansive definition which gives some indication of the groups that could come into consideration when conceiving of hate crime victims. She identifies a set of common characteristics from within the existing body of American hate crime literature to suggest that:

> (a) most victims are members of distinct racial or ethnic (cultural) minority groups ... (b) most victims are decidedly less powerful politically and economically than the majority ... and last, (c) victims represent to the perpetrator a threat to their quality of life (i.e. economic stability and/or physical safety). ... These common factors suggest the following base definition of hate crime: the victimisation of minorities due to their racial or ethnic identity by members of the majority.

As Petrosino goes on to note, her definition gives substance to the imbalance of power between the perpetrator and the victim who most commonly, though not always, will belong to the majority and minority groups respectively within a given society. Using a framework of power relations to describe this kind of victimisation is certainly a more constructive way of viewing hate crime as it allows us to recognise hate crimes not as an extraordinary category of offences *per se*, but rather as an extension of the types of prejudice, marginalisation and oppression experienced by minority groups within the structure of everyday society. However, Petrosino's conceptualisation of hate crime is constrained by two important limitations. At one level, it explicitly acknowledges the victimisation of ethnic minorities but does not recognise any other minority groups who conceivably could be vulnerable to the imbalance of power to which she refers. Secondly, her definition neglects to show how hate crime itself contributes to the subordination of the less powerful. In some respects Sheffield's (1995: 438) definition offers a more advanced account of hate crime:

> Hate violence is motivated by social and political factors and is bolstered by belief systems which (attempt to) legitimate such violence … it reveals that the personal is political; that such violence is not a series of isolated incidents but rather the consequence of a political culture which allocates rights, privileges and prestige according to biological or social characteristics.

As noted by other scholars (Perry, 2001; Hall, 2005a), this definition is helpful in the way it addresses both the political and social context through which hate crime develops and the significance of entrenched hierarchies of identity that underpin hate crime. In a similar vein to Petrosino, Sheffield points to the hierarchical structure of power relations within society and suggests that hate crime is an expression of power against those without the rights, privileges and prestige referred to above. Unlike Petrosino, though, Sheffield's framework does not limit her conceptualisation of hate crime victimisation to minority *ethnic* group membership, but instead extends this to include a potentially much broader range of groups marginalised on the basis of their 'biological or social characteristics'. Nevertheless, Perry (2001) argues that Sheffield's definition still fails to account for the impact of hate crime upon the actors involved in the process, namely the victim, perpetrator and their respective communities, and indeed this oversight is addressed within Perry's own comprehensive definition (2001: 10):

> Hate crime … involves acts of violence and intimidation, usually directed towards already stigmatised and marginalised groups. As such, it is a mechanism of power and oppression, intended to reaffirm the precarious hierarchies that characterise a given social order. It attempts to re-create simultaneously the threatened (real or imagined) hegemony of the perpetrator's group and the 'appropriate' subordinate identity of the victim's group. It is a means of marking both the Self and the Other in such a way as to re-establish their 'proper' relative positions, as given and reproduced by broader ideologies and patterns of social and political inequality.

In common with other definitions, this framework acknowledges the relationship between hierarchies and hate, and gives primacy to the notion of violent and intimidatory behaviour being somehow different when it involves an act motivated by bigotry and manifested as discrimination towards marginalised populations (see also Jenness, 2002). Moreover, like Sheffield, Perry's understanding of such groups extends not only to minority ethnic people but to 'all members of stigmatised and marginalised communities' (2001: 1). However, Perry's conceptualisation of hate crime would appear to offer several distinct advantages over other definitions. Crucially, it recognises that hate crime is not a static problem but one that is historically and culturally contingent, the experience of which needs to be seen as a dynamic social process involving context, structure and agency. In this regard, Perry takes her lead from the pioneering work of Bowling (1993, 1999), whose thoughts on framing racist violence are acknowledged by Perry as being directly relevant to the way in which we should conceive of hate crime victimisation. For Bowling (1993: 238) racist victimisation should be understood as a process, and not as an event:

> Conceiving of racial violence … as processes implies an analysis which is dynamic; includes the social relationship between all the actors involved in the process; can capture the continuity across physical violence, threat, intimidation; can capture the dynamic of repeated or systematic victimisation; incorporates historical context; and takes account of the social relationships which inform definitions of appropriate and inappropriate behaviour.

If we extend these ideas to hate crime more generally, we can see that the experience of hate crime does not simply stop and end with the commission of the offence, nor does it occur in a cultural or social vacuum. Therefore, by recognising the various features of the process referred to by Bowling above, and by incorporating this within the framework of power, hierarchy and oppression outlined in her own definition, Perry highlights the inescapable complexity associated with hate crime and the need to think of it 'in such a way as to give the term "life" and meaning' (2001: 9).

Another key factor within Perry's conceptualisation of hate crime is her emphasis on the group, and not individual, identity of the victim. She sees the specific victims as almost immaterial in that they are interchangeable; indeed, hate crimes, for Perry, are acts of violence and intimidation directed not only towards the victim but towards the wider community to which he or she belongs, and thereby these crimes are designed to convey a message to this community that they are somehow "different" and 'don't belong' (see also Hall, 2005a). As 'message' crimes, acts of hate reach 'into the community to create fear, hostility and suspicion' and in so doing reaffirm 'the hegemony of the perpetrator's and the "appropriate" subordinate identity of the victim's group' (Perry, 2001: 10). Moreover, and perhaps not surprisingly given the symbolic status of hate crime within Perry's conceptual framework, she regards these offences as most commonly perpetrated against strangers with whom the offender has had little or no personal contact, with the victim simply representing the 'other' in generic terms through their membership of the demonised group (ibid: 29).

Official definitions

It is evident from this initial inspection of academic definitions that hate crime has proved to be, if not elusive, then certainly a somewhat slippery notion and one that is difficult to fully conceptualise. Its ambiguity is such that definitions of hate crime can vary from academic to academic, from country to country and, at least within the USA, from state jurisdiction to state jurisdiction (Petrosino, 2003), and we should be mindful of this when seeking to define the parameters of what is and what is not recognised as a hate crime. However, while hate crime scholars have sought to grapple with what they see as the complexity associated with the term, official classifications have tended to be significantly less intricate in their interpretations of hate crime. Although the development of academic definitions like those presented above is central to our conceptual understanding of hate crime, such broad and elaborate definitions are rather less useful in a practical sense to criminal justice practitioners and legislators (Hall, 2005a). Consequently, practitioner constructions may in some respects appear more straightforward when compared to their academic counterparts.

Within the UK the key source of policy guidance on hate crime would appear to derive from the Association of Chief Police Officers (ACPO), whose operational definition is enshrined within their guidelines for police forces in England, Wales and Northern Ireland (ACPO, 2000, 2005). Produced in consultation with the Home Office, ACPO's initial piece of strategic guidance, their *Guide to Identifying and Combating Hate Crime*, published in 2000, came at a time of increasing and unprecedented focus upon the victimisation of minority groups. Indeed, as McGhee (2005: 125) observes, this document cited homophobic and racist hate crime as the two most high-profile forms of hate perpetuated in the UK chiefly on account of their association with the media publicity afforded to the Stephen Lawrence Inquiry and the nailbombing of the Admiral Duncan, a Soho-based public house frequented by London's gay community. This recognition of homophobic hate crime is significant, as is ACPO's reference to other group identities such as physical disability, religion and transgender status, because it is illustrative of a shift in thinking during this period beyond just 'race' to broader issues of diversity. Consequently, according to the ACPO guidance of the time, hate crime was defined as 'a crime where the perpetrator's prejudice against any identifiable group of people is a factor in determining who is victimised' (ACPO, 2000: 13). Explicit reference is made within the ACPO guidance to racist and homophobic incidents, which are defined consistently with the definition of a racist incident recommended by the Macpherson report to read, respectively, as 'any incident which is perceived to be racist by the victim or any other person' and 'any incident which is perceived to be homophobic by the victim or any other person' (ibid: 13).

In 2005 a revised set of hate crime guidelines were produced by ACPO. For the most part, these follow the guidance offered in the 2000 strategy, particularly in giving primacy to the perception of the victim or any other person as being the defining factor in determining a hate incident (ACPO, 2005: 9). However, there are some notable features within the 2005 guidelines that have important implications for the way in which we conceive of hate crime. In seeking to provide conceptual clarity, ACPO offer the following definitions of a hate incident and a hate crime (2005: 9):

A hate incident is defined as:

Any incident, which may or may not constitute a criminal offence, which is perceived by the victim or any other person, as being motivated by prejudice or hate.

A hate crime is defined as:

Any hate incident, which constitutes a criminal offence, perceived by the victim or any other person, as being motivated by prejudice or hate.

By distinguishing between incidents and crimes in such a manner, the ACPO guidelines make clear that there is an important difference between the two: while all hate crimes are hate incidents, some hate incidents may not constitute a criminal offence in themselves and therefore will not be recorded as a crime, but simply as incidents. We shall consider more fully in Chapter 7 the implications that this distinction has for the policing of incidents and crimes, but for the purposes of the present discussion it is important to note that ACPO's guidelines require all incidents to be recorded by the police even if they lack the requisite elements to be classified as a notifiable offence later in the criminal justice process. At the recording stage, any hate incident, whether a *prima-facie* 'crime' or not, should be recorded if it meets the threshold originally laid down by the Macpherson definition of a racist incident – namely, if it is perceived by the victim or any other person as being motivated by prejudice or hate – and not the stricter, evidential threshold required under criminal law for notifiable offences. Clearly then, if we consider hate 'occurrences' as opposed to just crimes *per se*, the scale of the problem, at least in terms of sheer numbers, becomes much more sizable than we may initially have imagined.

A further significant aspect of the ACPO definitions relates to the emphasis on prejudice, and not simply hate. By explicitly stating that hate crimes or incidents are not always concerned with hate but rather prejudice, ACPO's guidelines follow the line pursued by Gerstenfeld (2004) above by suggesting that the presence of hate is not necessarily central to the commission of a hate crime and that in reality crimes need not be motivated by hatred at all in order to be regarded as a hate crime. In essence, then, hate would appear to be a distinctly unhelpful term in many respects. Leading practitioner and academic definitions would appear to be consistent in drawing our focus towards behaviour motivated by certain forms of prejudice, which in itself is a much more expansive notion than hate, covering many varieties of human emotion of which hate may be only a small and extreme part (Hall, 2005a). Again, we shall return to this point in due course, but in seeking to offer conceptual clarity at this juncture of the book, this inspection of definitions underlines the need to recognise the centrality of prejudice within our conception of hate crime.

Finally, the ACPO guidelines offer some important assistance in framing our understanding of hate crime victimisation. Rather unhelpfully, the guidelines do not offer a definition of prejudice, and consequently this leaves considerable uncertainty around the distinction between 'acceptable' and 'unacceptable' prejudice and creates grey areas, as Hall (2005a: 10) suggests, with regard to 'how strong those prejudices must be in order to become unacceptable, how they must be expressed, whether someone is prejudiced or whether they are not, or indeed how we can ever know for certain'. However, despite failing to explain what they mean by the term prejudice, ACPO's guidelines do provide some degree of clarification by alluding to particular grounds for prejudice or hatred (2005: 10):

> For data recording purposes the police are obliged to record hate incidents where the perception of the victim or any other person that the motivation for the prejudice or hate is based upon:
>
> • Race
> • Sexual orientation
> • Faith
> • Disability

This reference to specific group identities is in itself a clarification of any ambiguity that may have surrounded ACPO's initial definition of hate crime in 2000, which, as we have seen, referred to 'the perpetrator's prejudice against *any identifiable group of people*' (emphasis added). As such, the 2005 guidance suggests that it is not just any prejudice that could form the basis of a hate crime, but rather prejudice against particular groups of people or based upon on particular grounds, namely 'race', sexual orientation, faith or disability. On the one hand, placing restrictions on the types of 'unacceptable' prejudice that can constitute a hate crime is critical to the viability of hate crime as an operational tool. At the same time, limiting the applicability of hate crime to certain groups and not others is inherently problematic as this requires difficult decisions to be made on who should be deserving of 'special protection'. As above, we shall return to this contentious issue in due course, but the potential for hate crime to create a hierarchy of victims, whereby some groups may be seen as being more important or deserving than others, is a problem that is central to debates over the conceptual basis of hate crime.

As mentioned earlier, the definitions of hate crime followed by criminal justice agencies, policy-makers, and practitioners will vary from place to place, and therefore it should be recognised that the ACPO guidelines are but one set of definitions that govern people's understanding of hate crime. That said, ACPO's guidance is significant because it represents the official, Home Office-endorsed interpretation of hate crime that dictates the way in which police forces conceive of and respond to the problem domestically, and it is for that reason that it needs to be considered alongside the key academic definitions examined earlier. While it is not directly applicable to Scotland, the Scottish *Working Group on Hate Crime Consultation Paper* of 2003 indicates a similar line of thinking to that developed in ACPO's guidance to police forces in England, Wales and Northern Ireland. This document puts forward a slightly different definition of hate crime – 'crime motivated by malice or ill-will towards a social group' (Scottish Executive, 2003: 11) – but the parallels between the two sets of guidance soon become evident in the Scottish Working Group's discussion of prejudice, vulnerability and motivation, which echoes the points presented by ACPO with regards to the centrality of prejudice on the grounds of 'race', religion, sexuality or disability.

The legal framework for hate crime

When mapping the contours of hate crime it is important to be familiar with the laws that exist to regulate its status. In this respect the situation in the UK differs markedly from that in the USA where a corpus of legislation has been enacted to give hate crime a substantially firmer legal footing. The first American federal law relating specifically to hate crime was introduced in 1990 under the auspices of the Hate Crimes Statistics Act (HCSA), which required the US Department of Justice to collect hate crime data from local law enforcement agencies nationwide. Subsequently, in 1994, the Hate Crimes Sentencing Enhancement Act was enacted, enabling penalties to be augmented in cases where an individual is being tried for a federal crime and where the victim was targeted on the basis of their group identity, although as Gerstenfeld (2004: 29) observes, this law has had limited scope in practice on account of the fact that federal criminal prosecutions are relatively rare in comparison with state prosecutions. A more recent bill – the Local Law Enforcement Hate Crimes Prevention Act – received approval from the Senate in September 2007 after a protracted passage through Congress of approximately ten years, expanding federal hate crime coverage to incorporate crimes committed on the grounds of sexual orientation, gender, gender identity and disability. In addition to these federal acts, many US states have developed their own set of hate crime laws. While this gives added complexity to official definitions in that country in the sense that the scope of hate crime legislation will inevitably vary from state jurisdiction to jurisdiction, it is also illustrative of the extent to which the concept of hate crime is firmly enshrined within American law.

Unlike America there is no explicit corpus of hate crime legislation within the UK, and this is arguably reflective of the different origins of hate crime within the two countries and the more established status of hate crime within the lexicon of US policy-makers and politicians. That said, the rationale behind the concept of hate crime have been recognised by legislators in the UK, and as a result a number of laws have been introduced which adhere to the principle that crimes motivated by hatred or prejudice towards particular features of the victim's identity, such as their ethnicity, faith, sexuality or disability, should be treated differently from 'ordinary' crimes. This legislation will be examined in greater depth during later chapters, but for the purposes of clarity at this stage we shall briefly examine the current legal framework for hate crime.

A significant piece of legislation within the context of the present discussion is the Crime and Disorder Act 1998. Introduced by the Labour government that came to power in 1997, sections 28–32 of the Crime and Disorder Act instituted provisions relating to racially aggravated offences, in essence creating a 'penalty enhancement statute' (Lawrence, 1999: 92) which enables higher penalties to be attached to crimes that are racially aggravated. As we shall see in Chapter 2, this Act was designed to provide the criminal justice system with a clear indication of the importance of identifying and dealing with racist crime by establishing a set of new racially aggravated offences based upon the existing offences of assault, public order, harassment and criminal damage (Burney, 2002).[1] Although the original framing of the Crime and Disorder Act provisions suggests that enhanced penalties can be imposed only in cases that fall under the remit of those particular four categories of violence, public order, harassment and criminal damage, section 153 of the Powers of Criminal Courts (Sentencing) Act 2000 (replacing section 82 of the 1998 Act) requires the courts to treat evidence of racial aggravation as an aggravating feature when deciding upon the sentence for *any* offence, including cases where offences are not specifically charged under the 1998 Act.

The principle that substantially higher sentences can be imposed in instances where there is evidence of aggravation was also extended to include religiously aggravated offences through the Anti-Terrorism, Crime and Security Act 2001. This amendment to the original Crime and Disorder Act provisions makes comparable provision for offences which are considered to be religiously aggravated, and as such, under section 39 of the 2001 Act evidence of religious aggravation is regarded as a factor which increases the seriousness of particular offences for the purposes of sentencing. Similarly, section 146 of the Criminal Justice Act 2003 empowers courts to impose increased sentences for offences aggravated by the victim's sexuality or their mental or physical disability. As Hall notes (2005a: 124), this Act stopped short of creating specific offences for these two aggravating factors in the same way that the Crime and Disorder Act 1998 does for offences relating to 'race' and religion, but it does ensure that the manifestation of prejudice on the grounds of sexual orientation or disability, expressed however strongly or in whatever way, is taken into account at the sentencing stage.

The principle of hate crime as a meaningful concept is also protected in law, though not recognised as a distinct category of crime in its own right, by the various strands of incitement legislation. Protection against the incitement of racial hatred, originally enshrined within provisions of the Race Relations Acts of 1965 and 1976, can be found in its most recent guise within the Public Order Act 1986. Section 17 of this Act prohibits the use of words, whether oral or written, or behaviour which is deemed 'threatening, abusive or insulting', and puts in place both a subjective standard of guilt where there is either intention to stir up hatred and also an alternative objective threshold where 'having regard to all the circumstances racial hatred is likely to be stirred up thereby'.

More recently, the Racial and Religious Hatred Act 2006 extends protection to the incitement of religious hatred by amending the Public Order Act to outlaw the use of threatening words or behaviour intended to incite hatred against people on the basis of their faith. Although similar in many respects to the incitement to racial hatred laws, the more recent offence has a higher legal threshold, for reasons that will be discussed in Chapter 3, in that it applies only to threatening (and not abusive or insulting) words or behaviour, and it requires the prosecution to prove that the perpetrator intended to stir up religious hatred. Furthermore, the government signified its determination to develop the scope of incitement laws through the Criminal Justice and Immigration Act 2008, which contains provisions creating fresh offences of inciting hatred against gay and lesbian people under a similar threshold to that specified in the Racial and Religious Hatred Act.

Another piece of legislation that should be mentioned within this context is the Protection from Harassment Act 1997.[2] Although this Act was originally conceived as a response to the problem of stalking, it also provides civil and criminal remedies for forms of conduct associated with hate crime. Indeed, as Mason observes (2005a: 842), the government of the time framed the Act around the concept of harassment, as opposed to stalking, on the basis that this would enable the legislation to provide redress for activities constituting harassment on the basis of 'race' as well as other related grounds. Harassment is not explicitly defined under the 1997 Act but is described in general terms as a course of conduct (i.e. conduct that occurs on at least two occasions) which causes alarm or distress, and which a reasonable person in possession of the same information would consider as amounting to harassment of another. As such, the Act offers victims of hate a further possible source of protection against the types of distressing behaviour and conduct for which prosecution under other offences might be difficult to achieve (ibid: 842). In a similar vein, the Malicious Communications Act 1998, as amended by the Criminal Justice and Police Act 2001, makes it an offence to send a letter or any form of electronic communication (including telephone calls, text messages or emails) which contains an indecent or grossly offensive message, or which conveys a threat or false information, which is deliberately designed to cause the recipient distress or anxiety.

As we shall see in due course within subsequent chapters, the effectiveness, legitimacy, scope and interpretation of these various pieces of legislation have all been called into question to varying degrees, and these areas of debate are central to our understanding and usage of the notion of hate crime more broadly. For the time being though, it is important to acknowledge the existence of these laws as this itself illustrates a crucial point: namely, that despite the absence of explicit hate crime legislation, a number of laws have been enacted in the UK which enshrine the conceptual principle of hate crime and which afford protection to the groups identified through ACPO's official guidance. In this respect, there is consistency in the message conveyed both by the law and by official policy documents in alerting criminal justice agencies, sentencers and the general public to the significance of hate crime.

Core constituents of hate crime offending and victimisation

It is worth pausing a moment at this stage to reflect upon what we know about hate crime from this inspection of definitions and legal provisions. Certainly, the range of policies, laws and campaigns that have emerged over the past 20 years or so in relation to issues of hate crime are indicative of the increased diversification of British society, and as McLaughlin (2002: 497) notes, should be seen as 'part of the ongoing process of identifying and articulating the values, sensibilities and ground rules of vibrant, multicultural societies, including the public recognition and affirmation of the right to be different'. But aside from representing society's condemnation of victimisation on the basis of such 'difference', why has hate crime assumed such significance? What does the term 'hate crime' represent and what are its key characteristics?

In many respects the emergence of the concept of hate crime is synonymous with the rise to prominence of 'the victim'. While victims of crime as a generic group are widely recognised as being important, newsworthy and deserving of public and criminal justice support, their concerns have only relatively recently formed a central feature of academic and political discourse having spent years on the fringes of criminological and sociological debate (Zedner, 2002; Goodey, 2005; Spalek, 2006). Although early studies of victimology were typified by a tendency to attach some degree of blame or responsibility to victims of crime through their reliance on notions of victim-precipitation and victim-proneness (for further discussion see Walklate, 1989; Zedner, 2002), recent decades have seen the emergence of a more critical stance which has examined in greater depth the wider social and cultural context of victimisation.

This increased standing for victims clearly has implications for the development of hate crime, for it is within this context that we have begun to appreciate the differential impact of certain forms of crime upon particular groups of victim. Indeed, this would appear to be one of the key underlying premises of hate crime: that crimes motivated by hatred or prejudice against certain groups of people deserve particular attention and protection. Specifically, it is minority groups who are recognised by most, if not all, definitions as being the groups to whom victims of hate crime must belong; groups who are stigmatised or marginalised on the basis of their perceived subordinate position within society. But equally there are a number of additional key elements to account for when conceiving of a hate crime. Crucially, as Hall (2005a: 4) asserts, there is nothing specifically 'new' about the crime element of hate crime as the offences themselves are already outlawed under existing legislation: to use his words, it is 'society's interest in the motivation that lies behind the commission of the crime that is new'. Indeed, we have seen from the broad interpretation offered by ACPO's official guidance that at face value *any* incident or crime could potentially form the basis of what we classify as hate crime, and as such it is clearly the 'hate' element of hate crime that requires conceptual clarification in order for us to comprehend the implications of the term.

On consideration of the motivation that lies behind the commission of a hate crime, several important features emerge. First, most definitions of hate crime are consistent in arguing that the identity of the individual victim is largely irrelevant as the victim is chosen on the basis of their membership of a particular minority group. Under this framework hate crimes are seen as 'message crimes'; crimes which are designed to tell not just the victim but the entire subordinate (as perceived by the perpetrator) community to whom they belong that they are different or unwelcome, thereby extending the impact of hate crime beyond the actual victim to create a sense of apprehension, vulnerability and tension among all members of that particular community. By implication, and as discussed above, it is commonly assumed that hate crimes are acts perpetrated against strangers with whom the offender has had little or no personal contact, and that the victim simply represents the 'other' through their membership of the subordinate group (see, for instance, Perry, 2001).

However, while this construction of hate crime helps us to understand the way in which the commission of hate crime may act as a way of reinforcing social hierarchies, it does restrict our conception of how hate crime can operate by suggesting that victims and perpetrators will almost invariably be strangers to each other. Mason (2005a), for instance, contests this assumption by drawing from

British Crime Survey data and other research evidence to show that a substantial proportion of racially motivated and homophobic incidents are committed by perpetrators who are in fact *not* strangers to their victims (see also Ray and Smith, 2001; Moran, 2007). Using this evidence as a backdrop to her own research data drawn from hate crime incidents reported to the Metropolitan Police Service, Mason's findings challenge the popular image of hate crime as a form of 'stranger danger' and the 'one size fits all' method of describing perpetrator–victim relationships (2005a: 856). Clearly, hate crimes may often take the shape envisaged by Perry and others of message crimes directed at the wider subordinate community, but by the same token they may also include acts where the perpetrator is familiar to the victim. This reality is an important but often overlooked feature of hate crime discourse that will be explored further in the chapters that follow.

Another key feature relevant to the motivation that lies behind the commission of a hate crime is the nature of the term 'hate'. The term itself would appear to be somewhat misleading since definitions consistently refer to a broader range of motivating factors than hate alone. As Jacobs and Potter point out (1998: 11):

> 'Hate' crime is not really about hate, but about bias or prejudice ... essentially hate crime refers to criminal conduct motivated by prejudice. Prejudice, however, is a complicated, broad and cloudy concept. We all have prejudices for and against individuals, groups, foods, countries, weather, and so forth. Sometimes these prejudices are rooted in experience, sometimes in fantasy and irrationality, and sometimes they are passed down to us by family, friends, school, religion and culture.

Underlining the point made earlier, the ideas expressed here by Jacobs and Potter confirm that the presence of hate is not necessarily central to the commission of a hate crime, but rather it is criminal behaviour motivated by *prejudice* that constitutes the key causal factor in the classification of a hate crime. However, as the authors go on to argue, this creates conceptual and operational ambiguity with regards to distinguishing between acceptable and unacceptable prejudices. Unless we impose limits on the types of prejudice that can form the basis of a hate crime then conceivably any type of prejudice could constitute a hate offence; conversely, making such distinctions requires difficult moral judgements to be made with regards to choosing which prejudices are more offensive, and therefore more deserving of increased punishment, than others.

This point notwithstanding, we also know from the ACPO guidance that officially there are certain prejudices that are considered to be more 'punishable' than others, and this is another key feature of hate crime that will be considered during the course of this book. Under this guidance, hate crimes constitute prejudice based upon on particular grounds, namely 'race', faith, sexual orientation or disability. By implication therefore, the damage or 'hurt' associated with offences perpetrated on such grounds is distinct from that created by other 'ordinary' crimes, and this justifies the 'special attention' that comes with their inclusion under the umbrella category of hate crime. But as with other core aspects of the hate crime concept, assessing how legitimate it is to make choices over which beliefs, attitudes or prejudices to class as unacceptable is a precarious process. Do offences based on racially or religiously motivated prejudice, or on homophobic or disability bias, 'hurt' more than other crimes? Are there other groups of peoples who deserve the special protection afforded to the officially recognised four minority groups? Are there important differences within these four related but distinct categories of hate crime and if so does the employment of umbrella terminology mask these differences for the sake of drawing attention to the commonalities in offenders' motivation and victims' experiences?

Conclusion

Ultimately, all of the points raised above are thorny but important issues which will be examined extensively in the chapters that follow. We have seen that the term 'hate' is a problematic, ambiguous, and in many cases inaccurate label used to describe the offences with which it is commonly associated, and there is considerable disparity between the various academic and official interpretations of what constitutes a hate crime. The ensuing lack of consensus over the conceptual and operational boundaries of hate crime has major implications for our usage and indeed for the legitimacy of the term, as well as for our responses to minority group victimisation.

Equally, we must not lose sight of the positive developments that have taken place in the years since hate crime discourse has gained salience within the UK. Taking its lead from the USA, where the shared realities of hate crime victimisation have united disparate social movements and directed attention towards the problems suffered by a variety of marginalised groups, the adoption of the hate crime label in this country has rightly given emphasis to the collective experiences of all minorities and the commonalties in their victimisation. An increasing number of laws have been passed during recent years which provide added protection to groups especially vulnerable to acts of hate and prejudice, and this has underlined the significance of hate crime to criminal justice agencies, sentencers, researchers, the media and the general public. Such unprecedented progress has been important to the governance of diversity and community cohesion in the UK and should not be under-valued. Therefore, when seeking to make sense of the concept of hate crime we should be mindful of its origins, and continued utility, as an umbrella construct designed to combat a range of prejudices. Whether its social and political importance in this context outweighs its conceptual ambiguities is a difficult question for hate crime scholars to address and one to which we shall return in later chapters, but to further our understanding the book now turns from a generic conceptual analysis of hate crime to consider specific forms of hate offences.

Guide to further reading

The subject of hate crime has been explored much more extensively in the USA than in the UK and, as such, the work of leading American scholars has retained a strong influence on the development of hate crime discourse. In particular, Perry, *In the Name of Hate* (2001), Perry (ed.), *Hate and Bias Crime: A Reader* (2003a), Jacobs and Potter, *Hate Crimes: Criminal Law and Identity Politics* (1998), and Gerstenfeld, *Hate Crimes: Causes, Controls and Controversies* (2004) all provide valuable insights into the conceptual basis of hate crime. This subject is a nascent area of study among British scholars and Hall, *Hate Crime* (2005) and Iganski, *'Hate Crime' and the City* (2008) are both useful texts for readers seeking an overview of hate crime in a UK context.

Notes

1 Assault, public order, harassment and criminal damage are all existing criminal offences under the Offences Against the Person Act 1861, the Public Order Act 1986, the Protection from Harassment Act 1997 and the Criminal Damage Act 1971.
2 Legal protection against harassment can also be found in section 5 of the Public Order Act 1986, which makes it an offence to use words, engage in conduct or display representations within the sight or hearing of a person who is likely to be caused 'harassment, alarm or distress'. In addition, under section 42 of the Criminal Justice and Police Act 2001 the police can direct someone to leave the vicinity of the victim's dwelling if they are causing distress or alarm and can arrest them if they fail to leave.

2

RACIST HATE CRIME

──────────────────────────── Chapter summary ────────────────────────────

Developing an understanding of racist victimisation is important to our overall understanding of hate crime: not only are crimes motivated by prejudice against the victim's ethnic identity the most common type of hate crime, they are also arguably the most recognised type of hate crime. As such, and unlike other less researched branches of minority victimisation, there is an extensive body of literature within the UK devoted to issues of 'race' and ethnicity, to the relationship between 'race' and the criminal justice system, and to the experiences and perceptions of victims of racist crime.

   This chapter seeks to address some of the salient points to have surfaced from this body of literature that have implications for our understanding of the conceptual basis and practical application of hate crime. It begins by examining 'race' within the context of its emergence as an issue of significance in the UK over the past century, before moving on to explore the problem of racist hate crime in greater depth. In particular, the chapter examines the scope and dimensions of this problem, together with the legal framework in place to address racist victimisation and the ways in which research in this field has shaped conceptions of racist hate crime.

──────────────────────────── Introduction ────────────────────────────

Racist hate crime is arguably the most widely recognised form of hate crime; indeed, politicians, journalists, practitioners and academics often fall into the trap of describing hate crime exclusively in terms of racist crime, thereby failing to acknowledge the broader dimensions of hate crime as a concept. This common mistake of equating hate crime with racist crime is indicative of the dominant status that 'race', ethnicity and racist prejudice have assumed within hate crime discourse. The sheer weight of literature devoted to these issues in comparison to the relatively small number of texts on other recognised categories of hate crime is illustrative of how racist victimisation has a more established standing within academic study, and it is only in recent times that other forms of targeted prejudice have begun to receive the recognition that they deserve.

The breadth, depth and scale of 'race'-related research conducted over the past 30 years or so is far too extensive to summarise within the confines of this particular chapter. There are a number of excellent texts that provide a comprehensive overview of the salient points from this research and their implications for our understanding of 'race' and racism, and these are acknowledged in the guide for further reading that follows this chapter. However, in terms of developing our understanding of hate crime, we need to consider the links between racism and crime and the way in which 'race', or more pertinently ethnicity, is used as a tool to victimise people on the basis of their 'difference'.

The term ethnicity has been used in this context as a way of drawing attention to broader ideas of culture and identity, and away from the biological notions of difference associated with 'race'. Again, a discussion of the conceptual debates and ambiguities surrounding the usage of this terminology is beyond the scope of this chapter (see, *inter alia*, Ratcliffe, 2004 and Webster, 2007 for a more detailed account), but it is worth noting that the notion of 'race' has traditionally been used to distinguish between groups on the basis of supposed biological differences. As such, this social construct is said to lack scientific validity (and hence the common inclusion of inverted commas around the term) on account of the dangers associated with differentiating between groups in such a deterministic manner. Ethnicity, meanwhile, refers more broadly to groups possessing some degree of solidarity based on culture, descent and territory, and this recognition of the role and influence of cultural identity enables us to transcend crude and contentious biological distinctions by acknowledging other important markers of differentiation. Similarly, the term racism is used fairly expansively within this chapter as a way of describing the beliefs and practices that can result in people being discriminated against on the basis of their perceived ethnic or racial origin. As we shall see shortly, problems of racism and perceptions of ethnic difference are complex, constantly evolving and contingent on global, national and local contexts. Conceiving of 'race', ethnicity and racism in a broad sense, therefore, can help us to chart more accurately the nature and impact of racist hate.

The development of the UK's 'race' agenda

While differentiation on the grounds of skin colour, bodily features or cultural practices has a long history, it is only relatively recently that the idea of 'race' has emerged as an explanatory device to justify such differentiation. As Bowling and

Phillips (2002) observe, the concept can be traced back to the philosophies of the European Enlightenment and to the ascendancy of science and reason within the work of writers such as Hume, Kant and Hegel. For many of these philosophers, 'race' was seen as a way of distinguishing the cultural superiority of white Europeans from the savagery associated with non-whites from outside Europe, a view that became entrenched during the expansion of the transatlantic slave trade over the course of the seventeenth and eighteenth centuries (Bhavani, Mirza and Meetoo, 2006). The acquisition and rule of far-away territories, and the ensuing sub-jugation of colonial subjects described by Bowling and Phillips (2002: 3) as 'being akin to children or animals, needing care, nurture and improvement under a civilised and beneficent rule', was reflective of the biological basis for racial supremacy during this period of empire building, and was central to the emergence in the mid-nineteenth century of the scientific discourse of Social Darwinism and its emphasis on the superiority and preservation of the European white race.

Similar lines of thinking developed during the nineteenth and twentieth centuries, most notably through the form of the eugenics movements which forcibly sought to control the perceived purity of the 'races' and also through the widespread promotion of laws across many countries designed to enforce racial segregation. However, it is the post-Second World War context that arguably has the most significant implications for the way in which the UK's recent 'race' agenda has developed. Although migration to and from the country had occurred quite extensively prior to this point, the post-Second World War influx of migrants into the UK (that occurred primarily as a way of filling labour shortages) quickly resulted in a noticeably different demographic profile. Approximately 11,000 West Indians arrived in Britain in 1954, with the figure more than doubling the following year, while the rate of migration from India and Pakistan rose dramatically from the comparatively low figure of 7,350 in 1955 to equal that from the West Indies after 1960 (Hiro, 1992).

While immigration during this post-war period was not confined solely to incomers from the Caribbean and Asia,[1] it is the migration of former inhabitants of New Commonwealth countries that appears to have shaped subsequent debates and policy-making on race relations. Specifically, the racial disturbances of 1958, first in Nottingham and then in Notting Hill, acted as a trigger for the now-familiar politicisation of 'race' and its association with crime, the economy and nationhood (Bowling and Phillips, 2002). The sustained violence directed towards black people during these disturbances, together with the sizable increase during the late 1950s and early 1960s of New Commonwealth immigrants, resulted in the Conservative administration taking a firmer stance on the issue of immigration. This was manifested in the Commonwealth Immigrants Act 1962, whose provisions were to differentiate unashamedly between the rights of white and non-white settlers by placing onerous restrictions on the rights of settlement for New Commonwealth would-be migrants, while allowing much greater freedom of entry to Old Commonwealth migrants from countries such as Canada, Australia and New Zealand.

The Labour Party's return to power in 1964 signalled a convergence of Conservative and Labour policy in favour of immigration control (Sales, 2007). Despite the tighter controls introduced through the 1962 Act anti-immigrant sentiment remained strong among many sections of the public, as Labour learned to their cost during the general election campaign of 1964. In the West Midlands constituency of Smethwick, Patrick Gordon Walker, a Labour shadow cabinet minister, lost what had been assumed to be a safe seat for his party to the Conservative candidate and local headmaster Peter Griffiths, whose campaign had been largely based around the threats posed by immigration to the local white population. Griffiths' campaign is perhaps most infamous for its use of the slogan 'If you want a nigger neighbour, vote Liberal or Labour', a rhyme which was described by the victorious MP as a 'manifestation of popular feeling' (Hiro, 1992).

The notorious 'rivers of blood' speech of Conservative MP Enoch Powell in 1968 helped to shape the future direction of immigration policy in the UK. Within this speech, Powell used highly emotive language to plea for an end to immigration and to criticise the government's perceived betrayal of the 'British' electorate through its open-door policies. Utilising provocative language that echoed images of slavery, Powell predicted that: 'In this country in fifteen or twenty years' time the black man will have the whip hand over the white man.' If existing levels of 'coloured' immigration were maintained, he continued, then: 'Like the Roman, I seem to see the River Tiber foaming with much blood' (Sandbrook, 2007: 679). Though the speech resulted in his removal from the Conservative shadow cabinet, his continued influence as an active backbencher, allied with the extensive media coverage devoted to the issues he raised, laid the foundations for the implementation of further legislation curbing the rights of New Commonwealth migrants through the Commonwealth Immigrants Act 1968 and the Immigration Act 1971 (Bowling and Phillips, 2002). A decade later the Conservative administration led by Margaret Thatcher issued the British Nationality Act 1981. Its main thrust reflected Thatcher's publicly declared fears of Britain being 'swamped' by an 'alien culture' by, among other things, removing the automatic right to citizenship of those born on British soil. A similarly tough stance on New Commonwealth migrants appeared in the Immigration Act 1988, signifying the continuing racialisation of immigration policy on the lines of skin colour (Sales, 2007).

These developments are important in the context of our understanding of racist hate crime: despite the extensive levels of violent racism directed towards minority ethnic communities from the Second World War to the late 1970s – a phase described by Bowling and Phillips (2002: 13) as being 'among the most viciously racist periods in British domestic history' – depictions of these communities tended be framed mainly in terms of their disorderly characteristics, with little attention given to their experiences as victims of racist hate (see also Hall et al., 1978). Even when the fractious relationship between the police and black communities collapsed with the outbreaks of public disorder and rioting during 1981 in Brixton, Toxteth, Moss Side and other inner-city neighbourhoods across the country, explanations for this disorder gave relatively little consideration to black experiences of oppressive policing and social and economic exclusion. Although the public inquiry into the disturbances chaired by Lord Scarman gave some recognition to the problems of minority ethnic deprivation and disadvantage, it stopped short of explicitly locating the black communities' grievances within their experiences of racist stereotyping and oppression, and failed to stave off the potential for future rioting which duly occurred in the areas of Handsworth in Birmingham and the Broadwater Farm estate in London during 1985.[2]

However, if 1981 was a landmark year in the context of British race relations because of the inner-city rioting, in other ways it was also an equally significant year for the recognition of ethnic minorities as victims. In this year the Home Office published *Racial Attacks*, its inaugural report highlighting evidence of the racist harassment directed at minority ethnic communities. This important first sign of official recognition for the vulnerability of minority ethnic communities laid the foundations for the systematic collection of evidence on various facets of racist victimisation that has taken place since. Indeed, it is only since 1981 that local and central government agencies have kept records of racist violence and have begun to develop policies in response to the problem (Bowling, 2003: 64). Equally, the murder of Stephen Lawrence in 1993, or more specifically the implications that accrued from the flawed Metropolitan Police investigation into his murder, has had a profound impact upon the way in which racism is perceived and policed (see Case Study 2.1). The tragic circumstances of Lawrence's murder – an unprovoked, racially motivated attack on a defenceless teenager – attracted widespread (and unprecedented in the context of victims of murderous racism) media coverage, even from newspapers such as the *Daily Mail* whose concerted campaign to name and shame the killers ran in stark contrast to their traditionally antipathetic stance towards issues of racism.

Case Study 2.1: Key events following the murder of Stephen Lawrence

April 22 1993
Stephen Lawrence is stabbed to death in an unprovoked attack by a gang of white youths as he waits at a bus stop in Eltham, south-east London, with his friend Duwayne Brooks.

April 26–30 1993
A surveillance operation on four prime suspects is carried out.

May 4 1993
The Lawrence family complains that the police are not doing enough to catch Stephen's killers.

May 7 1993
Searches are carried out at the homes of brothers Neil and Jamie Acourt, and David Norris and Gary Dobson. Norris is not at home but the Acourt brothers and Dobson are arrested, then released on bail.

May 10 1993
Norris surrenders to the police and is arrested and interviewed.

May 13 1993
Identification parades are done for Neil Acourt, Dobson and Norris. Neil Acourt is identified by Duwayne Brooks as one of the gang responsible. Acourt is charged with the murder of Stephen and the attempted murder of Stacey Benefield a month earlier. Norris is charged with the attempted murder of Benefield.

June 23 1993
Luke Knight is charged with Stephen's murder and remanded in custody.

July 29 1993
Committal proceedings are scheduled for Neil Acourt and Knight but the Crown Prosecution Service formally discontinues the prosecution after a meeting between the CPS and the senior investigating officer.

December 22 1993
The Southwark coroner, Sir Montague Levine, halts an inquest into Stephen's death after the family's barrister, Michael Mansfield QC, says there is 'dramatic' new evidence.

April 16 1994
The CPS says the new evidence is insufficient to support murder charges.

September 1994
The Lawrence family begins a private prosecution against the prime suspects.

April 18 1996
The murder trial begins against Neil Acourt, Knight and Dobson at the central criminal court.

April 25 1996
The case collapses after Mr Justice Curtis rules that identification evidence from Duwayne Brooks is inadmissible. All three are acquitted.

February 13 1997
The inquest into Stephen's death ends and the jury decides he was 'unlawfully killed by five white youths'.

July 31 1997
A judicial inquiry is announced by the Home Secretary.

(Continued)

(Continued)

December 15 1997
A Police Complaints Authority report on the original police investigation of Stephen's murder identifies 'significant weaknesses, omissions and lost opportunities'.

February 24 1999
The Macpherson report is published. It accuses the Metropolitan Police of incompetence and of being institutionally racist.

May 5 2004
The CPS announces there is 'insufficient evidence' to prosecute anyone for Stephen's murder.

April 2005
The double jeopardy legal principle, preventing suspects being tried twice for the same crime, is scrapped.

July 2006
A BBC documentary alleges police corruption in the Lawrence case. It is suggested that Clifford Norris, the gangland father of one of the prime suspects, might have paid the former detective sergeant John Davidson to be kept one step ahead of the investigation.

October 14 2007
The Independent Police Complaints Commission finds no evidence of police corruption and no evidence of dishonest links between Davidson and Clifford Norris.

November 8 2007
Police confirm that they are investigating new forensic evidence in the case.

Source: The *Guardian*, November 8 2007: 1, reprinted with the permission of the Press Association

The post-Macpherson upsurge of interest in the victimisation of ethnic minorities (and indeed in hate crime more broadly) has given rise to an extensive package of reforms that have inexorably shaped police–minority relations during this past decade. As McGhee (2005: 17–18) observes in reference to the impact of these developments:

> ... the impact of this murder and the inquiry can be described as the aperture through which so-called 'hate crimes', and the inadequate policing of them, came to public attention as social problems simultaneously. According to Jenness and Broad (1997), social problems such as hate crime and the discriminatory practices of public institutions in relation to minority groups targeted by hate crime are rarely fully constituted until its victims are made apparent. The Stephen Lawrence murder fits with Jenness and Broad's description of the emergence of a symbolic victim associated with a social problem ...

These events, and the governmental response to them, have given greater public, academic and political prominence to issues of racist victimisation than ever before.[3] Unlike the riots of 1981, the Lawrence case acted as a catalyst for change not only in the context of police–minority relations but also with respect to public attitudes towards issues of 'race', discrimination and racist violence (Bourne, 2001). Consequently, the post-Macpherson era has seen concerted efforts being made to understand, quantify and tackle racist victimisation and the chapter now turns to consider key aspects of this victimisation in more detail.

The scale and scope of racist hate crime

Official interpretations of racist victimisation are invariably informed by the broad definition of a racist incident provided through Recommendation 12 of the Macpherson report which has subsequently been adopted by the police and other criminal justice agencies. According to this definition, a racist incident 'is any incident which is perceived to be racist by the victim or any other person' (Macpherson, 1999: 328). This definition acts as a refinement to that previously used by the police by giving primacy to the interpretation of the victim, as opposed to the judgement of the recording or investigating officer, as was the case with the earlier definition (Clancy et al., 2001). Racism itself is also defined in fairly broad terms in the Macpherson report as consisting of 'conduct or words or practices which disadvantage people because of their colour, culture or ethnic origin' (Macpherson, 1999: 20).

The relatively wide-ranging scope of such definitions is illustrated by the substantial number of racist incidents recorded each year by the police, which had grown from 4,383 in 1985 (when such figures were first collected) to a pre-Macpherson report high of 23,049 in 1999 (Phillips and Bowling, 2002: 583). By 2006 the number of police-recorded racist incidents had risen significantly to 59,071, a rise of 4 per cent from the previous year (Ministry of Justice, 2008). While it cannot be said with any certainty which of a number of factors, such as an actual increase in racist crime, improved reporting and recording practices or the revamped definition of a racist incident, is responsible for the increase in the number of recorded racist incidents, it is well documented that official statistics provide only partial insights into the extent and nature of racist crime on account of the joint problems of under-reporting among ethnic minorities and under-recording by the police (Fitzgerald and Hale, 1996; Bowling, 1999; Webster, 2007). As such, alternative sources of information have been valuable in helping to establish a clearer picture of racist victimisation.

In recent years the picture has been clarified to some extent by the compilation of a further set of statistics. In addition to recording racist incidents, the police are also obliged to record racially and religiously aggravated offences under the penalty enhancement provisions introduced by the Crime and Disorder Act 1998, as amended by the Anti-Terrorism, Crime and Security

Table 2.1   Numbers of racist incidents recorded by police forces in England and Wales between 1999/00 and 2006/07

Year	Number of recorded incidents	Percentage change from previous year
1999/00	47,614	+108[1]
2000/01	52,638	+10.6
2001/02	54,858	+4.2
2002/03	47,810	−12.8
2003/04	53,113	+11.1
2004/05	56,654	+6.7
2005/06	59,071	+4.3
2006/07	61,262	+3.7

1 The substantial rise in the numbers of racist incidents recorded by the police in 1999 is likely to reflect changes practices following the Macpherson report rather than an increase in the number of incidents.
Source: Ministry of Justice (2008: 14)

Act 2001. According to recent published statistics, the police recorded 41,382 racially or religiously aggravated offences in 2006, an increase of 12 per cent from the previous year (Ministry of Justice, 2007). While this source of data provides us with useful supplementary information about the extent of police-recorded racism, it rather crudely conflates racist and religious aggravation despite the important distinctions between the two (as discussed more fully in Chapter 3) and again tells us little about those offences which are not reported to the police.

Successive sweeps of the British Crime Survey (BCS) have facilitated a more detailed examination of the different dimensions of racist victimisation. Recent estimates have suggested that the number of racially motivated incidents taking place in 2006 was approximately 139,000 (Ministry of Justice, 2007), a much larger figure than that recorded by the police in that year (59,071, as noted in Table 2.1). Although this represents a not insignificant fall from the previous year's BCS estimate of 179,000 incidents, it is nonetheless suggestive of high levels of racist victimisation. In this regard, the BCS has been a useful tool not only in charting a more accurate picture of people's experiences and fear of racism, but also in helping to explain the relationship between racist harassment and other forms of victimisation. As Fitzgerald and Hale (1996: 54) found, while only a relatively small proportion of offences against minority ethnic groups are instigated solely on the basis of ethnicity, a substantial number of such offences are likely to have an additional racist element attached to them. Moreover, not only are the most disadvantaged members of visible minority ethnic groups, at least in socio-economic terms, more likely than white people to be the victims of personal offences (ibid: 53; Zedner, 2002: 422), but ethnic minorities have also been found to be at greater risk of personal crime and to have a far greater overall fear of crime than white people (Salisbury and Upson, 2004).

Findings such as those discussed above have gone some way towards highlighting the seriousness of racist crime. However, despite the growing body of research on issues of racism and victimisation, much of this work has arguably failed to account for the particularities of the individual experience (Gilroy, 1990; Garland, Spalek and Chakraborti 2006). Instead, there has been a tendency to bracket together ethnic minorities as one seemingly homogeneous group for whom racism is a problem, thereby dismissing, or at best underplaying, the differences in experience and perception between the persons grouped together within such a framework, or for that matter persons typically excluded from such a framework. This can be the case even where attempts have been made to analyse victimisation by ethnicity, for the influence of various other factors, be they socio-demographic, religious or geographic, may not be sufficiently appreciated.

Consequently, attempts to quantify racist hate crime must be wary of assuming that the patterns and trends identified by a particular study are collectively applicable to all who fall under the umbrella of minority ethnic group 'membership' without acknowledging the differences in individual experiences. Gunaratnam (2003: 28–29) notes below how the research process itself can sometimes merely reproduce dominant conceptions of 'race' and ethnicity as a result of the common tendency to 'essentialise' the experiences and practices of individuals and groups into neat categories:

> A glance through journal articles concerned explicitly with 'race' and ethnicity – nearly always in relation to groups racialised as 'ethnic minorities' – provides numerous examples. There are articles that claim knowledge about 'the perceptions of Pakistani and Bangladeshi people', or 'the needs of the Chinese community', or 'the African experience' where the narratives/experiences of some individuals are used to represent all of those in the racial/ethnic category, erasing differences within the categories.

An appreciation of the broader dimensions of racist hate crime is also necessary in recognising the experiences of groups who can often be overlooked by researchers and policy-makers. The experiences of mixed-race families and relationships are a case in point, with what little research evidence there is suggesting that those from a mixed-heritage background face a markedly higher risk of crime in comparison to all other groups (Salisbury and Upson, 2004) and that white partners in mixed-race relationships face a real, but seldom recognised, risk of being the recipient of racist abuse (see, for example, Bowling, 1999; Garland et al., 2006). Studies have also tended to overlook the particular issues facing people of mixed heritage, whose ethnicity has been found to pose problems in terms of confusing perceptions of belonging and challenging apparently established boundaries of 'race', identity, custom and religion (Olumide, 2002; Tizard and Phoenix, 2002).

The experiences of groups such as Gypsies and Travellers have also remained largely obscured from mainstream enquiry. Though Gypsies have formally been recognised as a distinct ethnic group,[4] they have been subjected to a considerable amount of restrictive legislation from as far back as the sixteenth century designed to control their presence and activities. Meanwhile, different groups of Travellers, whose very identities are often homogenised within the general category of 'Gypsy' despite their differences in ethnicity and cultural identity, have tended to be regarded with fear and suspicion rather than as 'normal' people living an alternative lifestyle to much of the population. Interestingly, though, research has highlighted how abusive language and behaviour directed towards these groups is not always equated directly with racism *per se*, in the way that such acts towards other 'recognised' minority ethnic groups would be (Hester, 1999; James, 2007).

Clearly, then, it is not just visible minorities who can fall victim to racist hate. Indeed, while BCS data suggest that prima-facie white people face the lowest risk of racially motivated victimisation among all ethnic groups, this data does not disaggregate groups according to age, area of residence or social class (Webster, 2007: 83–84). Racism experienced within white working-class communities has received relatively little academic attention and may be an especially fruitful area of study for researchers, particularly as this is likely to have a quite different qualitative dimension from that experienced by visible minority ethnic groups. The failure to recognise prejudice directed towards 'undesirable forms of whiteness' (Neal, 2002) is also evident in the case of asylum seekers and Eastern European migrant workers. Despite hopes for a greater anti-racist consensus across society in the aftermath of the Stephen Lawrence report, issues of asylum and immigration have provided a vivid illustration of popular racism. Since the late 1990s press hysteria has generated a succession of headlines warning against the supposed dangers of allowing asylum seekers to enter the country, which has triggered increasingly punitive government responses restricting the entry, freedom and public acceptance of the asylum seeker (McGhee, 2006). Similarly, following the expansion of the European Union on 1 May 2004, the sizeable migration of workers from Eastern Europe has reignited age-old debates about Britain's allegedly 'soft' immigration policies and the supposed erosion of national identity (Hudson et al., 2007).

Inevitably, the continued political and media preoccupation with these issues has helped to foster an environment in which increasingly hostile and prejudicial sentiments are allowed to prosper, but at the same time the notion of Britain being a tolerant, 'anti-racist' society remains largely unchallenged within popular thought. Kundnani (2001: 50) uses the distinction between racism and xenophobia to suggest how such a situation has arisen:

> ... whereas racism denotes a social process of exclusion based on colour (or, latterly cultural) difference, xenophobia suggests a natural psychological reaction against 'strangers'. The first is an indictment of a social system, the second taken to be a normal part of human nature. Hence it appears that those who propound the view that 'too many are coming' are not racists to be cast out of the political mainstream – they are merely fearful of the impact that large numbers of new arrivals will have on the

nation, and that is considered a legitimate political viewpoint. As such, xenophobia provides an alibi for racism, legitimating it by making it seem natural.

Therefore, through the guise of adopting a xenophobic, as opposed to overtly racist, stance towards groups such as asylum seekers and migrant workers, popular discourse can maintain the hegemonic state of affairs that perpetuates the 'othering', and in some instances criminalisation, of particular 'undesirables'. Not surprisingly, the considerable suffering experienced by asylum seekers and economic migrants that results from ongoing moral panics has tended to receive little mainstream public or political sympathy, and yet it seems perverse not to recognise this process of demonisation as a form of racist hate. A broad and sufficiently inclusive conceptualisation of what racist hate entails is therefore all the more important in the context of this book to capture the experiences of those who can find themselves excluded from the narrow framework often employed in such debates.

Legal protection from racist hate crime

Given the complex nature of racism and wide range of potential targets of racist hate crime, the establishment of suitably robust legal protection is an important way of demonstrating society's condemnation of racism and offering support to victims. As intimated above, the main impetus for legislative change was the murder of Stephen Lawrence in 1993, itself the third killing in a sequence of racist attacks committed in the area of south-east London,[5] and the subsequent inquiry and report into the circumstances which led to that murder. The Macpherson report, published in 1999, was hailed as a watershed in British race relations, not least for placing the issue of racist crime high upon the agenda for criminal justice, political and other organisations by officially recognising the problem of 'institutional racism', for broadening the definition of a 'racist incident', and for supposedly leading the way for a more victim-oriented approach to dealing with racist incidents (Bridges, 2001; Burney and Rose, 2002).

Legal recognition of the seriousness of racist crime is evident in the changes introduced by the Crime and Disorder Act 1998, which established a series of new 'racially aggravated' offences structured on the basis of existing offences of violence, criminal damage, public order and harassment. Under section 28 of that Act offences are classed as racially aggravated if:

> at the time of committing the offence, or immediately before or after doing so, the offender demonstrates towards the victim of the offence hostility based on the victim's membership (or presumed membership) of a racial group; or the offence is motivated (wholly or partly) by hostility towards members of a racial group based on their membership of that group.

This definition of racial aggravation essentially relates to hostility based upon ethnicity which the prosecution must show to have been present in the immediate context of the basic offence (Burney, 2002: 105), with the result being the imposition of an enhanced sentence if the aggravated element can be proved. A 'racial group' under the 1998 Act refers to persons defined by reference to their race, colour, nationality or ethnic or national origins, and now, following the amendment introduced by section 39 of the Anti-Terrorism, Crime and Security Act 2001, section 28(3) covers membership of any religious group. Similar provisions on racial aggravation are available in Scotland under section 50 of the Criminal Law (Consolidation) (Scotland) Act 1995.

Further post-Lawrence legislative protection against racism can be found in the Race Relations (Amendment) Act 2000. Hailed at the time as the most significant post-Macpherson piece of anti-discrimination legislation (Bowling and Phillips, 2002; Bhavani et al., 2005), this Act was designed to outlaw direct and indirect racist discrimination in all public bodies not covered by the Race Relations Act 1976, including the police, prisons and the immigration service, by obliging organisations to proactively work towards eliminating unlawful discrimination and promoting equality of opportunity between persons of different ethnic groups.[6] Moreover, it should be noted that legislation addressing the promotion of racial hatred existed long before the Stephen Lawrence case in the form of the Race Relations Acts of 1965 and 1976, and more recently the Public Order Act 1986. Section 17 of the Public Order Act prohibits the use of words or behaviour which is 'threatening, abusive or insulting' and which is either intended 'to stir up racial hatred' or where 'having regard to all the circumstances racial hatred is likely to be stirred up thereby'. More recent provisions governing the incitement of religious hatred have been introduced under the Racial and Religious Hatred Act 2006, and will be the subject of closer scrutiny in Chapter 3.

Undoubtedly, changes to the law such as those described above have signified the government's desire to enshrine anti-racist principles within its legislative framework. However well intentioned these changes may have been though, there is evidence to suggest that some of the legislation may be not be having the effect that was originally intended. For instance, Burney (2002) has suggested that one of the major implications of the two-tier structure for demonstrating racial aggravation in the Crime and Disorder Act is its propensity to lead to guilty pleas for the basic offence, as opposed to establishing the added racist dimension evident in many crimes committed against members of minority ethnic groups. As Burney puts it, '... people will plead guilty to ordinary offences that they would probably have contested, for fear of a heavier sentence for a racist crime and of being labelled a "racist"' (2002: 106).

Bowling and Phillips (2002: 121) have also identified another potential concern relating to the imposition of harsher penalties for racially aggravated offences, namely that it could provoke a 'white racist backlash' among those who believe that minorities receive preferential treatment. While in reality there may not have been a 'backlash' as such in the years that have passed since the introduction of these laws, Dixon and Gadd's (2006: 311) research into the impact of the Crime and Disorder Act provisions has led them to conclude that the introduction of laws on racial aggravation 'may encourage those involved in this type of offending to believe that they are not so much hate crime perpetrators as the unfortunate victims of law enforcement agencies biased in favour of minority ethnic groups'. The resentment that can exist among majority communities as a result of additional legislative protection afforded to minority communities is an issue relevant not just to 'race' legislation but to hate crime laws in general and will be examined further during the course of this book.

Further problems have been identified with that Act with regard to its wording and implementation. For example, section 28 defines racial aggravation essentially in terms of hostility based on ethnicity, and one of the key advantages of using a broad term such as 'hostility' is that it enables a wider range of prejudices to be taken into account. Indeed, in noting that only 41 cases involving the incitement of racial hatred were brought for prosecution between 1990 and 1997 under the Public Order Act 1986, Hall (2005a: 123) highlights the limited effectiveness of that Act and in particular the overly restrictive nature of the word 'hatred' for the purposes of prosecution when compared to the flexibility of 'hostility' (see also Iganski, 1999). At the same time, though, no attempt is made within the Crime and Disorder Act to explain what 'hostility' actually entails, thereby rendering the boundaries of unacceptable behaviour ambiguous, notwithstanding its establishment through case law.

This ambiguity has left open the possibility that the Crime and Disorder Act could be casting its net of racist aggravation too wide by capturing a different type of offender from that originally envisaged through the creation of aggravation laws. Dixon and Gadd (2006), for instance, suggest that convictions for racially aggravated offences are not necessarily reliable indicators of racist attitudes, noting that some of whom they felt to be the least racist interviewees among their sample of perpetrators had prior convictions for racially aggravated crimes whereas some of the most racist had none. Similarly, for commentators such as Burney (2002) and Jacobs and Potter (1998), aggravation provisions – if interpreted literally – run the risk of capturing low-level, superficial expressions of racism and not deep-seated ideological hatred, while Bourne (2002) has expressed related concerns over the paucity of racially aggravated crimes brought to court by the Crown Prosecution Service because of the difficulties associated with proving the subjective element of racial motivation.

Other attempts to address racism have also been subjected to criticism. For example, despite the widespread praise received for the Macpherson report's recognition of institutional racism, it has been suggested that such a focus has allowed individuals to hide their own culpable racist behaviour behind the collective failings of a particular organisation (Bridges, 2001: 62), an assertion that has been lent further credence through the continuing debates about racism in the police force (see, for example, Ahmed and Bright, 2003; Fresco and O'Neill, 2008). Meanwhile, Bhavani et al. (2005: 75–76) have cast doubt over the impact of the amended Race Relations legislation by referring to the minimal progress made within organisations beyond the drafting of policies and action plans, and to the distinct lack of empirical evidence showing any real change to the social and discursive practices of racism following the 2000 Act. What little evidence there is on the impact of this Act points to institutional uncertainty over the integration of equality and diversity into service delivery (Office of the Deputy Prime Minister, 2003), organisations failing to implement their race equality obligations (Commission for Racial Equality, 2003), and an absence of race equality monitoring (Mills, 2002).

Therefore, although a number of steps have been taken in recent times to address problems of racism by strengthening the available legal protection, the reality is that members of minority ethnic groups may actually conclude, quite legitimately in many respects, that they face no lesser risk of, and no greater protection from, victimisation than before (Bowling and Phillips, 2002: 110). Research has indicated that such groups face a greater risk of being the victim of certain crimes, are more likely to perceive a racist dimension in the crimes that they experience and have concerns about the equitable operation of the criminal justice system (Clancy et al., 2001; Chakraborti and Garland, 2003). These factors will inevitably undermine the potential impact of any legal protection against racism. Notwithstanding the limitations of the existing legislative provisions, however, we should not underestimate the important declaratory role performed by this combined mass of legislation. This point is neatly articulated by McGhee (2005: 29) in reference to the racially aggravated provisions introduced by the Crime and Disorder Act 1998:

> This legislation also performs a symbolic role in attempting to modify or correct undesirable behaviour in society not only in the name of greater protection for certain groups who are 'injured' by hate, but also in the name of protecting wider society from the negative impacts of a hate incident in the form of institutional mistrust, and the potential polarization between social groups. The legislation also emphasizes the destructive and often marginalizing impact of hate crimes such as racist incidents on the victim, family, neighbourhood, community and ultimately the nation.

Through highlighting the symbolic importance of the laws on racial aggravation, McGhee makes reference here to one of the central justifications for hate crime laws in general: namely, that the higher sentences awarded to their perpetrators are an important way of denoting society's condemnation of such crimes, preventing future attacks upon the individual victim and their broader community, and protecting society at large from the destructive elements associated with the commission of hate crimes. Such sentences are therefore seen as justifiable on moral, utilitarian and consequentialist grounds (see also Bowling and Phillips, 2002: 121). At the same time this line of argument has been contested by critics of hate crime laws. Dixon and Gadd (2006: 324), for example, have cast doubt over the capacity of the racial aggravation provisions to deliver a symbolic message without unnecessarily criminalising significant numbers of already marginalised people whose 'racism' has surfaced not from a commitment to racist beliefs or ideology, but through an inability to control language in moments of stress and/or inebriation. Debates over the effectiveness or otherwise of hate crime legislation in terms of their declaratory and deterrent impact have been a central theme in academic discourse on hate crime (see, for instance, Jacobs and Potter, 1998; Iganski, 2002; Perry, 2002) and they shall be explored more extensively later in the book.

Conclusion

This chapter has limited its analysis to key areas of debate which have implications for our understanding of hate crime more broadly. While there has been welcome progress made in the field of race relations in the UK, there remain grounds for concern in a number of contexts. Following an initial examination of the emergence of 'race' as an issue of political and criminological significance, the chapter went on to discuss the scope of racist hate and suggested that official accounts paint an incomplete picture of the true extent and nature of this problem. It was argued that some groups' experiences can be overlooked as a result of oversimplified attempts to quantify racist hate crime and through the narrow frameworks and terms of reference used by researchers and policy-makers. This chapter has also drawn attention to some of the problems inherent to legislative provisions covering racist hate which have impacted upon the potential effectiveness of these laws.

In some respects, much of the difficulty surrounding the provision of legal protection stems from the continued reliance on 'incidents' as a means of distinguishing racist behaviour, which detaches the lived experience from its wider context of racism and racist exclusion (Bowling, 1999: 286). Such an incident-driven approach fails to appreciate the impact of racism on victims' lives beyond the actual incident itself, and goes some way towards explaining why victims can feel unprotected despite apparent improvements in policy, as suggested by Bowling (1999: 285) in his analysis of violent racism:

> Becoming a victim of any crime – particularly one as complex as violent racism – does not occur in an instant or in a physical or ideological vacuum. Victimisation – with the emphasis on the suffix 'isation' – denotes a dynamic process, occurring over time. It describes how an individual becomes a victim within a specific social, political, and historical context.

For Bowling, recorded crime statistics provide an unreliable measure of actual experiences of racism in their misconceived attempt to count so many complex events occurring over time and space. Rather than working to this narrow conception, Bowling has advocated a similar stance to that proposed by Kelly (1987) in her research into women's experiences of sexual violence, which sees victimisation as a continuum where the commonplace forms of this abuse can be connected with the more extreme acts of violence. Understanding the process, as opposed to simply the singular event, of racist victimisation requires an examination of the lived experiences of those affected, including the nature, extent and impact of racist behaviour, the wider context that gives rise to different forms of racism and the effectiveness of support provision for victims. It also requires an understanding of the routine, everyday nature of many experiences of racism; experiences which in themselves may not appear especially serious but which cumulatively, and when considered in the context of repeat victimisation and broader patterns of 'othering', can impact upon the victim (and their community) in a variety of corrosive ways, be it as Spalek (2006: 68) describes 'psychologically, emotionally, behaviourally, financially and physically' (see also Chahal and Julienne, 1999).

For instance, in their studies of rural racism, the authors of this book found that 'low-level' forms of racist harassment were reported to be commonplace by the vast majority of their minority ethnic research participants and formed part of a continuum of incidents that were a constant feature of day-to-day life, reflecting patterns of racist harassment noted in other contexts (Garland and Chakraborti, 2006b; see also Bowling, 1999; Rowe, 2004). While disturbing incidents of 'high-level' racism were also reported by minority ethnic participants, including physical assault and attempted petrol bombing, it was the cumulative 'drip-drip' effect of so-called 'low-level' incidents – examples of which included verbal abuse, unnecessary or persistent staring, the throwing of eggs or stones, 'knock-down ginger', the blocking of driveways with cars, being sprayed with air freshener and being the subject of racist 'humour' – which caused the greatest degree of concern to rural minority ethnic households despite this seldom being recognised as racist behaviour by other members of local communities or by agencies and policy-makers.

Recognising the significance of these more mundane experiences of racism raises important questions over the legitimacy, or otherwise, of the term 'hate' as a collective descriptor of such offences. As we saw in the previous chapter, while the term more often than not evokes graphic images of high-profile crimes, in reality the nature of racist victimisation, and indeed most hate crime victimisation, is rather less dramatic than the terminology suggests. At the same time, the process of racism does correspond with the framework of hierarchy and oppression associated with some of the leading academic constructions of hate crime offered in Chapter 1. For instance, for writers such as Essed (1991) the integration of racism into the fabric of everyday practices are reflective of underlying power relations in society, whereby the othering of ethnic minorities on the basis of their skin colour is embedded within our consciousness and incorporated into the way in which people live their day-to-day lives. The implications of this normalisation of prejudice in terms of our understanding of hate crime will be further explored in later chapters.

Guide to further reading

The body of literature on racist hate and victimisation is sizable, particularly when compared with the availability of texts on other forms of hate crime. For an insightful discussion of the historical development of race relations in the UK readers should refer to Hiro, *Black British, White British* (1992), Bowling and Phillips, *Racism, Crime and Justice* (2002) and Webster, *Understanding Race and Crime* (2007). The latter two books also provide comprehensive accounts of the relationship between 'race' and crime and the criminal justice response to racist crime. Hall et al.'s classic text *Policing the Crisis* (1978) has influenced our understanding of racist stereotyping and criminalisation while Bowling, *Violent Racism* (1999) remains a seminal text on core aspects of racist victimisation.

Notes

1   In excess of 121,000 former Polish soldiers came to the UK with their families following the 1947 Polish Resettlement Act, and these numbers were augmented by the arrival of 24,000 German, Ukrainian and Italian former prisoners of war and over 25,000 other immigrants (Somerville, 2007)
2   The riots of September 1985 in Handsworth resulted in the deaths of two Asian men, injuries to 74 officers and 35 locals and just under 300 arrests. A month later the death of a black woman during a police raid on her home triggered the disturbances on the Broadwater Farm estate in north London during which more than 250 people were injured and a police officer PC Keith Blakelock was fatally stabbed.
3   The Macpherson report was published in 1999 and produced 70 recommendations designed to reform relationships between the police and minority ethnic communities. There are a number of excellent texts that discuss the implications of the Macpherson report in greater depth than is possible in this chapter, as indicated within the guide for further reading.
4   As upheld in the case of Commission for Racial Equality v. Dutton (1989) 2 WLR 17.
5   The two high-profile racist murders to have occurred in south-east London prior to the death of Stephen Lawrence involved the killings of Rolan Adams in 1991 and Rohit Duggal in 1992.
6   Anti-discrimination legislation has since been bolstered through the introduction of a Single Equality Bill.

3

RELIGIOUSLY MOTIVATED HATE CRIME

---------------------------------- **Chapter summary** ----------------------------------

Since the turn of the millennium an increased focus has been placed upon the issue of religious identity in the UK, and with this has come greater scrutiny over the extent to which particular religious values and practices are compatible with constructions of British national identity. Although this growth in attention has in some respects been constructive in promoting an enhanced awareness of religious diversity and distinctions between religious and ethnic identity, it has also had rather more negative implications for faith communities targeted on the basis of their religious beliefs.

To begin with this chapter examines the relevance of religion to British criminology and discusses events which have seen religiously motivated hate crime emerge as a source of academic and political concern. As we shall see, the levels of legal protection available to defend faith communities from attacks upon their religious identity has increased significantly over the past decade, and the chapter also seeks to explore the underlying factors behind the introduction of this legislation. In so doing, attention is given to two particular examples of religious intolerance – Islamophobia and antisemitism – by way of illustrating the escalating problem of religiously motivated hate crime, before the chapter draws its analysis to a close by exploring the controversies surrounding the most recently enacted piece of hate crime legislation, the Racial and Religious Hatred Act 2006.

---------------------------------- **Introduction** ----------------------------------

Faith-related issues have assumed greater salience to social scientists in recent years. While such issues may in the past have been overshadowed by the propensity to focus predominantly, and sometimes exclusively, upon 'race' and ethnic identity, events over the past decade or so have seen religion now occupy a much more significant role within political and academic thought. In an age in which the terrorist attacks of September 11 2001 in the USA and July 7 2005 in the UK loom large in the British public's imagination, discussions of the activities of radical Islamic terrorists have overshadowed analysis of other conflicts, such as that within Northern Ireland, which have been driven in whole or part by religious affiliation. Religion was by no means the sole driving factor behind the 'complicated and multi-faceted phenomenon' of sectarianism in Northern Ireland (Cramphorn, 2002: 13), and for this reason sectarianism is not discussed at length in this particular chapter. Nevertheless, religiously-motivated prejudice did play a key part in the conflict in Northern Ireland, and this is discussed in Case Study 3.1.

Case study 3.1: The Troubles

The 30 year period of violence in Northern Ireland between the late 1960s and the late 1990s is generally known as the 'Troubles'. These three decades were characterised by sectarian intimidation, violence and murder by nationalists who wished to create an independent, united Ireland, and loyalists who wanted to maintain the status quo. Over 3,500 people were killed during the Troubles, and many thousands more injured. Many of the atrocities were committed by paramilitary groups such as the Provisional Irish Republican Army (PIRA) and the Ulster Volunteer Force who felt that violence was the only route by which they could achieve their goals (English, 2003).

The historical roots of the Troubles are significant, as perceived injustices within the republican (mainly Catholic) and loyalist (mainly Protestant) communities over events that occurred hundreds of years ago impacted upon the escalation of violence at the end of the 1960s and beginning of the 1970s. In addition, the Government of Ireland Act 1920, which partitioned the island of Ireland into Southern Ireland (with a majority Catholic population) and Northern Ireland (with a majority of Protestants), was bitterly resented by the outnumbered and disadvantaged minority Catholic community in the north. Loyalist paramilitary activity in the mid-1960s provided the catalyst for outpourings of Catholic anger that manifested themselves in ferocious rioting, and confrontation between those communities and the Royal Ulster Constabulary and British troops. This period also saw the formation of the PIRA (English, 2003).

At the same time though, the relevance of religious prejudice to the Troubles should not be underestimated. Cramphorn (2002), for instance, suggests that some Protestant paramilitary groups justified their violence by citing religious scriptures and viewed Catholics as the anti-Christ, while Collins (with McGovern, 1997) acknowledges the influence of Catholicism within the nationalist movement. However, the latter describes the growth of a radical Marxist element within the PIRA in the 1970s, and intense Irish nationalism and Ulster loyalism were also vital in fuelling community division, hostility and violence. Therefore, the Troubles can be seen to have been driven by a host of factors flavoured by extreme left-wing politics, national identity, feelings of anger and bitterness generated by perceived and actual injustice, the legacy of historical incidents, and intense identification with particular religious and ethnic community identities.

(Continued)

(Continued)

While the signing of the Good Friday Agreement in April 1998 marked the beginning of the end of the Troubles, some have suggested that sectarian divisions have in fact become more entrenched since the start of the peace process (Ellison 2002; Jarman, 2005); indeed, recent estimates indicate that sectarian hate crime accounts for over half of all hate crimes recorded by the Police Service of Northern Ireland (CJINI, 2007: 9). Thus, even though the cultural and social isolation of Northern Ireland during the Troubles may now be disappearing, the resultant diversification of the population has been accompanied by a rise in racist, religious and homophobic hate crimes (see Chapter six).

In the post 9/11 climate religious identification – and specifically the extent to which such identification is reconcilable with the secular values associated with contemporary national identity – has been the source of extensive conjecture. This has given rise to what Hunt (2005: 123–124) describes as a perceived clash of cultures between the visibility of faiths and the values of a secular culture, as evidenced, for instance, through disputes over faith schools, religious dress and custom and intra-faith attitudes towards gender and sexuality. In terms of criminological literature, researchers' propensity to view diversity through an ethnic lens may have resulted in the marginalisation of religious affiliation and in us overlooking important divisions within ethnic communities. For instance, use of the secular term Asian to describe people from the Indian subcontinent can overshadow the differences in history, perception and experience between the Hindu, Sikh or Muslim faiths, while Caribbean communities are often divided by their respective loyalties to various Christian traditions (Hunt, 2005; Spalek, 2008).

Distinguishing religious from ethnic identity is all the more important within a plurally constituted society such as the UK. The increased social significance of religious identity in this country is illustrated by the inclusion for the first time of a question about religion in the 2001 Census, and this has highlighted the broad range of different faith communities based within the UK. As can be seen in Table 3.1, Christianity is the most common religious affiliation in Britain by a considerable distance, with 71.8 per cent of the population declaring themselves to be Christian. Islam is the next most common religion with 2.8 per cent describing themselves as Muslim, while the Hindu and Sikh faiths are followed by 1 per cent and 0.6 per cent respectively (Office for National Statistics, 2006). This picture, however, may change quite dramatically in the future. According to recent estimates published by Christian Research, the number of active churchgoers is expected to decline by 2050 to a little under 900,000 whereas the active Hindu population is predicted to climb to around 855,000 and the active Muslim population to as high a number as 2,660,000 (Gledhill, 2008). Although these forecasts are based solely on an analysis of membership and attendance of religious bodies

Table 3.1   Population of Great Britain by religious group

Religion	Numbers	Percentage
Christian	41,014,811	71.8
Buddhist	149,157	0.3
Hindu	558,342	1.0
Jewish	267,373	0.5
Muslim	1,588,890[1]	2.8
Sikh	336,179	0.6
Any other religion	159,167	0.3
No religion	8,596,488	15.1
Religion not stated	4,433,520	7.8
All groups	*57,103,927*	*100*

1 In April 2008, Home Secretary Jacqui Smith disclosed that revised government estimates put the total Muslim population at around 2 million (Travis, 2008).

Source: Office for National Statistics (2006)
Note: Due to percentages being rounded up to the nearest decimal point the overall percentage figure totals 100.2

and therefore present only a partial picture of religious affiliation, they help to illustrate the evolving nature of religious practice within the UK.

Moreover, further analysis of the Census data in terms of the geographic distribution of faith communities conducted by Furbey et al. (2006) has revealed a varied picture with regards to the extent to which people of different faiths interrelate. For those authors, the data point to a significant degree of neighbourhood separation between different faith communities and a risk of these communities leading 'parallel lives' within local neighbourhoods, a finding which chimes with the fears raised by Trevor Phillips in 2008 (speaking in his capacity as head of the Equality and Human Rights Commission) that there existed a 'cold war' between Britain's different minority communities due to their inability or reluctance to interact with others of different faiths and ethnicities (*BBC News*, 2008a). These kinds of concerns relating to a perceived lack of inter-faith connectivity, together with the heightened tensions surrounding debates over religious ideology, citizenship and extremism, have inevitably placed greater scrutiny upon members of faith communities, and in particular British Muslims, as shall be discussed shortly.

Legal protection from 'faith-hate'

With faith being such a central, and in many instances *defining*, feature of people's self-identity, the need for effective legislative protection against attacks upon religious identity is clearly extremely important. Until relatively recently the main source of protection for faith groups in the UK could be found in the blasphemy provisions of the Criminal Libel Act 1819. To quote McGhee (2005: 96), these provisions preclude 'the publication of contemptuous, reviling, scurrilous or ludicrous matter relating to God as defined by the Christian religion, Jesus, the Bible or the Book of Common Prayer, intending to wound the feelings of Christians or to excite contempt and hatred against the Church of England or promote immorality'. However, while these provisions cover the Christian faith, they do not extend to those from other religious denominations. As such, the blasphemy laws of 1819 have limited relevance to today's multi-faith society, nor do they offer explicit protection against the incitement of religious hatred directed towards faith communities, Anglican or non-Anglican, or against any harassment, violence or criminal damage to property that accrues from such incitement (Forum Against Islamophobia and Racism, 2002: 12).

With respect to more recent legislation offering protection to faith groups, the Public Order Act 1986 and the Crime and Disorder Act 1998 have some relevance with, respectively, their incitement to racial hatred and racially aggravated provisions. Though these Acts were designed to cover ethnicity and not religious identity *per se* in line with the definition of a racial group under the Race Relations Act 1976 (which refers to race, colour, nationality and national or ethnic origin), case law has extended the scope of this definition to include religious groups commonly described as mono-ethnic, such as the Sikh and Jewish communities; communities whose membership, it is argued, has historically been drawn from just one cultural group (McGhee, 2005). Consequently, the framing of a racial group within both civil anti-discrimination legislation and criminal law created a significant distinction between the level of protection afforded to different faith groups, a point noted by the Forum Against Islamophobia and Racism (2002: 10), which described this distinction as 'an iniquitous anomaly in the law producing a hierarchy of protected faith communities'.

To some extent the Anti-Terrorism, Crime and Security Act 2001 helped to address the anomaly referred to above through the introduction of new religiously aggravated offences. Though this Act is arguably more renowned for its counter-terrorism measures, its creation of sentence enhancement provisions on the grounds of religious aggravation presents faith communities with similar levels of protection to those extended to ethnic groups under the racial aggravation provisions of the Crime and Disorder Act 1998. Under the 2001 Act therefore, the provisions of the Crime and Disorder Act are extended to all faith groups, allowing the courts to impose higher penalties in cases of harassment, violence or criminal damage to property motivated by religious hatred or where there is evidence of the additional element of religious-based animosity in connection with the offence. Moreover, section 153 of the Powers of Criminal Courts (Sentencing) Act 2000 obliges courts to consider evidence of racial or religious hostility as aggravating factors when deciding the sentence for any offence, and not just those specified within the Crime and Disorder Act.

In terms of sheer numbers very few prosecutions have been brought under the religious aggravation legislation, particularly in comparison to the equivalent number of prosecutions brought under the racial aggravation provisions.[1] According to Crown Prosecution Service (CPS) figures for 2006/07, religiously aggravated cases fell by approximately 37 per cent from the previous year with as few as 27 defendants received, whereas prosecutions for racially aggravated offences rose by 23 per cent with 9,145 defendants received. Of these 27 cases, it would appear that the majority of known victims were Muslim, although the victim's actual or perceived religious identity was unknown in four cases. In the 23 known cases, 17 victims were identified as Muslim, three as Christian, two as Jewish and one as Sikh (CPS, 2007a).

While the introduction of religiously aggravated provisions brought the protection available for faith communities in line with that provided to ethnic groups in one respect, measures on incitement to religious hatred were ultimately dropped prior to the passing of the 2001 Act, leaving faith groups, and particularly British Muslims, unprotected in this regard during what has since been recognised as an especially anti-Islamic period in British history (McGhee, 2005: 102). The incitement laws have since been revisited and incitement to religious hatred is now an offence under the Racial and Religious Hatred Act 2006. However, the controversies surrounding the passing of this legislation have significant implications for our understanding of religious hatred and will be explored in more depth later in this chapter.

This statutory recognition of the offence of incitement to religious hatred follows an especially fractious period of debate on the issue. In particular, the events of February 2006, a month described by Bunting (2006) as a *mensis horribilis* for British Muslims, provide a stark illustration of the way in which faith-hate has attracted unprecedented attention in recent years. During this month an extraordinary series of contemporaneous but coincidental stories centring around aspects of religion hit the news headlines and served to intensify post-9/11 and -7/7 tensions surrounding the relationship between religious identity and secular 'British' values (Chakraborti, 2007). The first of these news stories revolved around the rejection of the government's renewed attempts to create a new offence of incitement to religious hatred through 'abusive' or 'insulting' behaviour. These proposals were defeated by just one vote in the House of Commons, and in their place the decision was taken to approve House of Lords amendments restricting the applicability of these provisions to only 'threatening' behaviour. It is not entirely clear which of a variety of factors made this story especially newsworthy at the time – the contentious nature of the legislation in the eyes of the media, the narrow margin of the defeat or the illustration of governmental fallibility at a time in which other areas of policy-making by the Labour administration and its leadership were proving to be distinctly unpopular – but the limiting of the incitement provisions received considerable, and broadly favourable, media coverage.

Meanwhile, the debate between freedom of expression and protection of religious sensibilities, central to arguments put forward by supporters and opponents of the government's incitement proposals, was intensified only a few days after the defeat of these proposals by worldwide protests against the publication of satirical cartoons in a Danish newspaper depicting the prophet Muhammad in a variety of 'terrorist' guises (see Case Study 3.2). Though these cartoons were widely condemned as being offensive to the Islamic faith, their publication raised questions over the legitimacy or otherwise of repressing opinions, however insulting and repellent, while the nature of subsequent Muslim protests against the cartoons – which in some instances took the form of violent demonstrations and visible support for future suicide bombings in the West – served to reinforce stereotypes about the over-sensitivity of Muslim communities and the suspected incompatibility of Muslim and non-Muslim values (Joseph, 2006).

Case Study 3.2: The Danish cartoon affair

On September 30 2005 the conservative Danish newspaper *Jyllands-Posten* published 12 caricatures of the prophet Muhammad in what the paper described as an attempt to contribute to the debate regarding criticism of Islam and self-censorship. Despite, or arguably because of, the opposition in Islamic law to any portrayal of the prophet, even favourable, for fear it could lead to idolatry, *Jyllands-Posten*, Denmark's largest-selling broadsheet newspaper, used a series of cartoons to depict Muhammad, with the most offensive portraying the prophet carrying a bomb (replete with lit fuse) in his turban. The initial publication of the cartoons resulted in a series of protests by Muslim groups in Denmark but had relatively little impact outside that country until the cartoons were reprinted in newspapers in other countries. The cartoons first resurfaced in January 2006 within a Norwegian newspaper, and by the following month publications based in France, Germany, Italy, Spain, the USA and the Netherlands had decided to publish some or all of the cartoons, with publishers in Argentina, Australia, Canada, Costa Rica, Honduras, India, Ireland, New Zealand and South Korea soon following suit (Hansen, 2006).

The reprinting of the cartoons triggered a furious reaction from Muslims across the world. The ensuing protests were particularly heated across the Middle East and other predominantly Muslim countries, and included boycotts of Danish products, the burning of Danish flags and effigies of the Danish Prime Minister, and increasingly violent clashes between demonstrators and police authorities outside European embassies. Even after the issuing of a statement of apology to the 'honourable citizens of the Muslim world' by the editor-in-chief of the *Jyllands-Posten* on January 30, the violence showed little sign of abating. In some countries Muslim protests took the form of retaliatory violence against other faiths, including the burning of Christian churches in Pakistan and the publication of images satirising the Holocaust in Iran's best-selling newspaper, while in the West hundreds of thousands of demonstrators continued to rally against the perceived demonisation of Islam. Ultimately, as many as 140 people are known to have died as a result of the violence which followed the publication of the satirical cartoons (Hansen, 2006).

Debates surrounding the cartoons and their legitimacy centred essentially around the principles of freedom of expression and the protection of religious sensibilities. Many have supported the right (if not necessarily the decision) of *Jyllands-Posten* to publish the cartoons on the grounds of freedom of expression, while those outraged by the cartoons' publication have tended to base their arguments around the Islamophobic intent behind the depiction of Muhammad and the capacity of the cartoons to incite religious hatred. Although the furore has since subsided, events related to the cartoons' publication have continued to make the news. In 2007, two British Muslim protesters were found guilty of soliciting murder (with one also convicted for inciting racial hatred) following their behaviour at a demonstration in London during February 2006 and use of inflammatory placards calling for future acts of terrorism against the West, while several young Muslims were convicted in Denmark of planning terrorist attacks partially in protest at the cartoons. Also in 2007, cases brought against *Jyllands-Posten* and the Paris-based newspaper *Charlie-Hebdo* were rejected respectively by a Danish and French court, which both ruled that there was insufficient proof that the publication of the cartoons in each newspaper was intended to be insulting to Muslims. Meanwhile in February 2008 a number of Danish newspapers reprinted the cartoon depiction of the prophet Muhammad wearing a turban shaped like a bomb as a way of reiterating their commitment to free speech following the arrest a day previously of three people for allegedly planning to kill the man who drew the original cartoons (Popham, 2008).

These issues stayed in the spotlight following the conviction later that month of Abu Hamza al Masri, the radical Muslim cleric. Viewed in many quarters as the epitome of Islamist extremism in Britain (Campbell, Dodd and Branigan, 2006), his conviction on 11 out of 15 charges of soliciting murder and inciting racial hatred was widely welcomed by both non-Muslims and Muslims alike, although accusations of double standards did emanate from within some Muslim communities when drawing comparisons between the verdict reached in the Hamza trial and the different outcome of another racial hatred trial which had reached a conclusion only a few days earlier. In this trial Nick Griffin, leader of the British National Party (BNP) and his co-defendant and fellow BNP member Mark Collett, walked free from court having been partially acquitted of incitement to racial hatred charges,[2] despite having been filmed by an undercover BBC documentary team making openly inflammatory remarks about Muslims and the Islamic faith in speeches during the build-up to local and European elections in West Yorkshire. The overlapping timing of these two high-profile trials, together with the headlines generated by the Danish cartoon affair and the government's defeat in the Commons, gave even greater focus to the contentious nature of the incitement debate, and fuelled British Muslims' concerns over the ambiguous, and in some respects contradictory, legal provisions governing the 'preaching of hate' (Bunting, 2006). This chapter has already alluded to the heightened scrutiny directed towards

Muslims in the West since the turn of the century, and it now considers the position of Muslims as targets of religiously motivated hatred in more depth.

'Faith-hate' in action: Islamophobia

Though it may be tempting to conceive of anti-Muslim, or Islamophobic, prejudice as something of a new phenomenon that emerged in the aftermath of the 9/11 attacks in the USA, it is important to recognise that Muslims have faced forms of prejudice based upon their religious identity over the course of many centuries. Most other ethnic faiths, as Hunt (2005: 126–127) observes, lend themselves rather more readily to assimilation when transplanted to alien soil, and historically Muslims have seldom found it easy to adapt to the challenges of living within Western societies characterised by political and moral change, pluralism and a culture of disbelief and doubt. Key difficulties include the widespread misunderstanding and misrepresentation of Islam which has served to accentuate the differences between Muslims and non-Muslims; the extensive economic, political and social marginalisation suffered by Muslim communities; and the publicity given to the more extreme and purportedly barbaric practices of south Asian Muslims such as forced marriages and honour killings, as opposed to positive elements of their faith (see, for instance, Hudson, 2007).

The term Islamophobia, defined by the Runnymede Trust (1997: 4) as the expression of unfounded hostility towards Islam (including Muslims' experiences of unfair discrimination and political and social exclusion), gained salience towards the end of the 1980s following the infamous Salman Rushdie affair. This highly publicised chain of events centred around Rushdie's controversial novel *The Satanic Verses*, first published in 1988, and the affair is perhaps best remembered for the issuing of a *fatwa* by Ayatollah Khomeni, the then ruler of Iran, calling for the death of Rushdie because of the blasphemous content of his novel. This *fatwa*, together with the frenzied protests, demonstrations and book burning led by outraged Muslims, created or bolstered what Vertovec (2002: 23) describes as 'an image of a Muslim population that was homogeneous in its anti-modern values and dangerous in its passions, posing a challenge both to nationalist ideologies of "Britishness" and to liberal notions about freedom and human rights'. Such imagery has been heavily influential in the negative stereotyping of Islam in Western countries and has contributed to their perceived and actual susceptibility to attack even before the culmination of more recent events had increased the focus upon Muslim communities. Prior to 9/11, for example, Clancy et al.'s (2001) analysis of the British Crime Survey 2000 found that Pakistani and Bangladeshi households faced the highest risk among all ethnic groups of being the victim of a racially motivated offence.

Clearly, the problem of Islamophobia is not solely linked to the post-9/11 era, although the terrorist attacks of the past decade appear to have accelerated the process of what Werbner (2004: 464) terms the 'spiralling progressive alienation' of Muslims in the West. This has been highlighted by McGhee (2005: 102), who notes that there was a four-fold increase in the number of racist attacks reported by British Muslims and other Asian, ostensibly 'Muslim-looking', groups in the UK during the months immediately after 9/11, with Asians based in the Tower Hamlets district of London experiencing a 75 per cent increase in attacks during the same period. Similarly, in the three weeks following the July 7 bombings, police figures showed a six-fold increase in the number of religiously motivated offences reported in London, the vast majority of which were directed against Muslim households and places of worship, while during the same three-week period over 1,200 suspected Islamophobic incidents were recorded by police forces across the UK (*BBC News*, 2005; Dodd, 2005). Other evidence to illustrate the links between the terrorist attacks and the 'othering' of Muslim households has come from Spalek's (2002) research into British Muslim women's fear of crime, where she found that all of her research participants had felt more vulnerable to harassment and victimisation as a result of the 9/11 terrorist attacks, and from the similar contentions made by Muslim households in Garland and Chakraborti's (2004) studies of racism in rural England.

Of course, these difficulties are not confined solely to the UK. Perry (2003b: 184), for instance, refers to the surge in violence directed towards Muslims in the USA in the immediate aftermath of 9/11 to illustrate the scapegoating of the Muslim 'other'. She notes that by September 18 2001 the FBI was investigating more than 40 possible hate crimes believed to be related to the terrorist attacks; by October 3 this number had risen to more than 90; and by October 11 it had grown to 145, with groups such as the American-Arab Anti-Discrimination Committee (ADC) recording in excess of 1,100 such cases by mid-November of that year (see also Welch, 2006). Similarly, Modood (2003: 100) has referred to an 'anti-Muslim wind blowing across the European continent', with anti-Islamic feeling manifesting itself through widespread violence, mass demonstrations and reactionary governmental policy in places such as France, Italy, Germany, Spain and Scandinavia (Bremner, 2004). Following the events of 9/11, the European Monitoring Centre on Racism and Xenophobia (EUMC) reported an increase in the number of verbal attacks against Muslims in all 14 member states and a perceptible rise in physical attacks, particularly in the Netherlands, Sweden and the UK (EUMC, 2001, cited in Quraishi, 2005), while in Australia Poynting et al. (2004) have highlighted the post-9/11 emergence of the 'Arab Other' as the pre-eminent folk-devil of the present age.

In some respects these problems are illustrative of the suspicion that surrounds the 'alien' characteristics of the Islamic faith and its perceived threat to secular, and often monoculturalist, images of national identity. Said's writings on Islam (1978,

1997) refer to a process of 'Orientalism' to describe the sweeping generalisations made about the Islamic faith, which are based upon extravagant, media-driven distortions that are connected with terms such as fundamentalism, radicalism or extremism rather than any enlightened or scholarly understanding of the subject. Consequently, Islam presently finds itself conceived of in a way unlike that of any other religious identity, whereby its meaning goes beyond that of personal faith and instead takes the shape of a fiercely politicised construct. For commentators such as Kundnani (2002) and Fekete (2004), Muslims now find themselves in a position not dissimilar to that of black communities in 1970s' Britain, as described by writers such as Hall et al. (1978), whereby alarmist media narratives have combined with punitive political rhetoric to amplify the threat posed by Muslims and to create a new folk-devil, an object of hostility who bears the brunt of social anger and whose alien characteristics concretise moral anxieties.

Moreover, these constructions may have furthered Muslims' alienation from not only the white non-Muslim world, but increasingly from their minority ethnic counterparts and fellow targets of hate crime. In the same way as British Muslims have tended to identify themselves through their faith and not their ethnic identity, a similar trend has recently emerged among other south Asian groups, with the secular term 'Asian' often now replaced as a means of self-identification by reference to religious identity as a means of setting groups such as Sikhs and Hindus apart from Muslims, and thereby enabling such groups to escape the increased stigmatisation directed towards Muslim communities.[3]

'Faith-hate' in action: Antisemitism

The escalating levels of prejudice directed towards Muslim communities has not surprisingly given a higher profile to faith-hate, and has been a significant factor in the creation of explicit legislative protection against attacks upon religious identity. However, Muslim communities are not the only faith group to have experienced rising levels of prejudice. That there has been a discernible rise in the number of antisemitic incidents within the UK and other European countries may come of something of a surprise given that Jewish communities have been settled in many Western societies for a much longer period than most other religious groupings and have been found to be less stringent – and by implication less 'different' – in sustaining religious beliefs and practices than other minority groups, most notably Muslim communities (Hunt, 2005). Nonetheless, antisemitism remains a particularly significant and pervasive problem which has implications for our understanding of religiously motivated hate crime.

Antisemitism has a strong historical legacy which has been heavily influential upon the nature of prejudice directed towards Jewish communities in the present-day. Gerstenfeld (2004: 151–152) offers a number of examples of how antisemitism has flourished over time, citing, for instance, the persecution of Jews by Egyptians, Greeks and Romans during the pre-Christian era, the massacre of Jews who refused to convert to Christianity during the Crusades and the demonisation of Jews advocated by Martin Luther, the founder of Protestantism, and by the Catholic church. She suggests that this history of antisemitism is largely attributable to the fact that Jewish communities were a minority in every country in which they lived, and notes that their perpetual 'outsider' status, reinforced by their different religion, customs, language and manner of dress, has been particularly significant in Europe where ethnic identity has been regarded as especially important. The persecution of Jewish communities has also taken the form of expulsion from, and refusal of entry to, numerous countries and even large-scale extermination: for example, estimates indicate that as many as 100,000 Jews were killed in Eastern Europe between 1648 and 1658 alone (ibid: 151).

However, the most infamous illustration of antisemitic persecution in recent history is undoubtedly the Holocaust, a period which began in Nazi Germany with a carefully crafted campaign of bigoted rhetoric that escalated during the 1930s and culminated in the mass slaughter of Jews in the 1940s. As part of this systematic process of demonisation, millions of European Jews were stripped of citizenship and property and subjected to widespread sanctions and forms of discrimination as a way of enforcing their economic deprivation and social castigation, before being forced into ghettoes and then concentration camps during the later stages of the Nazi atrocities (Zukier, 1999). Approximately 6 million Jews – two-thirds of Europe's Jewish population and one-third of the global Jewish population – lost their lives during this period, prompting some hate crime scholars to describe the Holocaust as the most significant hate crime of modern centuries (Gerstenfeld, 2004; Levin, 2004). Equally, Holocaust denial – the denial or distortion of the historical facts of the Holocaust – has commonly featured within the antisemitic rhetoric expressed by extremist groups and far-right political parties and has helped to promote anti-Jewish sentiment in both America and Europe (Iganski, 1999; Levin,2004).

The rise in levels of antisemitic activity over recent years is well documented. According to the Community Security Trust (CST), a total of 532 antisemitic incidents were recorded in the UK during 2004, a figure that represented a 42 per cent increase on the number recorded the previous year and a considerable increase from the previous record figure of 405 in 2000 (Jinman, 2005). By 2006 this figure had risen to 594 and included a range of antisemitic offences including stabbings, assaults and malicious phone calls (CST, 2007, cited in Vasagar, 2007). Other countries too have experienced high levels of antisemitism in recent years. The significance of this problem within the USA has been highlighted by surveys undertaken by the Anti-Defamation League (ADL) in 2002, which revealed that as many as 17 per cent of Americans held hardcore antisemitic beliefs and an additional 35 per cent were moderately antisemitic (ADL, 2002, cited in Gerstenfeld, 2004: 153). Similarly, increases in the numbers of antisemitic incidents during this past decade have been recorded in countries with a long history of prejudice against Jewish communities, such as France and Russia, and in countries like Canada which do not share this historical intolerance (Altschiller, 2005).

Explanations for antisemitic hate crime have often been based around the ideologies and activities of far-right groups. Motivated by their belief in the superiority of the 'white' (Aryan) race over all 'others', many far-right groups and white supremacists have perpetuated violence against Jewish communities on the basis of the perceived threat that such communities pose to the sanctity of the white race. Indeed, this threat is seen not only to legitimate but to require the violent repression or elimination of Jews as enemies of the white race (Perry, 2003c). This line of thinking has been present within the ideology of a number of established neo-Nazi groups and extremist movements across the world, and has unquestionably been a factor behind the spread of antisemitic sentiment and commission of antisemitic hate crime. At the same time, though, one must be wary of overplaying the influence of organised far-right activity in the context of antisemitic hate crime. Ironically, it would appear that as the numbers of antisemitic incidents have risen, incitement against Jewish communities from the far-right has decreased as a result of successful criminal prosecutions and a post-9/11 change of strategy towards the Muslim community (McGhee, 2005). Sibbitt (1997) has questioned the influence of far-right groups in the UK, arguing that such groups play a marginal role in the perpetration of hate offences in terms of direct involvement, while Levin and McDevitt (2002) have also suggested that extremists are likely to be responsible for only a small proportion of antisemitic incidents (see Chapter 8 for an expanded discussion of these issues).

Therefore, to explain the apparent rise in antisemitism over recent years it may be necessary to examine the influence of other factors. Certainly, for Iganski, Kielinger and Paterson (2005), antisemitic incidents tend to occur as part of the unfolding of everyday life as opposed to being a result of political extremism, with their analysis of incidents recorded by the Metropolitan Police Service indicating that most experiences of antisemitism take the form of so-called 'low-level' crime, such as damage to property, theft and name-calling committed during the course of everyday interactions. As we saw in the previous chapter, the cumulative impact of these 'everyday' encounters should not be underestimated, nor should they be disassociated from the wider cultural context of bigotry in which they occur.

Anti-Jewish sentiment may be embedded within the cultural fabric of many societies across the world and Gerstenfeld (2004: 155–156) identifies a range of factors that have shaped such ill-feeling, including, for instance, the deep-rooted religious mistrust between Jews and other faith groups, resentment of the perceived socio-economic success enjoyed by Jewish communities in the West, and a confusion between anti-Zionism and antisemitism. This last point is perhaps particularly significant in the context of events that have taken place in recent years, such as the war between Israel and Hizbullah in Lebanon, and may be an especially telling factor behind the rise in levels of prejudice directed towards Jews. While those opposed to the basic proposition of Zionism – namely, support for a political movement to establish a national homeland for Jews in Palestine – should be distinguished from those who are opposed to Jewishness *per se* or who advocate the persecution of or discrimination against Jews, in practice the two positions may often become conflated. Consequently, Jewish people may commonly be the victims of attack where the perpetrator in fact has nothing against Jewishness, just the principles of Zionism (ibid: 156). This has been acknowledged by the CST, which has suggested that the 'transfer of tensions' from the Middle East to Britain and an increase in anti-Zionist or anti-Israeli sentiment have been major factors behind the rise in antisemitic activity within the UK (Jinman, 2005; Vasagar, 2007).

Inciting religious hatred

In light of the rise in religiously motivated hate crime and the heightened sense of vulnerability among certain faith groups, it is not altogether surprising that fresh legislation has been introduced to offer further protection to faith communities from attacks upon their religious identity. This has come in the form of the Racial and Religious Hatred Act 2006, an Act which by its very title highlights an explicit statutory recognition of 'hate crime' (Goodey, 2007). However, just as significant to our understanding of hate crime as the legislation itself is the controversy that has surrounded the introduction of this legislation. Indeed, prior to the 2006 Act there had been six attempts within the previous 12 years to make incitement to religious hatred unlawful, with each attempt in turn greeted with fierce criticism (Goodhall, 2007).[4] It is worth reflecting upon the reasons behind this controversy and the way in which this has affected the formulation of the provisions.

The enhanced protection for faith communities offered under the 2006 Act centres around the creation of a new offence of incitement to religious hatred. As alluded to previously, prior to the passing of this Act there had been earlier demands to create such an offence which would give victims of religiously motivated hate crime the same level of protection as provided to victims of racist hate crime under the incitement to racial hatred provisions of the Public Order Act 1986. The Runnymede Trust (1997: 60), for example, called for the Public Order Act to be amended to outlaw incitement to religious hatred, making reference to the anomalous situation whereby incitement of hatred towards Jewish and Sikh communities can fall within the incitement to racial hatred provisions whereas incitement directed towards other faith communities cannot.

In addition to addressing this anomaly, a further justification for extending the laws on incitement relates to the message conveyed by such a move. For McGhee (2005), the declaratory value of incitement to religious hatred legislation resides in its capacity to send out a clear message to society denouncing faith-hate as not only unacceptable, but also criminal. Moreover, he suggests that such legislation would be designed to target a specific audience, namely the far-right, and a specific legislative problem, namely the exploitation by the far-right of the existing lack of protection for religious groups (ibid: 110). This point is particularly relevant for Muslim communities in the context of the anti-Islamic propaganda that has followed the high-profile acts of terrorism during the past decade. For instance, by explicitly focusing upon the alleged threat posed by Muslims and the Islamic faith, it is argued that groups such as the BNP have been able to incite hatred while circumventing the racial hatred provisions of the Public Order Act, thereby exploiting the distinction between racial and religious hatred (Goodall, 2007; Jeremy, 2007).

Certainly, the acquittal of the BNP's Nick Griffin and Mark Collett on incitement to racial hatred charges in 2006 is illustrative of the way in which explicit attacks upon religious identity have been deliberately and carefully framed in religious and not racial terms so as to reduce the chances of prosecution. However, in addition to deterring the Islamophobic hatred perpetuated by far-right groups, the potential for incitement to religious hatred provisions to influence the activities of extremists *within* the Muslim community may have been an equally persuasive factor behind the government's determination to press ahead with the legislation. Introducing provisions that would help to deter and prosecute incitement from so-called Muslim 'hate clerics' has arguably been especially relevant in the post-7/7 climate, where allaying public fears over the preaching of anti-Western sentiment and the radicalisation of Muslim youth has assumed greater political significance.

These were some of the central justifications for introducing incitement to religious hatred provisions; incitement which, under the original framework of the Religious and Racial Hatred Bill, would include words, behaviour or material which were threatening, abusive or insulting, and which would constitute a criminal offence if the words, behaviour or material were likely to be seen or heard by any person in whom they were likely to stir up such hatred. However, from the outset the Bill was subjected to a barrage of criticism from MPs of all parties, large sections of the media and freedom of speech campaigners, chiefly on the grounds that the government's original proposals unfairly curtailed freedom of speech and in so doing criminalised 'fair comment' and 'religious humour'. Fears over the extent to which the proposals – and in particular the criminalisation of not just threatening but also abusive or insulting words, behaviour or material – would stifle freedom of expression formed a central component of the powerful (and ultimately successful) lobbying effort to derail the proposals.

A further limitation of incitement legislation has been outlined by Iganski (2004), whose criticisms of the deterrent effects of the Public Order Act provisions on racial hatred are equally pertinent in the context of religious hatred. According to Iganski, the capacity for incitement provisions to deter the expression of hatred is compromised by the stringency of the terms 'incitement' and 'hatred' and the failing therein to recognise that inflammatory language can be more coded than such terms suggest and yet equally powerful at the same time. Consequently, perpetrators of hate can side-step incitement safeguards simply by utilising more subtle forms of expression and by avoiding sending out obviously illegal material. In some respects this might lend support to the notion of criminalising abusive and insulting words, behaviour or material as advocated by the original provisions of the Racial and Religious Hatred Bill, though in practice even this broad threshold is likely in itself to be insufficient. Indeed, the forms of propaganda that are commonly used to fan the flames of racial or religious intolerance tend to rely more upon mistaken facts and emotive imagery rather than explicit 'hate' language to convey their provocative message.

Following the House of Lords amendments to the Bill, the incitement to religious hatred provisions now enshrined within the Racial and Religious Hatred Act 2006 represent a watered-down version of those originally proposed. The amended provisions restrict the scope of the original proposals in several key ways. Under the 2006 Act, which has created a new Part 3A of the Public Order Act 1986, for incitement to religious hatred to constitute a criminal offence the prosecution need to prove that the perpetrator's words, behaviour or material were threatening (and not merely abusive or insulting) and that the perpetrator intended to stir up religious hatred. In both respects the provisions represent a departure from the equivalent protection against incitement to racial hatred under section 17 of the 1986 Act which, as we have seen, criminalises words, behaviour or material deemed to be threatening, abusive or insulting and which is either intended to stir up racial hatred or where racial hatred is likely to be stirred up. In addition, the 2006 Act inserts an explicit defence clause for freedom of expression into the Public Order Act through the creation of section 29J, which makes it clear that the 'discussion, criticism or expressions of antipathy, dislike, ridicule, insult or abuse of particular religions' is not enough to constitute incitement.

The rationale behind the tightening of the threshold on incitement to religious hatred has been discussed above: allied with the practical necessity of finding a compromise solution that would appease critics of the original proposals, the new provisions in their more restricted guise offer extended protection from hatred to faith communities while adhering to the principles of free speech. However, some important issues remain unresolved. By limiting the scope of the legislation to threatening words, behaviour or material, the Act is clearly intended to govern the more extreme forms of incitement, and yet, as we have seen, incitement does not need to be framed in explicitly 'threatening' terms to convey its message. In all likelihood perpetrators of religiously motivated hatred will have little trouble in keeping their incitement within the boundaries of the law by claiming that they intended 'only' to abuse, insult or express antipathy towards the practices of a religious community.

Moreover, the inclusion of only a subjective burden of purposive intention (and the removal of the more objective 'likely to' test of intention) makes it even harder in practice for prosecutors to bring a case of incitement to religious hatred. As Goodall (2007: 111) observes, the 'likely to' test was included as part of the incitement to racial hatred provisions precisely because research had shown that prosecutions were likely to flounder under the restrictive threshold of proving purposive intention. Consequently, she argues, the requirement under the incitement to religious hatred laws for proof of intention to be an essential prerequisite for successful prosecution renders the new legislation almost unenforceable because of the difficulty involved in proving purposive intention.

Conclusion

We have seen in this chapter how the problem of religiously-motivated hate crime has become an issue of considerable academic, political and social significance. Far from being simply an adjunct to issues of 'race' and ethnicity, religious identity, and more specifically the perceived threat posed by particular faith communities to secular constructions of cultural and national identity, has become a major source of debate and a recognised factor behind the commission of hate crimes. Especially contentious in this post-9/11 age has been the position of Islamic identity within British society, with British Muslims becoming ever more vulnerable to attack (both metaphorically and literally) not only through organised Islamophobic campaigns and far-right activity, but also through more routine and legitimised forms of prejudice and demonisation.

Indeed, to appreciate quite how emotive this subject is one only has to recall the furious response to the Archbishop of Canterbury Dr Rowan Williams' calls in February 2008 for there to be 'a constructive accommodation [within British law] with some aspects of Muslim law as we already do with aspects of other kinds of religious law'. Despite assurances from the Archbishop that he was in no way proposing Islamic law in Britain nor recommending its introduction as a parallel legal system, his comments attracted an alarmist response with politicians, Christian and secular groups and most sections of the media united in their criticism for what was commonly perceived as another nail in the coffin of 'British' values (Bunting, 2008). The *Sun* newspaper even went so far as to refer to the Archbishop's remarks as a 'victory for terrorism' and on February 8 ran a front page headline of 'What a Burkka' alongside a picture of a woman dressed in a burkka flicking a V-sign, an image one can only presume was intended to convey Islam's perceived defiance of, and victory over, 'traditional' 'British' values.

In light of the apprehension that surrounds aspects of religious identity, it is all the more important that Muslims, and indeed all faith communities, have recourse to adequate legal protection to guard against attacks upon their identity. As outlined above, the level of such legal protection has been significantly bolstered since the turn of the millennium through the introduction of penalty enhancement legislation under the Anti-Terrorism, Crime and Security Act 2001 and the creation of an entirely new substantive offence under the Racial and Religious Hatred Act 2006. While to all intents and purposes this statutory recognition of religiously-motivated hatred puts faith communities on the same footing as minority ethnic communities in terms of safeguarding their identity in the eyes of the law, the controversies surrounding the 2006 provisions – and the amendments made to these provisions – show how difficult it is to strike a balance between incitement to religious hatred and freedom of expression. While supporters of the proposals could quite justifiably argue that they represented a practical attempt to criminalise the expression of hate and to respond to the mounting problem of religious intolerance, critics would present equally powerful arguments to defend the principles of free speech and to highlight that religion should not be beyond criticism.

As discussed above, the balance that has ultimately been struck seeks to marry the two positions by making subtle but significant legal distinctions between the incitement to religious hatred provisions and the corresponding racial hatred laws, but in practice this is likely to mean that the 2006 legislation serves little purpose to faith communities in terms of increasing their chances of securing successful prosecutions against incitement. Certainly, in the context of faith-hate it would seem that the value or otherwise of hate crime laws lies not so much in the quality of protection they offer to minority groups but rather in their symbolic capacity to reassert society's condemnation of hate crime. We shall return to this point in Chapter 9.

Guide to further reading

Specific texts on religiously motivated hate crime are few and far between and readers will need to refer to a diverse collection of literature in order to fully appreciate the problem. Those seeking to develop an understanding of the role of religion in contemporary Britain will find helpful insights provided by Furbey et al., *Faith as Social Capital* (2006) and Hunt,

Religion and Everyday Life (2005), while more specific accounts of faith-hate can be found in McGhee, *Intolerant Britain?* (2005) and Spalek, *Communities, Identities and Crime* (2008).

The McGhee text also provides a useful account of issues relating to Islamophobia, as does Chakraborti, 'Policing Muslim Communities' (2007) and Fekete, 'Anti-Muslim Racism and the European Security State' (2004). Antisemitism is covered extensively within the American hate crime literature, with the leading British contributions on this topic coming from Iganski, 'Legislating Against Hate: Outlawing Racism and Antisemitism in Britain' (1999) and Iganski, Kielinger and Paterson *Hate Crimes against London's Jews* (2005).

Notes

1 Although legislation in England and Wales now distinguishes between racially and religiously aggravated offences, statistics published each year by the Home Office do not disaggregate information relating to these different types of crime. Consequently, disaggregated data on recorded crimes against specific religious communities are simply not available (Goodey, 2007).
2 Nick Griffin was acquitted on two charges relating to speeches filmed by the BBC undercover documentary team, and the jury failed to reach verdicts on two other charges. Mark Collett was cleared of four similar charges of stirring up racial hatred, and the jury failed to reach verdicts on a further four counts in his case. Both men were since cleared of all charges in a second trial held in November 2006.
3 Kundnani (2002: 72), for instance, illustrates the tensions between south Asian communities by describing how in January 2002 a leading Asian radio station, Sunrise Radio, went so far as to ban the word 'Asian' as a result of long-running campaigns led by Hindu and Sikh groups determined to disassociate themselves from Muslims.
4 As Goodhall (2007: 89) notes, two attempts to introduce incitement to religious hatred legislation were made in the Criminal Justice and Public Order Bill 1994, and again with the introduction of a Religious Offences Bill 2001. The Labour government that came to power in 1997 made three further attempts: in the Anti-Terrorism, Crime and Security Bill 2001, in the Serious Organised Crime and Police Bill 2004 and the Racial and Religious Hatred Bill 2005.

4

HOMOPHOBIC HATE CRIME

─────────────────────── Chapter summary ───────────────────────

This chapter presents an analysis of homophobic hate crime and victimisation. After discussing definitions of homophobia and heterosexism the chapter assesses how the outlawing of male homosexual behaviour, and its concomitant over-policing, has adversely affected the relationship between gay communities and the police. This lack of trust and confidence between the two parties has been a major factor in the reluctance of victims of homophobic crime to report incidents to the police. The chapter then discusses how legislative developments, such as the Criminal Justice Act 2003, Sexual Offences Act 2003 and the Criminal Justice and Immigration Act 2008 have brought more equality under the law for gay people and may well have helped to improve the confidence that such communities have in the criminal justice system.

The nature, extent and location of homophobic hate crime are also assessed, and it is suggested that low-level forms of harassment are commonplace for gay communities. The risk of experiencing violent assault in public places is also higher for these groups than it is for their heterosexual equivalents, while violent homophobic incidents tend to be more brutal and extreme than other forms of hate crime. The effects of this harassment can be deeply distressing for victims and it is argued that levels of homophobic violence are still worryingly high, although relations between gay communities and the police have improved over the last decade.

─────────────────────── Introduction ───────────────────────

The murder of Jody Dobrowski in London in 2005 was treated by the police as a homophobic crime from the outset. Unlike the racist murder of Stephen Lawrence in 1993, when the police had been slow to realise the true nature of the incident, the Metropolitan Police Service moved swiftly to arrest Dobrowski's killers who were subsequently successfully prosecuted. However, just as Lawrence's murder was only one in a succession of violent racist incidents in South London at that time, so too was Dobrowski's just one in a series of homophobic assaults in 2005. He was the 141st victim of a homophobic attack in the London borough of Lambeth alone in 2005 (Grove, 2005: 39) and one of 1,306 homophobic crimes reported to police in the capital during that year (Buckley, 2006). Some of these are worth noting here. In September 2005 a man survived after being garroted with a piece of wire by an attacker on Clapham Common, and two weeks later another was beaten unconscious in the same location. Five months after Jody Dobrowski's killing, a further violent attack on the Common left a gay man with severe facial injuries and a broken leg (ibid).

The extreme nature of these assaults reflects Perry's (2001) contention that homophobic attacks tend to be more violent than other forms of hate crime. Furthermore, one characteristic of the experience of gay communities (and especially male ones) that sets them apart from other minority groups is that, historically, their private sexual activities have been over-policed. This 'policing of the closet' (McGhee, 2005: 119) has been symptomatic of the criminal justice system's attitudes towards homosexual men and women in the post-war period and has been one of the reasons for the lack of trust placed in the police service by gay people. An understanding of how these circumstances have changed is vital for a full perspective of the gay communities' experience of hate crime, but before a brief historical analysis of the policing of gay sexual behaviour is conducted, this chapter will look at definitions of homophobia and homophobic hate crime.

Definitional issues

In a similar fashion to the label 'hate crime', 'homophobia' is itself a contested term. It implies a deep-rooted fear of homosexuals: a psychological condition that is involuntary and irrational but which denies a role for wider societal causes for the bias-related harassment faced by gay men and lesbians. It may therefore be misleading, for, as Tomsen and Mason (2001: 270) argue, 'few perpetrators of the violence directed at lesbians and gay men suffer from an exceptional and literal "phobia"'. Nevertheless 'homophobia' has become the accepted terminology used by statutory and voluntary agencies to describe such incidents, and its common currency demands that it is used here.

McManus and Rivers (2001: 3, cited in McGhee, 2005: 125) argue that homophobia is not just a fear but a hatred of, or prejudice towards, people who are lesbian, gay or bisexual, or who are perceived to be, while McGhee (2005: 119) suggests that: 'Homophobia is the umbrella term used to describe the form of prejudice expressed by societies, institutions and individuals who hate (and fear) homosexuals.' Interestingly, the definitions of both homophobia and transphobia provided by the Crown Prosecution Service (CPS) insist that they do not have to be predicated on hatred of gay or trans people, but instead can be based merely upon dislike:

> 'Homophobia' and 'transphobia' are terms used to describe a dislike of LGBT [lesbian, gay, bisexual or transgender] people or aspects of their perceived lifestyle. In other words, homophobia and transphobia are not restricted to a dislike of individuals; the dislike can be based on any sexual act or characteristic that the person associates with a LGBT person, whether or not any specific LGBT person does that act or has that characteristic. That dislike does not have to be as severe as hatred. It is enough that people do something or abstain from doing something because they do not like LGBT people. (CPS, 2007b: 6)

The CPS's notion also suggests that homophobia can be evidenced not just by someone's actions, but by their *inactions,* an interesting idea that has echoes in Macpherson's idea that institutional racism can be the result of *unwitting* attitudes or actions that disadvantage minority ethnic people (Macpherson, 1999: para 6.34 – see Chapter 2). The significance of broader institutional and societal prejudices – such as the dominant heterosexist popular culture in the UK – for the development of individual and institutional homophobia should not be underestimated.[1] The concept of heterosexism was first articulated in 1975 (Morin and Garfinkle, 1978, cited in Mason, 1997) and has since been expanded upon by a number of those who have studied homophobic harassment, including Herek (1992: 89), who argues that:

> Anti-gay violence is a logical, albeit extreme extension of the heterosexism that pervades American society. Heterosexism is defined here as an ideological system that denies, denigrates and stigmatises any non-heterosexual form of behaviour, identity, relationship or community.

As stated in Chapter 2, in the immediate aftermath of the 1999 Macpherson report the police service revised its definitions relating to hate incidents in order to give priority to the perceptions of the victim, rather than those of police officers. Consequently, ACPO produced a fresh definition of a homophobic incident:

> Any incident which is perceived to be homophobic by the victim or any other person. In effect, any incident intended to have an impact on those perceived to be lesbian, gay men, bisexual or transgender. (ACPO, 2000: 13)

Therefore in the post-Macpherson climate of understanding hate incidents, if the victim feels that their case is hate-related then the police are obliged to record it as such. Herek, Cogan and Roy Gillis (2003), in their study of the experiences of 450 sexual-minority adults in California, uncovered a range of factors by which victims could identify a homophobic incident, including:

the perpetrator making homophobic comments; that the incident had occurred in or near a gay-identified venue; that the victim had a 'hunch' that the incident was homophobic; that the victim was holding hands with their same-sex partner in public, or other contextual clues.

Herek et al.'s work is useful for supplying some context to the police's employment of a more victim-oriented approach to defining hate incidents. Interestingly, though, in the ACPO definition above, incidents relating to transgendered victims were included under the same 'homophobic' definition as lesbians, gay men or bisexual people, as presumably ACPO felt that such incidents had sufficient commonalities for them to be grouped together. This understanding had changed by 2005, when, in the revised version of the ACPO manual, homophobic and transphobic incidents were separated, with the former defined as: 'Any incident which is perceived to be homophobic by the victim or any other person' (ACPO, 2005: 11). This acknowledgement of the difference between transphobic and homophobic incidents reveals the improved police understanding of the subtleties of victims' experiences, and these will be explored in further detail below and in Chapter 5. Before a detailed discussion of the manifestation of homophobic harassment, what follows now is a summary of the struggle for gay communities to achieve equality under the law regarding sexual behaviour.

Legal protection from homophobic hate crime

Since the Second World War lesbians and gay men have had involvement with the criminal justice system in two main ways: first, because of the specific nature of the homophobic harassment and violence they have experienced, and secondly, because of the criminalisation of male homosexuality, which led to the policing of the private space of gay men in a way that heterosexual males have not experienced. Arguably, what links these two involvements is society's pervading homophobic and heterosexist prejudices, which fuelled acts of harassment and also exemplified the kinds of attitudes that justified the criminalisation of a sexual minority's behaviour. Between the early 1950s and the present-day there have been a number of key milestones that have challenged such attitudes, and a necessarily brief review of them begins with the Wolfenden report, which paved the way for the decriminalisation of homosexuality in England and Wales.

The report was produced by a Committee appointed by the government (chaired by Sir John Wolfenden) to examine the law and practice relating to homosexual offences (Home Office and Scottish Home Department (HOSHD), 1957: 1). In the mid-1950s, all male acts of homosexuality, whether committed in public or private, were illegal, although sex between females was left untouched by the law. The report appeared in 1957, and was a progressive document that made a number of key recommendations. For example, the Committee argued that, as homosexuality was 'a state or condition', then it 'as such does not, and cannot, come within the purview of the criminal law' (ibid: 11). The Committee therefore concluded, rather bravely for the times, that:

> Unless a deliberate attempt is made by society, acting through the agency of the law, to equate the sphere of crime with that of sin, there must remain a realm of private morality and immorality which is, in brief and crude terms, not the law's business. We accordingly recommend that homosexual behaviour between consenting adults in private should no longer be a criminal offence. (ibid: 24-25)[2]

The Committee did, though, support provisions in law for homosexual acts committed in public or with persons (such as young men or the mentally ill) who were thought of as 'vulnerable'. The eventual outcome of the report was that Parliament passed the 1967 Sexual Offences Act, which made homosexual acts between two adult males (over the age of consent of 21) in private no longer a criminal offence (it would take until 1980 for similar legislation to be passed in Scotland and 1982 in Northern Ireland). However, this new feeling of sexual freedom was marred by what McGhee (2005: 143) terms the 'even more rigorous policing' of acts of homosexuality, which meant that, in the immediate years following the passing of the Act, arrests for homosexual offences in public places actually increased, further damaging relations between gay males and the police. It would take until the Sexual Offences Act of 2003 for the offences of buggery and gross indecency finally to be removed from the statute book, thus effectively ending discriminatory law dating from the Victorian era that punished certain homosexual activities but not their heterosexual equivalents.[3]

Also in 2003, and significantly for the study of hate crime and its prosecution, section 146 of the Criminal Justice Act conveyed upon courts the capacity to increase sentences for offences that: 'At the time of committing the offence or immediately before or after doing so, the offender demonstrated towards the victim of the offence hostility based on the sexual orientation (or presumed sexual orientation) of the victim' or 'The offence was motivated (wholly or partly) by hostility towards persons who are of a particular sexual orientation' (CPS, 2007b: 10). This hostility can be displayed 'at the time of committing the offence, or immediately before or after doing so' (ACPO, 2005: 13). Also, importantly, the wording of the Act implies that the demonstration of hostility *or* motivation can be enough to secure conviction, which means that motivation (something notoriously difficult to verify) does not have to be proved in order to gain a conviction as long as there is evidence of hostility (CPS, 2007c). Also of note is the insistence of section 146 that the displaying of any other prejudice at the time of committing the offence is irrelevant to the enhancement of the sentence if bias based upon sexuality is evident (Hall, 2005a).

Prior to this Act, while the Crown Prosecution Service had collated annual statistics relating to offences it deemed to be motivated by homophobia, there was no legal provision for this type of offence to have an enhanced sentence.[4] Section 146 (which came into effect on April 4 2005) was therefore an important development as it provided gay victims of hate crime with similar provisions to those for victims of racially and religiously aggravated offences, although the Act did not create specific new offences that were 'homophobically aggravated' in the way that the Crime and Disorder Act 1998 had created 'racially or religiously aggravated' offences.[5] Therefore the prosecution has to prove that the crime was aggravated by homophobia in order for the court to enact its duty of sentence enhancement, and yet, unlike the case for racially aggravated offences where the offence and the aggravation are inseparable, the defendant can still be found guilty of the 'basic', non-aggravated offence (CPS, 2007c).

In Scotland, the Working Group on Hate Crime (2004) recommended that statutory provisions for aggravated offences be extended to include those predicated upon hostility towards a victim based on their actual or presumed sexual orientation, transgender identity or disability. This has taken the form of the Sentencing of Offences Aggravated by Prejudice (Scotland) Bill, which began its progress through the Scottish Parliament during the latter part of 2008.

Another important piece of legislation is section 74 of the Criminal Justice and Immigration Act 2008, which amended Part 3A of the Public Order Act 1986 (hatred against persons on religious grounds) to include a new offence of inciting hatred based upon a person's sexual orientation, thereby achieving similar legal provision for gay people to that already provided to minority ethnic and religious communities under previous incitement legislation. The aim of the Act is, in the words of gay rights organisation Stonewall (2008), to outlaw 'serious hatred against individuals defined by reference to their sexual orientation, with a high threshold for prosecutions which must be approved by the Attorney General and heard before a jury'. This high threshold means that abusive or insulting language directed against gay people is not considered to be illegal under the Act (thus allowing homophobic comedy to go unpunished, for example) and only words, behaviour or material that are *threatening* will be liable to legal sanction, as in the case for the incitement of religious hatred.

This high threshold reflected concerns expressed during parliamentary debates regarding section 74 that those whose religious views caused them to find homosexuality unacceptable would be subject to arrest and prosecution under the proposed new law, thus threatening the freedom of speech for those with deeply-held religious convictions (House of Lords, 2008). These objections largely prompted the final version of the Criminal Justice and Immigration Act to insert a new part in the original Public Order Act 1986, '29JA Protection of Freedom of Expression (Sexual Orientation)', which states 'for the avoidance of doubt, the discussion or criticism of sexual conduct or practices or the urging of persons to refrain from or modify such conduct or practices shall not be taken of itself to be threatening or intended to stir up hatred' (Office of Public Sector Information, 2008). However, Stonewall (2008) expressed concern that these concessions 'could mean that a very small number of people of extreme views attempt to avoid prosecution by citing a "religious defence"' when criticising or questioning minority sexual orientations, thus facilitating, in Stonewall's view, the expression of homophobic sentiment under the guise of religious conviction.

Nevertheless, despite these doubts, Stonewall was broadly supportive of the legislative developments discussed above, although, worryingly, the organisation's perception was that homophobic incidents themselves may have increased in frequency since the turn of the twenty-first century (ibid). It is to an analysis of these that this chapter now turns.

Nature and extent of homophobic harassment

The true extent of homophobic harassment is difficult to discern as it is estimated that only around one-in-four to one-in-five homophobic incidents is reported to the police (Jenkins, 2007: 13; Dick, 2008). However, victimisation surveys can help to give an indication of the extent of this form of hate crime. For example, both the Beyond Boundaries (2003) survey of lesbian, gay, bisexual and transgender people in Scotland and a 1996 Stonewall survey of lesbian and gay men in the UK found that around seven out of ten had been verbally abused or threatened by someone who assumed they were LGBT (Mason and Palmer, 1996, cited in Jarman and Tennant, 2003: 14), an almost identical figure to that in Moran, Paterson and Docherty's (2004: 22) research. Stonewall's more recent analysis of the experiences of 1,721 lesbian and gay men found that one in five had suffered a homophobic incident in the last three years and one in eight had been victimised within the past 12 months (Dick, 2008). A survey of gay men carried out in Edinburgh (Morrison and MacKay, 2000: 1) indicated that nearly 60 per cent of respondents had experienced some form of harassment over the last year and that three-quarters of these incidents were felt by the victim to be homophobic. Also, a quarter of those surveyed had experienced a homophobic physical assault and one in 20 a physical assault in the last 12 months. Furthermore, a House of Commons report stated that there had been 'a particularly dramatic increase in reported incidents of attack and intimidation' on people of an LGBT background in Northern Ireland in the mid-2000s (House of Commons Northern Ireland Affairs Committee, 2005: 3).

A useful summary of similar research is contained in Table 4.1, which is adapted from Jarman and Tennant's (2003) analysis of homophobic harassment in Northern Ireland.

Table 4.1   Comparison of homophobic victimisation surveys

Survey	Experience of violence (%)		Experience of harassment (%)	
	Females	Males	Females	Males
Stonewall[1,2]	24	34	75	72
GALOP (1998)[2,8]	44	49	89	82
Edinburgh (Morrison and Mackay, 2000)[3]		26		57
Beyond Boundaries (2003)[4,7]	23	23	68	68
LASI (Quiery, 2002)[5]	20			
ICR (Jarman and Tennant, 2003)	42	61	76	85
Stormbreak (2006)[4,6]	20	20	39	39
Moran et al. (2004)[9]	12	14	37	38

1 Refers to Stonewall's 1996 survey (Mason and Palmer, 1996).
2 Harassment here refers specifically to verbal abuse.
3 Survey only covered gay men.
4 No distinction given of male and female experiences.
5 Survey only covered lesbians and bisexual women.
6 Survey of 521 lesbians and gay men in London in 2003/04.
7 Survey also included transgendered people.
8 Survey focused on those aged 25 and under.
9 Results refer to experiences in the last 12 months.

Source: Adapted from Jarman and Tennant (2003: 39)

While methodological differences regarding how the surveys were carried out may explain some of the variance in these figures, there are broadly similar trends that can be picked out. For example, levels of harassment are consistently high for both sexes and demonstrate that being a victim of homophobic harassment is a persistent fact of life for most lesbians and gay men. Figures for being a victim of violence are much lower but also vary more widely, with 'only' 23 per cent of males reporting being such a victim in the Beyond Boundaries survey compared to 61 per cent for ICR. Again, methodological issues may explain some of this difference, but it is nevertheless worth noting that even the lowest figure (20 per cent for females in the LASI survey) indicates that as many as one in five lesbians had experienced homophobic violence.

Perry (2001) argues that lesbians suffer homophobic violence at a lower rate than males, something borne out by Stonewall's 2008 survey which revealed that gay men were two and a half times more likely to be the victim of a physical assault than lesbians (Dick, 2008). Perry explains that same-sex affection and physical contact between women are more acceptable for the general public than similar acts between men, making them less of a target for homophobic harassment. Kirkey and Forsyth's (2001: 433) study of rural gay communities in the USA may bear this out, as their gay male respondents pointed to the higher incidence of lesbian couples holding hands than their gay male equivalents as being evidence of greater tolerance of female public displays of homosexuality than male.

The work of Mason and Palmer (1996, for Stonewall) provides an insight into the many dimensions of 'queer bashing' in Britain. One-third of their respondents cited examples of harassment, including threats, blackmail, graffiti, vandalism and hate mail, and nearly three-quarters recorded incidents of verbal abuse. Typical of such abuse are terms including 'faggot', 'dyke', 'man-hater', 'queer' and 'pervert' (Namaste, 2006: 588), that are 'so loaded and considered derogatory, that even to be called it in jest is cause for alarm' (Ruthchild, 1997: 1–2).

It is also important to note the types of homophobic harassment experienced. Of the third of Herek et al.'s (2003: 243) sample of 450 lesbians and gay men who had experienced an actual or attempted bias crime, one in nine were victims of property crime (such as robbery or vandalism) and just under a quarter had experienced an assault, rape, or robbery. A survey of young lesbian, gay and bisexual people by GALOP (Gay London Police Monitoring Group) found that around eight out of ten respondents reported verbal abuse and half reported physical assault (GALOP, 1998, in Jarman and Tennant, 2003: 15). Jarman and Tennant (2003: 6) cite figures collated by the Police Service of Northern Ireland which show that the most common forms of homophobic harassment were verbal abuse and physical assault. Other forms of homophobic harassment included theft, being followed on foot or by car, having graffiti daubed on their property, phone calls, vandalism of property, being stalked, receiving hate mail, being spat upon, being raped or sexually assaulted, and being blackmailed.

As discussed in Chapter 2, a key aspect of understanding hate-related harassment is to recognise incidents as forming part of a continuum of such victimisation. Drawing upon Kelly's (1987) study of sexual violence, this continuum should not be seen as one with the most minor events at one end and the most violent at the other, for, as Kelly argues, *all* such incident cause alarm, hurt and distress to the victim. Instead, such a continuum of victimisation is based on the *frequency* of such events, and for many gay people these can be part of their daily lived experience. Moran et al. (2004: 38), for example, found that over three quarters of their survey respondents who had experienced violence within the last year had been the victim of more than one incident and just over a half had experienced more than two incidents in that period. Jarman and Tennant's (2003: 45) work in Northern Ireland revealed that, although 25 of those surveyed had experienced verbal abuse only once in the past two years, 76 had experienced it at least twice, and of those, 14 had been on the end of such abuse 21 or more times – a substantial figure. Other forms of repeat harassment included being followed on foot or by car, being stalked, receiving abusive phone calls, or suffering graffiti.

Violent harassment

Perry (2001: 107) argues that homophobic attacks tend to be among the most brutal acts of all hate crimes, citing work by the National Gay and Lesbian Task

Force in the USA, which found that over half of gay-related homicides show evidence of 'rage/hate-fuelled extraordinary violence … such as dismemberment, bodily and genital mutilation, use of multiple weapons, repeated blows from a blunt object, or numerous stab wounds'. This graphic violence reveals a frightening kind of 'overkill' typical of manifestations of violent homophobia (see also Herek et al., 2003). Research has also shown that on a significant number of occasions these violent episodes also involve an element of humiliation, perhaps revealing evidence of real *hatred*, rather than just prejudice, on behalf of the perpetrator (see Case Study 4.1). Perry cites Hassel's interview with another gay male victim (1992: 144–145, in Perry, 2001: 111):

> They made me address them as 'Sir'. They made me beg them to be made into a real man. They threatened to castrate me. They threatened to emasculate me. They called me 'Queer', 'Faggot'. One of them urinated on me. They threatened me with sodomy.

These threats are sometimes followed through. Ten per cent of those victims of homophobia surveyed in Northern Ireland had experienced a homophobic sexual assault (Jarman and Tennant, 2003: 46); around one in eight of the hate incidents experienced by gay men in Stonewall's 2008 survey had involved unwanted sexual contact (Dick, 2008); and Channel 4's survey uncovered events such as a respondent describing how he was gang raped in a public toilet 'by some straight guys' (Hickman, 2006: 14).

Case Study 4.1: The killing of Jody Dobrowski

The horrific murder of Jody Dobrowski in 2005 made national headlines. Dobrowski, who lived an openly gay lifestyle in London, was violently assaulted by two strangers on Clapham Common (a popular gay cruising haunt) on the night of October 16. His assailants, Scott Walker and Thomas Pickford, were heard by witnesses to scream homophobic insults as they rained punches and kicks upon their victim. Walker stuffed a sock into Dobrowski's mouth and smashed him around the head with a shoe, while Pickford broke a bottle over his head. A man on the common heard Dobrowski's screams and asked the assailants 'Are you trying to kill him?' One replied: 'We don't like poofters here and that's why we can kill him if we want to.'

In their later trial for the murder of Jody, Walker and Pickford were described by the prosecution as 'kicking and jumping on the man as if trying to kill an animal' (Kennedy, 2006: 4). Pickford's jeans became soaked in blood up to their knees. Officers who dealt with the case were badly shaken, with one commenting:

> [It was a] … terrible murder. Officers who are used to dealing with these sorts of injuries were shocked by what they saw. Jody Dobrowski died from severe head, neck and facial injuries. He was the victim of a sustained and violent assault. (O'Neill, 2005: 5)

After the trial the District Crown Prosecutor at the Old Bailey Trials Unit said: 'The Crown Prosecution Service treated this case as a homophobic killing from the beginning. In our view Pickford and Walker attacked Jody in such a brutal fashion simply because of his sexuality and he was a completely innocent victim of their extreme violence.' Both men received sentences enhanced to 28 years through the provisions contained in section 146 of the Criminal Justice Act 2003, whereby a judge, when faced with a murder motivated by the victim's sexuality, must consider imposing an additional tariff on top of the 15 years for most murders. The legislation came into force on the day that Pickford and Walker were sentenced.

Worryingly, the killing of Jody Dobrowski was not an isolated occurrence of such incidents. In 2007, for example, a man was jailed for life and another for nine years for a homophobic attack in Perth, Scotland, that took the life of James Kerr. The assailants repeatedly punched and kicked him in the face and head, and one of them shouted 'I hate gays and poofters' (Carrell, 2007). In July 2008, 18-year-old Michael Causer was battered to death by two assailants in Huyton, Merseyside, in what police described as a 'hate crime' (Rossington, 2008).

The complexities surrounding this area are highlighted by Tomsen (2002), whose study of the homophobic murders of gay men found two distinct categories: attacks on those perceived to be homosexual by groups of people in public spaces, and one-on-one attacks in private spaces, which give rise to allegations of unwanted sexual advances that somehow triggered the assailant's actions. Just over half of the victims in Tomsen's research 'did not know or barely know their assailants at their time of death' (Tomsen, 2002: 25), a finding that is consistent with Perry's (2001) notion that hate crimes are commonly committed by strangers rather than intimates of the victim. Bartlett's (2007) detailed examination of gay sexual homicide also sheds light on this complicated phenomenon. His research (an analysis of CPS files relating to the deaths of 77 people from 1976 to 1981) found that, in almost all of the cases, there had been no prior intent to kill; usually, only the victim and the perpetrator were present at the time of death, but exceptional violence in the deaths was commonplace (Bartlett, 2007: 582).

Thankfully murders of gay people in any context are rare, but there is evidence that assaults are more commonplace than many may recognise and that gay and lesbian people are more at risk of assault from a stranger in a public place than their heterosexual equivalents (Tomsen and Mason, 2001). It is also worth noting that the pair who murdered Jody Dobrowski had beaten up a gay man in woods on Clapham Common two weeks earlier. On the same common just a year later two assailants used a piece of wire to attempt to strangle their gay victim (Buckley, 2006).

In 2005, in another high-profile incident, a gay priest was called 'a queer' by his attacker who proceeded to hit him with a baseball bat. The following year the perpetrator was jailed for two years for what the presiding judge described as 'an extremely unpleasant assault ... [that] was premeditated ... [and] aggravated by homophobic motivation' (PinkNews.co.uk, 2006). Such incidents are not only frightening, but can also involve vandalism of property, arson and death threats, as one of Herek et al.'s (2003: 249) respondents testified:

> A Molotov cocktail was lobbed onto the second story front porch where I was at. ... And it immediately ignited the porch. ... As the building was burning I could hear the windows being broken out of the cars. And the people doing it laughing and screaming 'faggot' at the top of their lungs. ... There was a note attached to the windshield of my car: 'The faggot that lives here will be dead within a week.'

Location of incidents of harassment

In the Edinburgh survey of gay men (Morrison and MacKay, 2000), the three most common locations for homophobic physical assaults were 'in the street', at 'school or university' and 'outside a gay bar/club', broadly reflecting Herek et al.'s findings and also those from both of the Stonewall surveys of 1996 and 2008. The earlier Stonewall study found that around a quarter of attacks occurred in the street or in or near a club, and slightly less at or near home (Mason and Palmer, 1996, cited in Jarman and Tennant, 2003: 14). Namaste (2006: 589) suggests that the home is a significant site for homophobic assaults, with around a quarter to a third of lesbians and gay men reporting being assaulted there.

McNamee (2006) and Dick (2008) found that the workplace remains a significant setting for much of the violence and harassment gay people experience. As Morrison and Mackay (2000) point out, a lack of recognition of gay members of staff as a vulnerable group, coupled with a reluctance to report incidents, may cause employers to think that homophobia is not an issue in their organisation. A gay male reported the following to the 2008 Stonewall research (Dick, 2008: 15): 'I have in the past had windows broken and been assaulted, although these were not random acts but carried out by people who I have worked with and still work with.' The Beyond Boundaries survey also revealed that educational establishments were commonly the seat of homophobic harassment. This situation was also uncovered by the NSPCC, whose analysis of the nature of the calls they had received showed that the issue of homophobic bullying within schools accounted for a quarter of all the calls related to sexuality issues (Smithers, 2006). Cull, Platzer and Balloch's (2006) study of homeless lesbian, gay, bisexual and transgender youth revealed similar problems. Over two-thirds of people in their study had been bullied at school and in most cases there was a homophobic element to that bullying (Case Study 4.2).

Case Study 4.2: Homophobic harassment in schools

Schools and universities appear to be environments in which gay and lesbian students can experience frequent homophobic harassment. This can come from fellow pupils and students, but can also come from those in authority, such as teachers. Hunt and Jensen's (2006: 3) large-scale survey research of young lesbian, gay and bisexual people at secondary schools revealed that:

- almost two-thirds of lesbian, gay and bisexual pupils had experienced homophobic bullying;
- 30 per cent stated that adults were responsible for homophobic incidents in their schools;
- seven out of ten gay pupils who had experienced homophobic bullying stated that this had had affected their school work.

Such bullying can lead to feelings of isolation, depression and a sense of helplessness, particularly when it goes unchallenged or is tacitly endorsed by teachers (Trotter, 2006). Hunt and Jensen's work also uncovered the varied and complex forms that homophobic harassment can take in schools, ranging from verbal abuse to death threats, sexual assault and being ostracised. Typical of the experience of many lesbian and gay pupils is that of a female in Trotter's (2006: 295) research, who, in the words of one of her contemporaries, '... got tortured for it [her sexuality]. She ended up sitting on the front at dinner times and breaks for being called lesbian.'

Interestingly, the four most frequently experienced types of harassment in Trotter's research – verbal abuse, malicious gossip, intimidating looks, and being ignored and isolated – are so-called 'low-level' forms of abuse which can nevertheless be damaging. The effect of homophobic insults – such as 'poof', 'dyke', 'rug-muncher', 'queer' and 'bender' – can be devastating, and can lead to truanting and depression on the part of the victim (Hunt and Jensen, 2006: 3; see also Cull et al., 2006). Also worthy of note is the relatively new phenomenon of cyberbullying, which can occur via internet message boards, on social networking sites such as Bebo or Facebook, or via mobile phones, and which was experienced by over four out of ten respondents to Trotter's (2006) survey.

Over the last decade the term 'gay' has 'become embedded in popular usage, particularly among adolescents, as a term of insult or as a reference for things deemed "rubbish" or "lame"' (Johnson et al., 2007: 31). Such misuse of the term can damage the self-worth of gay people and has been a significant factor in low educational achievement or truanting among LGB pupils (Cull et al., 2006; Johnson et al., 2007). These studies also revealed that gay pupils often felt that teachers were unsympathetic to their homophobic victimisation and indeed there were occasions when pupils had witnessed teachers themselves being homophobic (Mitchell, 2004; NSPCC, 2006).

Effects of homophobic harassment

The impact of homophobic harassment can include feelings of lack of self-worth and depression, increased general psychological distress and anxiety, heightened sense of vulnerability and insecurity, a sense of helplessness and isolation, lack of self-esteem and confidence, and increased insecurity among other members of the local gay community (Herek et al., 2003). These can have a long-term effect on mental health, which can lead to relationship difficulties and break-ups, substance abuse and addiction, and homelessness (Cull et al., 2006). Many of these factors can affect the construction of a positive self-identity, in itself an important step for young people coming to terms with their sexuality.

Homophobic abuse, experienced either in the familial home or in rented accommodation, has resulted in a disproportionate number of homeless people of a minority sexuality (Cull et al., 2006). Of even more concern is that there is a higher prevalence of suicidal distress among LGB people than heterosexual people (Johnson et al., 2007). Another consequence of homophobic victimisation is the damage that it does to feelings of safety and security. Only a quarter of Jarman and Tennant's (2003) lesbian and gay survey participants stated that they felt safe on the street at night and almost half said they did not feel safe in a non-gay bar. These feelings of insecurity can seriously affect self-worth and confidence, and can restrict movements and behaviour (Dick, 2008). The Beyond Boundaries (2003) survey shows that feelings of insecurity are greatest in the street or in other public spaces such as bars or on buses and trains, where much 'low-level' harassment takes place.

Reporting incidents to the police

As discussed above, gay communities' perception of the police has been negatively affected by the over-zealous policing of the sexual behaviour of gay men. This wariness has helped to create the situation whereby, despite being more likely to be victims of crime, lesbian, gay and transgender communities are less likely to report crime to the police than the general population (McManus and Rivers, 2001). There is also a feeling among LGB communities that such institutional and individual police homophobia will manifest itself in active hostility towards them, and that officers are not inclined to take their hate incident seriously nor pursue their investigation with any urgency (Dick, 2008; Wolhuter et al., 2009). This lack of trust and confidence is exacerbated by low detection and clear-up rates for homophobic hate crimes and their infrequent successful prosecution (Williams and Robinson, 2004).

In the context of the USA, the reluctance of victims to report to the police is worsened by the remarkable suggestion that almost one-quarter of all anti-gay hate crimes in that country are perpetrated by police officers (Berrill, 1992, cited in Williams and Robinson, 2004: 215). In the UK, Williams and Robinson (2004: 214–215) suggest that there can be a:

> ... tendency for working groups of police officers to display hostile, negative and stereotyped views about LGB people. The occupational culture of police officers appears to instill negative attitudes about minority individuals, especially those identifying as lesbian, gay or bisexual.

Such an assertion helps to clarify why concerns about the police were the most significant factor in explaining the reluctance of victims of homophobia in Herek et al.'s (2003) study to report incidents to the police. Indeed, in a UK context, ACPO suggests that victims' views of the police are influenced by concerns that the individual officer assigned to their case may be homophobic, that victims may be 'outed' as a result of reporting, and that information regarding their sexuality will be recorded and stored by police against their will (ACPO, 2000, cited in McGhee, 2005: 129). These concerns may vary between different groups, with Herek et al. (2003) finding, for example, that reporting rates were higher among gay men than lesbians. However, one group that passes 'under the radar' by rarely reporting homophobic incidents is that of usually heterosexual men, who are victimised while having sex with other men but do not want to disclose this secret 'other side' to officers or anyone else (Williams and Robinson, 2004).

However, despite the historically troubled relationship between gay communities and the police, there is some evidence that in the post-Macpherson policing climate the police are trying to purge the service of homophobia, while also placing increased emphasis on the investigation of homophobic hate crimes (McGhee, 2005). For instance, in the period since the publication of the Macpherson report in 1999 the number of LGBT liaison officers in the Metropolitan Police Service has grown to over 200 (*BBC News*, 2008b) while organisations within the police service, such as the Gay Police Association, are also playing a proactive role in engaging with gay communities at a local level (Spalek, 2008). This more positive stance may be bearing fruit as there are signs to suggest that relations between gay groups and the police are improving. For example, less than 10 per cent of respondents to Mitchell's (2004) survey of LGBT communities stated that they would definitely *not* report homophobic or transphobic harassment to the police, and the majority of those in Stormbreak's (2006) survey who had reported such incidents to the police found them to be sympathetic. Similarly, almost half of Beyond Boundaries' (2003) respondents thought the police had handled their case well, while a fifth of the respondents to a Victim Support survey of hate crime victims felt that the police 'were the most helpful source of support' that they had received after their incident (Michael Bell Associates, 2006: 54). While these statistics show that there is still considerable scope for improvement in the police's handling of homophobic hate crime, they do offer some grounds for optimism.

Conclusion

This chapter has explored the nature, extent and effects of homophobic hate crime. It traced the history of problematic relations between gay communities (and especially gay males) and agencies of the criminal justice system, such as the police. It was suggested that the struggle for the decriminalisation of homosexuality was an important facet of challenging the hegemony of heterosexist ideas in society that foster homophobic attitudes. The chapter also examined the over-zealous 'policing of the closet' that has damaged the trust and confidence that gay men have had in the police. The chapter argued that legislative developments, such as the Sexual Offences Act 2003 and the Criminal Justice Act 2003, may have helped rebuild this trust by providing more equality for gay people under the law. The nature and extent of homophobic hate crime were also assessed, and it was suggested that so-called 'low-level' harassment was commonplace for LGB groups. Evidence was also cited of a worryingly high frequency of violent homophobic assaults, and it was argued that not only are lesbian and gay men more likely to be the victims of such attacks than their heterosexual counterparts, but that these assaults were likely to be of a more extreme nature than other forms of violent hate crime.

An interesting aspect of the research discussed in this chapter relates to how many of those conducting this research, or organisations responsible for helping victims of homophobia, utilise a framework which includes lesbian, gay, bisexual and transgendered people under one single banner, 'LGBT', which in itself suggests that the experiences of such populations are similar enough to group them under one banner. However, lesbians and gay men can suffer different levels and forms of hate crime victimisation and have variable experiences of policing (Tomsen and Mason, 2001; Williams and Robinson, 2004, Dick, 2008). As Moran and Sharpe (2004) argue, transgendered populations' experience of hate crime is different still, casting further doubt over the appropriateness of the LGBT 'umbrella'. These are complex issues which will be explored in the discussions of transphobic hate crime in Chapter 5, when further parallels and differences between homophobic and transphobic hate crime will be drawn.

Arguably, the progressive legislative developments mentioned earlier, coupled with a re-evaluation of the criminal justice system's attitudes towards minority communities in the post-Macpherson climate, have created an improved atmosphere within police–LGB relations. The successful prosecution of the perpetrators of high–profile homophobic crimes, such as the murder of Jody Dobrowski, may also have helped to reassure gay communities that the police are now according the investigation of homophobic hate crime the resources that it deserves. However, a series of violent homophobic assaults during recent years, such as the targeting of gay men in the city of Brighton in 2007 and the murder of a gay male in a public toilet in Surrey in 2008 (Staff Writer, 2007, 2008), serves as a timely reminder that homophobic hate crime is still a very serious issue that can have extreme consequences for victims.

Guide to further reading

Dick, *Homophobic Hate Crime* (2008) offers a comprehensive overview of both homophobic and 'general' crime suffered by gay communities. Herek, Cogan and Roy Gillis (2003), 'Victim Experiences in Hate Crimes Based on Sexual Orientation' provide an insightful analysis of the nature of homophobic hate crime, and Chapter 5 of McGhee (2005) *Intolerant Britain?* offers a summary of the gay communities' relationship with the police. The *Journal of Homosexuality* makes for informative reading and the 1957 Wolfenden report is an excellent historical document (Home Office and Scottish Home Department, 1957).

Notes

1 It is estimated that around 6 per cent of the United Kingdom's population is gay (Hickman, 2006: 15).
2 At the time of the publication of the Wolfenden report the *Sunday Express* was moved to refer to it as the 'Pansies' Charter' (Sandbrook, 2007: 487).
3 Sections 12, 13 and 32 of the Sex Offences Act 1956 (covering gross indecency, buggery and soliciting by a man) were all abolished under Sex Offences Act 2003. The Home Office acknowledged that these sections had been used in a discriminatory way in the past against gay men (McGhee, 2005: 202).
4 The first full set of annual CPS statistics relating to such incidents covered the year 2004/05, when it prosecuted 317 offences identified as having a homophobic or transphobic element. By 2006/07, this figure had risen to 822 (CPS 2005, 2007a).
5 Other significant legislation includes the Civil Partnerships Act 2004, which entitles same-sex couples to a union of 'civil partnership' that provides the same legal benefits as those enjoyed by married heterosexual couples, and the Sexual Orientation Regulations 2007, which forbade the non-provision of goods and services to someone based upon that person's sexuality.

5

GENDER, TRANSGENDER AND HATE

──────────────── Chapter summary ────────────────

This chapter discusses hate crimes motivated by issues related to gender. It examines the intersection of gender with sex and sexuality, and assesses the importance of their complex relationship within the context of understanding the rationale behind perpetrators' actions. Following a summary of theoretical ideas, the chapter examines the nature and extent of hate crimes where the victim is transgender. The various forms of this harassment are outlined, and it is suggested that their effect upon victims can be profound. Discussions of transphobic crime are often included with those relating to the victimisation of lesbian, gay and bisexual communities under the 'LGBT' label, suggesting implicitly that the experiences of these groups are similar. The chapter challenges this assumption by unpicking the differences between transphobic and homophobic hate crime. By asking whether the transgender experience of hate crime is unique the chapter will be touching upon one of the book's central conundrums: whether the umbrella term of 'hate crime' can actually be applied to the range of 'bias or prejudice' crimes experienced by such diverse groups as homosexual men, lesbians and transgendered individuals, who may not themselves feel part of a unified 'LGBT' grouping.

The chapter also debates the emotive topic of domestic violence. Part of this discussion will examine the suggestion that LGBT communities, and female victims of domestic violence, are targeted because they 'don't do gender properly'. These crimes are perpetrated by males who are seeking to reaffirm their position at the top of a hierarchical society ordered by gender, with heterosexual masculinity at the top of this structure, and with female and other minority forms of sex and gender subordinated below. It is argued by some theorists that heterosexual males reassert their powerful position through acts of violence, whether they are directed against homosexuals, transgendered people or women. It is within this context that comparisons are drawn between hate offences, such as homophobic and transphobic crimes, and domestic violence.

Introduction

Within the study of hate crime it is important to recognise the complexities of the relationship between gender, sex and sexuality, especially when the victim is of a minority sexuality or is someone who does not conform to 'standard' ideas of gender. For example, understanding how these facets, so central to a person's identity and sense of self, interrelate with each other can help uncover any commonalities between homophobic and transphobic victimisation. Furthermore, knowledge of how these two issues link with another emotive offence, domestic violence, is also important for understanding why it is that the latter is commonly thought *not* to be an example of a hate crime yet the former *are*.

A useful starting point in this discussion is an analysis of the concepts of 'gender' and 'sex'. For Namaste (2006: 587), 'gender' refers to societal expectations of the 'roles and meanings assigned to men and women on their presumed biological sex'. Whittle (2002: 253) cites Zucker and Bradley's (1995) idea that gender roles are 'behaviours, attitudes, and personality traits that a society, in a given culture and historical period, designates as masculine or feminine'. 'Sex', on the other hand, refers to someone's biological characteristics at birth, with especial reference to their genitalia, which usually means that they are categorised as being either 'male' or 'female'. As we shall see below, however, this categorisation can itself cause problems if the recipient disagrees with it because they feel at odds with their biological sex. Also, the defining of someone's sex through the nature of their genitalia is, for Bettcher (2007), deeply entrenched in dominant societal notions of gender. Yet this method of definition is, for Kessler and McKenna (2000), merely 'a social construction' as 'virtually all of the time, gender attribution is made with no direct knowledge of the genitals or any other biological "sex marker"' (cited in Ekins and King, 2006: 15). Therefore, for Kessler and McKenna, it is how a person *performs* their gendered role (through behaviour and appearance) that governs how their gender identity is perceived by others, rather than their actual physiology. This framework thus provides the necessary space for the construction of a plurality of gender identities, rather than just the oppositional binary of male and female, and also challenges 'accepted' and traditional ideas of how men and women behave, function and present themselves (see Case Study 5.1).

Case Study 5.1: What do we mean by 'transgender' and 'transsexual'?

The lack of a consensus in the definitions of 'transsexual' and 'transgender' is due to the sheer complexities of the concepts involved – sex, gender, identity and sexuality – and the wide range of disciplines, from gender studies to feminism and from sociology through politics to psychology and psychiatry, in which they are discussed.

Often the debate centres upon the significance of gendered behaviour rather than the physical or surgical details of what actually constitutes a male or a female. There is therefore scope for someone who is physically male to behave and dress in a feminine fashion, and consider themselves female, and yet also for someone to have hormone treatment and surgery and *physically* become female.[1] One term for the former person could be 'transgendered' and for the latter, 'transsexual'. Bettcher expands these ideas (2007: 46, emphasis added):

> *Transgender* may be used to refer to people who do not appear to conform to traditional gender norms by presenting and living genders that were not assigned to them at birth or by presenting and living genders in ways that may not be readily intelligible in terms of more traditional conceptions. The term may or may not be used to include transsexual …

> *Transsexual* may be used to refer to individuals who use hormonal and/or surgical technologies to alter their body in ways that may be construed as at odds with the sex assignment of birth or which may not be readily intelligible in terms of traditional conceptions of sexed bodies. Traditionally, the term has been connected to psychiatric notions such as gender dysphoria and also associated with the metaphor 'trapped in the wrong body'. Yet *transsexual* has also been deployed in ways amenable to and possibly subsumable under the more recent term *transgender.*[2]

Abbreviations are often used to denote those who have 'transitioned' from one gender to another. A person who was male but has become female is often denoted as MTF ('male-to-female'), while someone who has undergone the opposite experience is frequently cited as FTM ('female-to-male'). This and all related terminology needs to be used with care and sensitivity, which is why surveys of such communities can include gender categories such as 'crossdresser, drag queen, drag king, transsexual man (FTM), transsexual woman (MTF), transgender man, transgender woman' (GenderPAC survey, in Lombardi et al., 2001: 93). Juang (2006: 711) goes further, citing Stryker's (1998) assertion that there is a 'wild profusion of gender subject positions' including 'FTM, MTF, eonist, invert, androgyne, butch, femme, nellie, queen, third sex, hermaphrodite, tomboy, sissy, drag king, female impersonator, she-male, he-she, boy dyke, girlfag, transsexual, transvestite, transgender, cross-dresser'. Furthermore, a trans person may move from one trans identity to another over time (Whittle, Turner and Al-Alami, 2007).

The sheer multitude of these positions can complicate discussions of transgender issues enormously. What is clear, though, is that transsexuality should not be confused with homosexuality, although this error is not uncommon among the general public (Namaste, 2006). While issues of sexuality are important and are interwoven with gender, transsexual people can be gay, straight or bisexual – just like 'ordinary' members of the public.

'Sexuality' is itself a concept distinct from both gender and sex, and 'refers to the ways in which individuals organise their erotic and sexual lives' (Namaste, 2006: 588). Again, though, (as discussed in Chapter 4) there are dominant ideas and expectations within most Western societies regarding sexuality and sexual behaviour that are usually based upon 'acceptable' conceptions of heterosexuality. This in turn can breed a climate of heteronormativity (the institutional privileging of heterosexuality), which devalues or denigrates other forms of sexuality, such as homosexuality. Just as with gender, however, sexuality can have a myriad of permutations that exceed hegemonic and rather restrictive societal expectations of sexual behaviour (see Beasley (2005) for an extended discussion of sexuality).

For Butler (1990), however, gender is 'performative' and is not based upon physical differences between people. Furthermore, Butler suggests that differences in male and female genitalia are no more important a physical characteristic than the colour of one's eyes (cited in Beasley, 2005). Butler therefore rejects the kind of feminist politics discussed in the 'Domestic violence' section below as, for her, such a stance promotes and supports the idea of oppositional binary genders, like male and female, whereas Butler's aim is to 'disrupt categories *per se*, to disrupt the fixity of identity by showing up its non-natural incoherence' (Beasley, 2005: 105). Butler's work concentrates upon those who may feel that they belong to neither gender or perhaps even to both, and are therefore marginalised from traditional constructions of gendered society. These 'gender outlaws' (Whittle, 1996) can often be the target of violence and intimidation, discussed in the 'Transphobic hate crime' section below.

Butler's work, and that of other 'queer theorists', is important for developing a framework that can include some of those who are the victims of homophobic and transphobic violence. Such a framework challenges commonly-held societal assumptions about the demarcation of gender, sexual desire and identity: it is, in the words of Whittle (2002: 67), a 'full frontal' attack on established notions of gender and sex roles. It questions the taken-for-granted assumption that male bodies, for example, automatically produce a certain kind of heterosexual masculinity. Instead, queer theory offers a model that allows for the fluidity and permeability of gender and sexual boundaries while questioning associated hierarchies.

Similarly, for Goffman, society places heterosexual masculinity in the dominant position in a gender and sexual hierarchy. Goffman (1963: 128, cited in Perry, 2001: 106) describes this ideal, or hegemonic, masculinity, as:

a young, married, white, urban, northern, heterosexual Protestant father, of college education, fully employed, of good complexion, weight and height, and a recent record in sports. … Any male who fails to qualify in any of these ways is likely to view himself – during moments at least – as unworthy, incomplete and inferior.

This structure exists not only between genders but also within them, meaning that all other types of masculinity that do not conform to this 'alpha male' image, and all forms of femininity, are subsumed under it. A contentious aspect of queer theory, though, is that in some respects it does *not* offer space that incorporates transgendered perspectives, but rather excludes them. It does this because it challenges the very notion of clearly defined genders, and yet for many in the transgendered communities the identification with a certain gender is the most important facet of their lives. Their sense of gender identity is so strong that it defines not only who they are but perhaps also who they want to become, i.e. it may be the catalyst for the process of transitioning from one gender to another. Thus, rather than 'queering' gendered boundaries, for some commentators, transgendered people actually reinforce them (see Beasley, 2005).

However, it is not just queer theory that offers challenges to the very notion of transsexualism. Feminism, for example, has, on a 'theoretical, political and cultural level ... been largely hostile to transgender practices' (Hines, 2007: 17). Some radical feminists, such as Janice Raymond, argue that it is patriarchal society that has generated such clearly defined notions of masculinity and femininity, and yet transsexuals, rather than offering a new and 'queered' version of gender, merely find themselves in the situation where 'uniquely restricted by patriarchy's definitions of masculinity and femininity, the transsexual becomes body-bound by them and merely rejects one and gravitates towards another' (1980, cited in Ekins and King, 2006: 76). She controversially argues that 'All transsexuals rape women's bodies by reducing the real female form to an artefact, appropriating this body for themselves' (Raymond, 1979: 49, cited in Whittle, 2002: 49). She also sees MTF transsexuals as 'pastiches' of women that reinforce male domination.

Such a rejection of MTF transsexuals by some radical feminists may undermine attempts to find similarities between different forms of hate-related violence, such as homophobic and transphobic violence, and domestic violence. In the case of transphobic violence, if its victims are nevertheless viewed as reinforcing the patriarchal society that is seen by many feminists as being the root cause of much domestic violence, then it becomes clear that victims of transphobic and domestic violence can have little in common. However, it could be argued that Perry's (2001: 107) suggestion that 'anti-gay violence [is] an active exercise in the construction of gender' has some similarities to Walby's (1990) view that heterosexuality is central to the patriarchal structure of society. If it is understood that the recipients of homophobic and transphobic violence are the 'gender outsiders' within a heteronormative society subject to a strict gender hierarchy that has *all* forms of gender identity subservient to that of heterosexual males, then victims of homophobic and transphobic hate crime may have more in common with victims of domestic violence than some feminist theorists may credit. It is to an analysis of transphobic violence that this book now turns.

Transphobic hate crime

As was discussed in Chapter 4, the phenomena of homophobia and transphobia have historically been treated by many academics and practitioners as issues with a number of shared characteristics. However, within the last decade transphobia has begun to receive attention in its own right, and is now more readily acknowledged as being a separate phenomenon from homophobia. Bettcher (2007: 46) sees transphobia as 'any negative attitudes (hatred, loathing, rage, or moral indignation) harboured toward transpeople on the basis of enactments of [their] gender' and Bornstein's (2006: 238) definition equates to the fear and hatred of anyone seen as a 'border-dweller' (someone who occupies a gender position that may be on the margins of the 'accepted' male/female dichotomy). Hill and Willoughby (2005: 533-534) offer a more detailed explanation:

> [Transphobia entails] emotional disgust toward individuals who do not conform to society's gender expectations; [and transphobia] involves the feeling of revulsion to masculine women, feminine men, cross-dressers, transgenderists, and/or transsexuals. Specifically, transphobia manifests itself in the fear that personal acquaintances may be trans or disgust upon encountering a trans person ... the 'phobia' suffix is used to imply an irrational fear or hatred, one that is at least partly perpetuated by cultural ideology.

This definition, by broadening the scope of negative feelings to include the revulsion and irrational fear of a range of gender 'non-conformists' (see Case Study 5.1), provides a more complete picture of transphobia. It is also particularly helpful as it incorporates the importance of wider societal attitudes and prejudices that dominate as a form of 'cultural ideology'. Meanwhile, a very succinct practitioner-oriented definition is supplied by ACPO (2005: 11), who classify a transphobic hate incident as: 'Any incident which is perceived to be transphobic by the victim or any other person.'

Nature and extent of transphobic hate crime

There is some evidence that transphobic hate crimes are more extreme than homophobic ones (Johnson et al., 2007: 15). The incidence of transphobic victimisation may be higher (Mitchell, 2004), with many transgendered people experiencing the 'pervasive and everyday presence of violence' (Moran and Sharpe, 2004: 396) which is 'grossly under-reported' (Lombardi et al., 2001: 91). Alarmingly, Bettcher (2007: 46) notes 14 murders of transsexuals in the USA in 2003 and 38 worldwide. According to Juang (2006), there are roughly two killings of transsexuals reported each month in the USA. Perhaps the most infamous of these (as it inspired the 1999 film *Boys Don't Cry*) was the 'execution style' shooting of Brandon Teena (a FTM transgendered person) in rural

Table 5.1   Transgendered people's experience of violence or harassment during lifetime

Victim of ...	Percentage
Harassment or violence	59.5
Street harassment/verbal abuse	55.5
Violence	26.6
Being followed or stalked	22.9
Assaulted without a weapon	19.4
Object being thrown at them	17.4
Rape/attempted rape	13.7
Assaulted with a weapon	10.2

Source: Lombardi et al. (2001: 96)

Nebraska in 1993 (Halberstam, 2005). However, such incidents are not unknown in the UK, as the 2007 murder of Kellie Telesford (a MTF trans woman) in her London flat illustrates (Grew, 2007).[3]

Like other forms of hate crime, the prevalence of transphobic incidents is hard to gauge as there are few official reported incidents in the UK, although many more are recorded in community surveys (Moran and Sharpe, 2004; Wolhuter et al., 2009). It is interesting, though, that a number of the surveys discussed in Chapter 4 were of 'LGBT' people (and not solely gay groups), meaning that the transgender experience is subsumed under the LGBT umbrella and consequently its specificities are lost. It therefore makes direct comparisons between the different minorities – based on sexuality, on the one hand, and gender/sex on the other – difficult.

There is also much less research on the transgendered experience of hate crime. A useful starting point is Whittle, Turner and Al-Alami's (2007: 52) finding from their online survey of over 870 trans people that over 70 per cent had had 'experienced comments, threatening behaviour, physical abuse, verbal abuse or sexual abuse while in public spaces'. Similar high rates of victimisation were uncovered in Lombardi et al.'s survey (2001) of 402 transgendered people, which found that almost 60 per cent of respondents reported having been a victim of violence or harassment.

Table 5.1 also shows that over a quarter of respondents had endured violence and over half had been harassed or verbally abuse in the street (and Lombardi et al.'s (2001) research also shows that a third had been harassed or verbally abused in the past year alone). One in five had been assaulted without a weapon and one in eight had experienced rape or attempted rape. Almost half had suffered assault at some point in their lives. These rates are similar to those for homophobic victimisation outlined in Chapter 4 and may hint at some commonalities between homophobic and transphobic hate crime. Certainly it appears that the forms these crimes can take are similar, and their incidence is also broadly comparable. However, while some of the research into homophobic harassment did not find the workplace to be a significant location for such incidents, Lombardi et al.'s analysis of transphobic abuse is less ambiguous, with its suggestion that 'workplace discrimination is so rampant that it is the norm amongst transgendered people' (2001: 98).

Educational establishments are also common sites for transphobic hate crime, as they were found to be for homophobic harassment in Chapter 4. Whittle et al. (2007: 17) found that over half of the young trans men, and just under half of young trans women, they surveyed had experienced harassment and bullying at school; higher rates than for comparable homophobic victimisation. The same authors found a significant problem within higher education, with the following being a typical experience of a MTF trans student:

> I was attacked in the Student Union at 'x' University for being 'A transgender cunt' and had a knife thrown at me which hit me just above my right eye. Our Student Union does not have a good record of upholding equal opportunities...

Bettcher (2007: 46) argues that around 80 per cent of transgendered people have been victims of verbal transphobic abuse and 30 per cent to almost half had suffered some form of physical assault, slightly higher than some of the surveys of homophobic harassment mentioned in Chapter 4. There is also the suggestion that rates of victimisation can vary according to the victim's MTF or FTM status. Participants in Moran and Sharpe's (2004) research felt that MTF transsexuals had worse experiences of transphobic hate crime than FTM, which could be due to the fact that they pose a more significant challenge to society's ideas of both heteronormativity and gender hierarchies than FTM transsexuals, a notion echoed by Whittle et al. (2007).

One FTM transsexual in Moran and Sharpe's (2004: 405) study reported suffering death threats, threats of rape, homophobic graffiti, the smashing of his windows and having bottles thrown at him after his transgendered identity was revealed on television. Dittman (2003: 284) spoke movingly of her experiences of being a victim of hate while transitioning from male to female:

> I have been given a beautiful black eye, had bricks thrown at me, drinks tipped over me in bars, and plenty of verbal abuse. I think verbal abuse is perhaps the more difficult and insidious form of what I consider to be a hate crime. It has been a revelation to me that people believe that they have, because of your nature, the right to abuse you, and you are expected to play the role of the cowering victim.

Thus, while being 'out' carries greater risk of violence for all LGBT groups, the risks may be worse for those transsexual individuals who do not visibly conform to society's accepted notions of how males and females should look, and therefore experience 'regular and extreme levels of physical and verbal abuse' (Johnson et al., 2007: 18; Spalek, 2008).

Such harassment may go unrecorded in official statistics as transphobic incidents may be misrecorded as homophobic ones or the victim's transgendered status may be misunderstood or ignored (Juang, 2006). Indeed, it was interesting to note that some of the tabloid reporting of the murder of Kellie Telesford in 2007 was infused with just such misunderstandings, with the *Sun*, for example, repeatedly referring to Kellie as a 'transvestite' despite her living full-time as a female for over seven years (Online Reporter, 2007). The reporting of the birth of a girl to a FTM transsexual in 2008 also received a degree of mischievous and salacious coverage from Britain's 'red tops' (Pilkington, 2008). As Bettcher (2007: 54) argues:

> It is precisely the fact that transpeople often do not have their self-identifications taken seriously that is so deeply bound up with transphobic hostility and violence. How can we ignore the fact that often 'transgender woman' simply means 'man disguised as a woman' to so many people?

These difficulties can be compounded by other factors that are unique to the transgender experience. For example, a victim's sense of self-worth can be further dented by the fact that those who want gender reassignment surgery are classified as having gender identity disorders, and therefore psychiatrists still regulate gender reassignment processes, which can damage self-esteem and self-acceptance (Johnson et al., 2007). The victim therefore has to cope with the trauma of experiencing a hate incident while also coping with the stigma of being 'pathologised'. It is no surprise, therefore, to note that studies that focus specifically on transgendered people have found elevated rates of suicide and self-harming behaviour in adolescents and adults (Lombardi et al., 2001).

Legal protection from transphobic hate crime

Transgendered victims of hate crime do not appear to enjoy the same provisions under the law as do other victims of hate-related harassment or violence. As already noted, while the Crime and Disorder Act 1998 and the Criminal Justice Act 2003 instruct courts to impose longer sentences for crimes motivated by homophobic, racist, disablist or religious hostility, there are no equivalent legal provisions for crimes motivated by transphobia. While courts do have 'a general power and discretion to increase sentences that are aggravated by transphobic hostility' (CPS, 2007c: 20), they do not have a statutory *duty* to do so, leaving victims of transphobic harassment on something of an unequal footing with victims of homophobic harassment, for example – a rather puzzling anomaly. [4]

This anomaly is also reflected in the provisions of section 74 of the Criminal Justice and Immigration Act 2008, which, as mentioned in Chapter 4, make the incitement of hatred on the grounds of someone's sexual orientation an offence.

This section, however, does not cover incitement based upon someone's transgendered status, illustrating that, once again, gay communities enjoy broader legislative protection than transgendered ones. This perhaps reflects Whittle et al.'s assertion that 'every legal gain made by the UK trans community has been through the courts rather than through the good will of a government pledged to equalities for all' (Whittle et al., 2007: 10), although other pieces of legislation paint a less gloomy picture. For instance, the Gender Reassignment Regulations 1999 offers trans people a degree of protection from discrimination while transitioning and the Gender Recognition Act 2004 enables trans people to obtain a birth certificate in their new gender, and also marrying in that gender. These developments have undoubtedly provided a step forward in the trans communities' struggle for equal rights under the law.[5]

Transphobic and homophobic victimisation compared

As has been mentioned above, often the specificities of the transgendered experience of hate crime have been lost due to the propensity of practitioners to employ the broad 'LGBT' category under which sexual and gender minorities are subsumed. By doing this, practitioners are assuming that the nature of the lesbian, gay, bisexual and transgendered populations' victimisation is broadly similar, and also that the groups themselves have enough in common for them to be thought of as a unified LGBT grouping. Indeed, there is some evidence that, by not 'doing gender properly' (Perry, 2001), LGB and transgendered people may be victimised for broadly the same reason: that they do not conform to gender or sexual norms (Moran and Sharpe, 2004). Namaste (2006) argues that the public often confuses gender and sexuality, and that if the perception of gender dissidence informs homophobic harassment, then those individuals who live outside normative sex/gender relations, whether they be lesbian, gay or transgender, will be most at risk of assault. Furthermore, Namaste (ibid: 588) contends that gay men behaving effeminately are at a much higher risk of homophobic violence than those who behave in a 'masculine' way.

McDonald (2006) and Tomsen and Mason (2001) argue that much homophobic violence directed against lesbians and gay men is *gendered* and is mainly perpetrated by men seeking to preserve the dominant status of masculinity within society's gendered hierarchy. Violence directed against lesbians and gay men is fuelled by perceptions that they are not performing gender roles 'correctly' (either by being 'butch' lesbians or effeminate men, for example), rather than by hatred against gay people *per se*. According to Tomsen and Mason (2001: 270), gender shapes 'much of the dynamics and commonality of homophobic violence'.

As the evidence in this chapter and Chapter 4 has suggested, the effects of transphobic and homophobic harassment may also be similar, with LGB and transgendered victims feeling isolated, depressed and anxious. However, Johnson et al. (2007) suggest that these feelings can be heightened for transgendered people, who can become more likely to be homeless, to self-harm or to feel suicidal. The same authors argue that, for those transgendered people who have difficultly passing in their chosen gender, the risk of hate-related harassment may be higher than for gay groups and may be more extreme (ibid). This may explain why transgendered young people have a greater likelihood of attempting suicide than other populations (Rogers, 1995, in Lombardi et al., 2001).

Whether it is appropriate to employ an all-inclusive LGBT banner under which homophobic and transphobic hate crimes can be grouped is somewhat unclear. Cahill and Kin-Butler (2006), for example, cite the 2006 US National Lesbian and Gay Task Force survey in which hate crime came out as the third most-mentioned policy priority for transgendered people, yet it was not in the top three for gay males. This may indicate that hate crime may be a more overt concern for transgendered communities or it may suggest that these communities have further to travel in their struggle for equality than gay male populations. Certainly, Dittman (2003: 287), herself a MTF transsexual person, is clear that the police and other agencies should recognise the important distinction between gender identity and sexuality, even if the consequences of hate crime are similar for sexual and gendered minority communities.

Another important implication of the broad LGBT category is that often the associated groups do not see themselves as one unified community. Indeed, there is evidence that transgendered women face discrimination from certain LGB groups, including gay men and feminist lesbians (Moran and Sharpe, 2004; Beasley, 2005). Stryker (2006: 245) asserts that some of this invective is so extreme that, if said of other minority groups, 'would see print only in the most hate-riddled, white supremacist, Christian fascist rags', and goes on to quote from one letter to a US gay/lesbian periodical:

> I consider transsexualism to be a fraud, and the participants in it ... perverted. ... When an estrogenated man with breasts loves a woman, that is not lesbianism, that is mutilated perversion. [This individual] is not a threat to the lesbian community, he is an outrage to us. He is not a lesbian, he is a mutant man, a self-made freak, a deformity, an insult.

Such prejudiced thinking reveals a rift within the LGBT 'community' which may indicate that it is unwise to perceive that much unity exists between the different groups within it. Meanwhile, Bettcher (2007) suggests that minority ethnic transsexuals suffer higher rates of transphobic victimisation than their white equivalents, an interesting point that also raises the issue of intersectionality: the idea that individual identities should not be understood and solely defined under one label based upon one aspect of that person (such as their sexuality or transgendered status), but rather it is the *intersection* of their many different identity aspects, including sexuality, age, disability and ethnicity, that is most important (Spalek, 2008). By doing this, Moran and Sharpe (2004: 400) argue that simplistic assumptions about the nature of transphobic victimisation can be avoided, and other factors, such as the victim's ethnicity, can also be taken into account. Their perspective may offer a way forward, as, for all the commonalities in the nature of hate-related victimisation suffered by the different lesbian, gay, bisexual and transgendered groups, their experiences can best be understood if the multiple facets of their identities are fully acknowledged.

Domestic violence

In 2001 an Open University television documentary examined the new methods of policing hate crime employed by the Metropolitan Police Service (MPS) in the wake of the 1999 Macpherson report. The programme-makers followed the work of officers assigned to a borough community safety unit responsible for handling hate crime incidents, which at the time included 'domestic violence, homophobic attacks and hate mail, as well as racist crime' (Open University, 2001). It is interesting to note, though, that just a few years later the list of offences freshly defined by ACPO as 'hate crimes' omitted domestic violence (ACPO, 2005), and in the years since the Open University documentary domestic violence has also appeared to fall outside the MPS's specific hate crime remit (Metropolitan Police Service, 2007). The remainder of this chapter will assess whether ACPO and the MPS were correct in deciding that domestic violence should not, after all, be considered as a hate crime.

While there are a number of competing ideas surrounding definitions of domestic violence, a lack of space prevents them from being discussed here (see Jackson, 2007). Instead, the Home Office's (2008b) definition will be adopted for the purposes of this chapter. This refers to domestic violence as: 'any incident of threatening behaviour, violence or abuse between adults who are or have been in a relationship together, or between family members, regardless of gender or sexuality'.

As Goodey (2005) suggests, domestic violence is a common and widespread problem that can involve repeat victimisation over a number of years. While commonly understood as an issue with mainly female victims, in fact domestic violence 'is experienced to a similar degree by both sexes' (ibid: 83). However, the British Crime Survey (BCS) has repeatedly shown that women are more likely than men to have been subjected to, or threatened with, physical or sexual violence. The 2004/05 sweep revealed that 20 per cent of women (aged 16 to 59) and 11 per cent of men in England and Wales had experienced, or been threatened with, domestic violence since they were aged 16. If the definition is extended to include financial, emotional and sexual abuse, these percentages increased to 25 per cent and 16 per cent respectively.[6] Although comparing different rounds of the BCS suggests that the number of men who admit victimisation appears to be growing, it remains the case that well over two-thirds of victims are women (Walby and Allen, 2004). There may also be other explanations for official statistics showing an apparent rise in male victimisation, such as the use of violence by female victims who are defending themselves against assault from males (Walklate, 2008).

As Walby's (2004) analysis of BCS data shows in Table 5.2, women constituted nearly six out of ten of those who had suffered 'non-sexual severe domestic force'. Victims reported a wide variety of assaults, with the most commonly cited in the severest category being 'kicked, bit, hit with fist', followed by 'threats to kill'. Interestingly (and alarmingly), over nine out of ten of those reporting being choked or being subject to an attempted strangulation were women, as were those who had experienced a threat to kill them.

Table 5.2   Estimate of number of victims of domestic violence by type of act

Type of domestic violence (violence from intimates)	Number of female victims	Number of male victims	Total number of victims
Domestic homicide	102	23	125
Non-sexual severe domestic force within which:	242,000	186,000	428,000
Choked or tried to strangle	65,000	6,000	71,000
Used a weapon	13,000	11,000	24,000
Kicked, bit, hit with fist	205,000	177,000	382,000
Threat to kill	82,000	13,000	95,000
Threat with a weapon	36,000	16,000	52,000
Non-sexual minor domestic force (pushed, held down, or slapped)	410,000	174,000	584,000

Source: Walby (2004: 30)

Mirrlees-Black and Byron (1999, cited in Goodey, 2005: 84) argue that women's experience is qualitatively worse, even if some statistics suggest that men and women may be equally frequent victims of domestic violence, inferring that, on average, men are: 'less upset by their experience; considerably less frightened; often less injured; less likely to seek medical help'. Walby and Allen (2004) found that women comprised nine out of ten of those subject to more than three incidents of domestic violence from the same perpetrator since they were aged 16. Nearly one in three had experienced domestic violence from this person on four or more occasions compared to only around one in ten of men. Spalek (2008) also suggests that domestic violence elicits a high level of fear in victims, with women especially nervous and fearful of future victimisation from male partners.

These findings are important within the remit of this book: if domestic violence is a form of *gendered* crime that impacts worst upon women, and if women are viewed as a disadvantaged group, then there may be some parallels with other forms of hate crime. For example, if a minority ethnic victim of a racist incident is also deemed to a victim of a hate crime – as they have suffered 'acts of violence and intimidation' due to their membership of a 'stigmatised and marginalised' group', as Perry's definition states (Perry, 2001: 10, see Chapter 1) – then there could be a case for arguing that female victims of domestic violence also fit that definition, as women have, historically, suffered discrimination and marginalisation economically, politically and socially.

Moreover, just as homophobic and transphobic violence can have a more profound impact upon victims than other forms of hate crime, so injuries sustained from domestic violence can be worse than those suffered during other forms of violent crimes (Morley and Mullender, 1994). Importantly, domestic violence can also have a long-term impact on the mental health of the victim, just as racist, religious, homophobic or transphobic hate crimes also can upon their victims. Such an impact can induce feelings of anxiety, fear, self-loathing and depression which leave the victim with a damaged sense of self-worth – something which undoubtedly links many victims of interpersonal violence, whatever its hue.

Also, as is the case with racist, homophobic and transphobic hate crimes, there is a high degree of repeat victimisation with domestic violence, with, for example, more than two in five of those reporting domestic violence having been victimised repeatedly (Dodd et al., 2004). As was discussed in earlier chapters, Kelly's (1987) concept of victims of sexual violence experiencing a 'continuum of violence' can be adapted and applied to victims of hate crimes too, as all of these varieties of victim can face actual and potential victimisation on an everyday basis. Kelly also suggests that one of the main aims of violence is the social control of the victim group, which in the case of her work refers to women. This may have parallels with the concept of hate crimes as 'message crimes' perpetrated not just to inflict physical harm on victims, but also in order to intimidate and subjugate members of their wider minority communities. These forms of violence are not idiosyncratic personal expressions but are mechanisms of 'power and oppression' (Perry, 2001: 10) enacted to reinforce publicly dominant discourses that support the subordination of historically marginalised groups.

This suggestion – that the perpetrator is part of a hegemonic group and the victim part of a subordinate one – may have resonance with theories of the 'patriarchal society' developed by some feminist thinkers. As Walby (1990: 128) comments, for example, 'male violence has all the characteristics one would expect of a social structure … it cannot be understood outside of an analysis of patriarchal social structures'. Thus male-perpetrated domestic violence has *meaning*, designed (in part) to intimidate and subordinate the social group of its victim while reinforcing the dominant societal position of its male perpetrators – just as hate crimes are intended to 're-create simultaneously the threatened (real or imagined) hegemony of the perpetrator's group and the "appropriate" subordinate identity of the victim's group' (Perry, 2001: 10). Perry draws further comparison by suggesting that violence targeted at lesbians could be an extension of broader patterns of male misogyny, enacted by males who feel that lesbians are not performing their gendered roles correctly and occupy a position that is independent of the kind of male-dominated social structures that perpetrators want to reinforce.

For Tomsen and Mason (2001), though, feminist explanatory models of patterns of violence towards women, which emphasise gender inequalities and dominant social constructions of masculinity, marginalise the issue of sexuality in anti-female violence. They argue that some feminist theories of violence are too rooted in the male/female binary, within which sexuality becomes synonymous with heterosexuality. As a result, the homophobic element of anti-lesbian violence is, in Tomsen and Mason's view, dismissed by many feminists keen to prioritise gender issues above those of sexuality, thereby inadvertently marginalising the experience of some female victims of violence perpetrated by males.

Another key aspect of Perry's (2001) conception of hate crime is that the victim should not be personally known to the perpetrator. For Perry, hate crimes are inherently 'stranger danger' offences in which the personal identity of the victim is irrelevant to the attacker, who has assaulted them merely because they are a member of a group that is despised and 'othered'. Victims are thus interchangeable with another member of the same minority group as it is the group itself that is under attack from the perpetrator. On face value, at least, domestic violence would not appear to fit this idea of a hate crime for, as Stanko (1990) suggests, women are most at risk of attack from the men they actually know as friends, neighbours and partners, rather than strangers. However, the picture is more complex than this, for, as discussed in more detail in Chapter 8, scholars such as Mason (2005b) and Ray and Smith (2001) cast some doubt as to whether hate crimes are really clear-cut 'stranger danger' crimes as there appears to be a significant proportion of acts of hate-related harassment, for example, in which the perpetrator and the victim know each other – at least to a certain degree. Indeed, there is evidence that a significant proportion of racist and homophobic harassment occurs in local neighbourhoods and even in the home, which is the location in which female victims of domestic violence are most at risk.

However, Tomsen and Mason's (2001) study of homophobic harassment may cast some doubt on these similarities between hate crime and domestic violence. Tomsen and Mason highlight the gendered differences in homophobic victimisation, with gay men less likely to be victims of 'privatised violence' than lesbians. They also suggest that lesbians are more at risk of attack from strangers than heterosexual women are. Lesbians may therefore be more frequent victims of the type of incidents that more easily fit the 'stranger danger' hate crime model than their heterosexual female counterparts, who are more likely to be victims of violence in the home, perpetrated by a male with whom they are intimate.

Conclusion

The chapter began by assessing issues of gender, sex and sexuality, and how their multifaceted relationships can have implications for the study of transphobic and homophobic hate crime. Of particular relevance was the idea that gender might not be a natural 'given' based upon biology, but instead may be a socially constructed and performative phenomenon that can be lived or enacted in many different ways. The challenge posed by queer theorists to traditional notions of gender, sex and sexuality was also discussed, especially within the context of those 'gender outlaws', like transgendered and transsexual people, who do not conform to conventional understandings of gendered and sexed roles. The impact of transphobic hate crime was then debated, and it was suggested that it can be more severe and more commonplace than other forms of hate crime, and an especially pertinent problem for those male-to-female transsexuals who have difficulty in passing as female.

The complexities of the emotive problem of domestic violence were also outlined, and parallels were also drawn between this form of interpersonal crime and others, such as racist or homophobic harassment, which are commonly regarded as hate crimes. We have seen that there are some similarities between domestic violence and hate crimes, such as the fact that patterns of violence tend to be broadly similar, with many victims experiencing a continuum of violence that involves repeat victimisation. Moreover, some feminist explanations of domestic violence (which suggest that it is a product of a hierarchal, male-dominated society and is enacted to maintain this structure) are similar, in some respects, to explanations of hate crime that also see its purpose as being to maintain one group's dominant position while simultaneously reinforcing the subordinate position of the victim's group.

Some commentators feel that gender is central to the perpetration of homophobic and transphobic violence, encapsulated in Bornstein's concept of the perpetrator as a 'gender defender', whose fear and hatred of anyone who contravenes gender norms causes them to 'lash out' at gender or sexual 'outsiders', thus perpetuating 'the violence of male privilege and all its social extensions' (Bornstein, 2006: 237). Both Perry (2001) and Halberstam (2005) also identify perpetrators' violent assertion of their own aggressive heterosexual masculinity as a motivating force behind homophobic and transphobic hate crime, which has some resonance with the theories of writers such as Walby (1990).

Stanko (2001) extends this debate by arguing that domestic, racist and homophobic violence have sufficient commonalities for them to be grouped together, but not as 'hate crimes' *per se*. Stanko finds the 'hate crime' label itself misleading and instead suggests a new term – *targeted violence* – which 'recognises the special vulnerability of individuals because they are in some relational "disadvantage" to the perpetrator without bracketing the kind of vulnerability into a category' (Stanko, 2001: 318). By adopting this term, hate crimes and domestic violence share a common factor: the vulnerability of the victim in relation to the perpetrator. They could also, Stanko posits, be linked by the 'historical, social and economic legacies' and 'popular discourses' that marginalise vulnerable groups (such as minority ethnic people and women) and justify their victimisation in the eyes of their assailant.

However, although there are some similarities between domestic violence and hate crimes, there are also differences. As mentioned in the earlier discussion of sexuality and also of transphobic crime, there is a body of heterosexual and lesbian feminists who do not recognise male-to-female transsexuals as being 'legitimate' females and thus would dismiss any commonalities shared between the victims of transphobic hate crime and domestic violence. Although Whittle (2002: 82) would see this as evidence of the 'homosexual and women's movement's ignorance of the real oppression trans people face', what it certainly does reveal is the schism in the solidity of the supposed 'LGBT' grouping. It is also harder to justify the inclusion of domestic violence under the hate crime 'umbrella' if there are such vocal opponents within those communities of the idea of unity between victims of domestic, homophobic and transphobic violence as those mentioned here.

Another aspect of this debate is whether victims of domestic violence can be deemed to be members of a 'stigmatised and marginalised group', as Perry (2001: 10) suggests they should be if they are to be considered to be victims of hate crimes. While there are some who would view female victims of domestic violence as fulfilling that criteria, what is more difficult to justify is that *male* victims of domestic violence can be considered so. This focus upon male victims may be unpalatable to some who emphasise the gendered nature of this offence, but it is argued here that the high proportion of domestic violence victims who are male – over 40 per cent of the total number of victims of 'non-sexual severe domestic force' and 30 per cent of those subjected to 'non-sexual minor domestic force' (Walby, 2004, see Table 5.2 above) – simply cannot be ignored, even if the female experience of domestic violence is qualitatively worse than the male. Within the context of our discussions, what this means is that if both females *and* males can be acknowledged as victims of domestic violence, and if domestic violence is considered to be a hate crime, then this implies that *anyone* can be a potential victim of a hate crime, something which broadens the concept out so far as to undermine any utility that it may have for highlighting the plight of minority groups that suffer hate-motivated harassment.

Guide to further reading

Beasley, *Gender & Sexuality* (2005) provides an in-depth survey of issues which underpin many of the discussions above. Stryker and Whittle, *The Transgender Studies Reader* (2006) and Ekins and King (2006) *The Transgender Phenomenon* are rich sources of research and opinion on issues of gender identity and sexuality. Whittle, *Respect and Equality* (2002) assesses the trans communities' struggle for legal rights and recognition. Jackson, *Encyclopedia of Domestic Violence* (2007) provides a comprehensive overview of the development of relevant theoretical perspectives.

Notes

1 It is estimated that there are between 5,000 and 6,000 trans people in the UK (Ashdown, 2008: 1).
2 As the debate surrounding these terms is so complex, and remains unresolved, they shall be used interchangeably.
3 In the subsequent murder trial, the person accused of killing Kellie was found not guilty, angering some transgender campaigners who viewed the portrayal of Kellie as some kind of 'deviant' in the trial as key to besmirching her character in the eyes of the jury.
4 In Scotland, the Sentencing of Offences Aggravated by Prejudice (Scotland) Bill proposes additional sentencing tariffs if the hostility towards the victim is based upon their transgendered status.
5 Unfortunately there is not enough room here for a detailed discussion of transgendered communities' struggle for equality under the law; see Whittle (2002) for further analysis.
6 These rates are broadly similar to those reported by victims of violent homophobic harassment.

6

DISABLIST HATE CRIME AND 'BORDERLINE' EXPRESSIONS OF HATE

Chapter summary

This chapter examines different forms of harassment and violence on the margins of the hate debate. It centres initially upon disablist hate crime, a form of hate crime which often finds itself on the periphery of academic and practitioner concerns. Through its assessment of the nature and impact of disablist hate crime, the chapter notes that unlike other forms of hate crime where the perpetrator and victim are often strangers to each other, violent disablist assaults are often carried out by 'friends' or 'carers' whom the victim knows well.

The chapter then turns to consider other forms of harassment and violence which are based upon prejudice but which are *not* routinely viewed as hate crimes, such as elder abuse, attacks upon members of youth subcultures and sectarianism. The disturbing murder in 2007 of Sophie Lancaster, a member of the goth subculture, by youths who attacked her for no other reason than that she was 'different', is of especial interest because the judge at the subsequent trial of her killers made a point of describing the assault as a 'hate crime'. While it is acknowledged that crimes like this do have much in common with other forms of hate crime, it is argued that to define them as such would be to make the hate crime umbrella too 'broad' to have much meaning and would also downplay the importance of the historical context for established forms of hate crime.

The chapter concludes by suggesting that the victimisation of disabled people is rightly classified by the criminal justice system as a hate crime as it shares several characteristics with other forms of this type of crime. Its continuing marginalisation from mainstream hate debates may be down to the fact that those who suffer disablist harassment are not commonly seen as 'ideal victims' deserving of sympathy, and only when this is rectified will disablist hate crime occupy the central place within the hate debate that it deserves.

Disabled people are viewed as being more at risk of hate-related victimisation than the non-disabled population (Miller, Gillinson and Huber, 2006) and are also more likely to be victims of other crimes, have a higher fear of crime but lower trust and confidence in the criminal justice system (Quarmby, 2008: 12). They are also subject to unique prejudice and responses from other sections of society, including 'horror, fear, anxiety, hostility, distrust, pity, over-protection and patronising behaviour' (Barton, 1996: 8).

The Disability Discrimination Act 1995 defines a disabled person as someone with 'a physical or mental impairment which has a substantial and long-term adverse effect on his [sic] ability to carry out normal day-to-day activities' (Office of Public Sector Information, 1995). Interestingly, the Criminal Justice Act of 2003 views disability as any physical or mental impairment, while the Disability Discrimination Act 2005's definition includes people living with HIV/AIDS, cancer or multiple sclerosis. Disabilities can be visible, non-visible, and can range significantly in severity (Disability Rights Commission, 2006), and like the non-disabled populations, disabled communities are diverse, complex and multi-layered. Any discussions of disablist hate crime therefore need to be informed with the understanding that disabled people's experience of such crime can vary according to their disability, and that it is unwise to assume that all disabled people experience the phenomenon in the same way.

There are 11 million people registered as disabled in the UK (Cook, 2007), with the likelihood of someone becoming disabled increasing with age. Yet, despite the possibility that non-disabled people may become disabled at some point in their lives, prejudiced attitudes towards disabled people are 'rife' within society (Miller, Parker and Gillinson, 2004), with commonplace labels such as '"invalid", "cripple", "spastic", "handicapped" and "retarded" all imply[ing] both a functional loss and a lack of worth' (Barton, 1996: 8). This range of negative attitudes and actions towards disability is captured in the term 'disablism', defined succinctly as 'discriminatory, oppressive or abusive behaviour arising from the belief that disabled people are inferior to others' (Miller et al., 2004: 28). It is a prevalence of all forms of disablism within society that can create an atmosphere in which disablist hate crime can flourish and yet remain widely unacknowledged (Barnes, 2006; Deal, 2007), and it is to an analysis of its forms, extent and impact that this chapter now turns.

The ACPO *Hate Crime* manual defines a disablist incident as: 'Any incident which is perceived to be based upon prejudice towards or hatred of the victim because of their disability or so perceived by the victim or any other person' (ACPO, 2005: 11). Therefore, and as is the case with other hate incidents, if the victim or anyone else believes an incident to have been motivated by disablism, then the police are obliged to record and investigate it as such. However, as yet there are no centrally collated annual statistics available to indicate the yearly number of disablist incidents reported to the police, reflecting the fact that accessing any sort of statistics about disablist hate crime is certainly more challenging than it should be. It is therefore very difficult to accurately comprehend the scale of disablist hate crimes (Lamb and Redmond, 2007).[1]

A survey of disabled people in Scotland conducted by Disability Rights Commission and Capability Scotland (DRCCS) revealed that nearly half of their respondents had experienced being frightened or attacked because of their disability, and many participants felt that being scared or victimised was a part of their everyday lives (DRCCS, 2004). Sobsey (1994) suggests that disabled people are at least one-and-a-half times more likely to be the victim of assault or abuse than others of similar age and gender, and typically experience more prolonged and severe abuse, with more serious effects.

In response to a survey on the subject of hate crime against those with learning disabilities, more than four out of five disabled advocacy groups and three out of four partnership boards said hate crime was a problem (Lamb and Redmond, 2007: 3). Miller et al. (2004: 24) cite evidence collated by Disability Awareness in Action which shows that since 1990 thousands of disabled people have suffered verbal, sexual and physical abuse, with hundreds more having been murdered or denied life-saving treatment. Worryingly, it appears that the incidence of disablist crime is rising (House of Commons Northern Ireland Affairs Committee, 2005; Rickell, 2007).

Among the most vulnerable disabled groups are those with mental health problems, learning difficulties and visual impairments (Iganski, 2008). The charity Mind's investigation into hate crime directed against people with mental distress indicates that over seven out of ten of their respondents had been a victim of crime or harassment in the last two years and felt this was related to their mental health history, while four out of ten were victims of ongoing bullying. Nearly a quarter of their respondents had been physically assaulted and one in ten had been sexually assaulted (Mind, 2007: 2). Mencap's analysis showed that nearly four out of five children and young people with a learning disability are verbally abused and that three out of five are physically hurt (Mencap, 2007: 5–6). Typical of these cases is the experience of a youth with learning difficulties, Ben, who:

> ... often returned home with spit on him or the tyres of his bike deflated. On some days he was chased by a group of children until he reached the safety of home. ... Ben was bullied wherever he went. He would return from the park with bruises and torn clothes. As far as the local kids were concerned, Ben was there for their entertainment. He was the butt of their jokes, an object to ridicule. (ibid: 8)

In a similar fashion to other hate crimes, the most common forms of disablist harassment are 'low-level' ones, such as name-calling, unnecessary staring or being made to feel unwelcome or even at risk (Rainbow Ripples and Butler, 2006: 207). Three-quarters of respondents to the DRCCS survey reported being verbally attacked, a third had been physically assaulted and another third harassed in the street (DRCCS 2004: 18). Mind's (2007) examination of hate crime targeted at those with a history of mental health problems also revealed that name-calling was the most common form, but that being 'bullied or continually targeted' was also a significant problem (see Table 6.1).

Table 6.1 Experience of crime or harassment in the community linked to mental health history over the past two years

Incident	Percentage
Called names or insulted	62
Bullied or continually targeted	41
Theft	34
Followed, pestered or chased, had things thrown at them	29
Sexually harassed	27
Home targeted	26
Physically assaulted	22
Hate mail or prank phone calls	17
Spat at	13
Sexually assaulted	10

Source: Mind (2007: 6)

It is especially disturbing to see that over a quarter of Mind's respondents had been sexually harassed, while as many as one in five had also been physically assaulted. Although physical assaults rarely result in the death of the victim, there has nevertheless been a spate of shocking murders of disabled people within the last decade. Perhaps the most high-profile of these was the killing of Brent Martin in 2007, which is summarised in Case Study 6.1.

Case Study 6.1: 'I'm not going down for a muppet': the murder of Brent Martin

In August 2007 Brent Martin, a 23-year-old male with a history of mental health problems and learning difficulties, bumped into William Hughes, Marcus Miller and Stephen Bonallie on their home estate of Sunderland's Town End Farm. He regarded the three young men as his friends. Unbeknown to Brent, however, the three had just had a £5 bet between them as to who could knock Brent unconscious first. In an ordeal which stretched for over a mile across the housing estate, Brent was kicked, punched, stamped upon and headbutted. For a while he was dragged along by his

(Continued)

(Continued)

belt. After each time he was beaten, he would try to shake the hands of his assailants and tell them they were his friends (Fletcher, 2008). In a final act of degradation he was stripped naked from the waist down, and left lying in a pool of blood, while his ecstatic attackers posed for photographs. He suffered terrible brain damage and later died in hospital, without regaining consciousness. A post-mortem showed he had suffered 18 blows to the head and neck (*BBC News*, 2008c).

Described during the subsequent trial at Newcastle Crown Court as being 'gentle, easily led and desperate to be liked' (Wonfor, 2008), Brent had spent the £3,000 he had saved during the nine years he had resided in psychiatric hospital by buying drink and cigarettes for Hughes, Miller and Bonnallie (*Disability Now*, 2008). Yet, as prosecutor Toby Hedworth QC told the court, the people against whom he had 'never lifted an aggressive finger' had killed him 'for their own sport' (ibid). While Hughes and Miller had pleaded guilty to the murder, Bonnallie denied his culpability, purportedly telling the other two, 'I'm not going down for a muppet' (Holt, 2008). All three were found guilty by the jury.

Judge John Milford described the attack as 'sadistic conduct on an extremely vulnerable victim' (*BBC News*, 2008c) and jailed Hughes for a minimum of 22 years, Miller for at least 15 years and Bonallie for at least 18 years. Surprisingly, though, despite senior police officers initially suggesting that Brent had been targeted because of his learning disabilities (Condron, 2007) and the availability of provisions in the Criminal Justice Act 2003 for extending sentences for offences aggravated by disablism, the judge did not use this opportunity to do so. This caused much anger and frustration among disability rights campaigners, and this was compounded when, in June 2008, the sentences were reduced on appeal.

Sadly, cases like that of Brent Martin are by no means isolated and Quarmby (2008) details seven other recent instances when disabled people have been tortured, sexually assaulted, beaten, robbed, humiliated and then murdered. Interestingly, though, Quarmby argues that there is a 'striking difference' between the profiles of those who perpetrate these disablist hate murders and those who commit homophobic or racist ones (ibid: 35), with the former being committed predominantly by 'friends' or carers of the victim, and the latter conducted mostly by strangers (conforming more to the 'stranger danger' hate crime model). As a number of these extreme disablist cases begin with low-level harassment, then escalate into abuse, physical violence and eventually murder, it is paramount that the victim's version of events is believed by police officers or others that the victim may inform. However, it may be difficult for the victim to convince criminal justice agencies that they are suffering at the hands of someone who is supposedly caring for them, while the problems that disabled people have had in convincing police officers that they are credible witnesses can, in these extreme cases, place their lives in danger (Higgins, 2006).

For 'lower-level' forms of disablist hate crime the picture is similarly complicated. While some evidence suggests that incidents are, more often than not, carried out by strangers (DRCCS, 2004; Mind, 2007), other research suggests that that the victim may actually know the perpetrator. For example, the Rainbow Ripples investigation found that perpetrators were often known to the victims 'as neighbours, work colleagues, frequent users of the same services, or even service providers' (Rainbow Ripples and Butler, 2006: 209). The DRCCS research found that around one in five respondents had been victimised by a friend or colleague and a similar proportion had experienced harassment from a teacher or carer (DRCCS, 2004). There is also some evidence that, generally speaking, perpetrators of disablist hate crimes may be older than other hate crime offenders (Higgins, 2006) and that some forms may also be more frequently perpetrated by women than other types of hate crime (Quarmby, 2008).

Not surprisingly, in the context of the preceding discussion, disablist hate crime tends to have a profound impact upon the victim. DRCCS (2004: 22) report that a high proportion of victims in their study felt 'scared, embarrassed/humiliated, lacking in self-confidence, lonely or isolated, helpless and worthless' and one in five disabled people in Scope's survey stated that they never felt safe and secure at home or in their local community (Scope, 2008a). Crucially, even minor incidents can be traumatic for victims as they may well be 'aware of the extreme violence that has been perpetrated on members of their group' (Boeckmann and Turpin-Petrosino, 2002: 221). This underlines the significance of high-profile murders, like that of Brent Martin, whose impact extends to the wider disabled community whose fear of victimisation, even of a 'minor' nature, is heightened. That such cases are not flagged by the criminal justice system as hate crimes is therefore significant, as these decisions can affect the feelings of security of the wider community. It is to a discussion of legal matters that this chapter now turns.

Legal protection from disablist hate crime

The last two decades have seen the disabled community gain legal recognition for its right to safeguards from discrimination, as well as a measure of equal protection under 'hate crime' law. In 1995 the Disability Discrimination Act, which outlawed direct discrimination against disabled people, was passed, and this Act has since been significantly supplemented and strengthened by the Disability Rights Commission Act 1999, the Special Educational Needs and Disability Act 2001 and the Disability Discrimination Act 2005. These pieces of legislation now grant disabled people new rights in areas such as employment, education, property, and accesses to services and facilities.

As discussed earlier in this book, the Crime and Disorder Act 1998 created provisions for racially aggravated offences, for which the perpetrator would receive a longer sentence than they would have had otherwise (the Act was later amended by the Anti-Terrorism, Crime and Security Act 2001 to include religiously aggravated offences). However, it was not until the Criminal Justice Act 2003 that disabled people were afforded similar legal protection. Section 146 of the Act, while not creating new and separate offences 'aggravated by disablism', nevertheless did decree that hostility based on a victim's actual or perceived disability could be seen as an aggravating factor when sentencing someone convicted of an offence.

The Crown Prosecution Service (CPS), in its *Guidance on Prosecuting Cases of Disability Hate Crime*, lists a number of factors to be considered when deciding whether hostility towards someone's disability is evident in the commissioning of an offence against them. These include 'serious aggravating factors' (CPS, 2007d: 24) including 'deliberately setting the victim up for the purposes of humiliation or to be offensive', 'if the victim was particularly vulnerable' and 'if particular distress was caused to the victim or the victim's family'.

These factors are especially significant in the case of Brent Martin. As noted above, the sentences handed to Brent's murderers were not enhanced by the provisions available under section 146, even though the three 'serious aggravating factors' listed above appeared to have been present. The fact that one of the killers referred to Brent using the disablist term 'muppet' seems to reveal contempt for, and disregard of, the lives of disabled people. A senior police officer admitted that there was a culture of bullying of people with learning difficulties on Brent's estate (Quarmby, 2008: 27). Despite the apparent weight of evidence, the opportunity to treat this murder as a disablist hate crime by various agencies was missed, prompting some to question whether disabled victims of hate crime are receiving the same treatment from the police, CPS and courts as those from minority ethnic, religious and gay communities.

These concerns are reflected in Quarmby's (2008) examination of 50 disability-related crimes that occurred in the 2000s. Quarmby argues that in the majority of these cases the police, judges and reporting journalists referred to them as 'senseless' and 'motiveless', seemingly unable, or unwilling, to acknowledge their disablist element. This was even the case in the five murders of disabled people in the 2000s – Rikki Judkins, Raymond Atherton, Barrie-John Horrell, Steven Hoskin and Kevin Davies – which, Quarmby argues, were not 'motiveless' at all, but instead had 'striking similarities':

> The victims were treated as sub-human by their attackers, four out of the five were attacked by 'friends', money was stolen from them and all were subjected to particularly vicious, sustained and unprovoked violence. In other cases victims were

deliberately targeted, many of them had been attacked or harassed before, and the perpetrators used explicit derogatory language like 'spastic', 'schizo', 'cripple' and 'muppet' to describe their victims. (ibid: 24)

One explanation for why section 146 of the Criminal Justice Act 2003 has been used so infrequently may be that there is another, less problematic legal route through which offenders who commit crimes against disabled people can be punished more severely. Advice from the Sentencing Guidelines Council (2004: 5) encourages courts to impose stiffer sentences upon those found guilty of crimes committed against certain vulnerable groups, including disabled people. Therefore, offences committed against disabled people can be punished with longer sentences without recourse to section 146, which demands the more 'onerous' proof of evidence of acts of disablist hostility or motivation (CPS, 2007d; Quarmby, 2008: 24). By taking this course of action, however, sentencers' reluctance to utilise section 146 represents something of a missed opportunity to 'flag up' genuine acts of disablist hate crime to wider society.

That agencies within the criminal justice system have little knowledge of, and negative attitudes towards, disabled people has been noted by a number of authors (Sobsey, 1994; Higgins, 2006; Spalek, 2008). This has helped to create problematic relations between the criminal justice system and disabled communities in a manner that is reminiscent of its relations with minority ethnic and gay populations, whether in terms of lack of trust, miscommunication and under-reporting. Equally problematic in the context of this relationship is the fact that disabled victims often intimately know the perpetrators of hate crimes against them, especially in the case of more violent and extreme forms of crime. Sherry (2003) argues that this may cause police officers to fail to recognise hate crimes as such because they hold the view that they are solely 'stranger danger' forms of crime. There may also be a reluctance to see carers as possible perpetrators of hate crimes (Quarmby, 2008), and in these cases also a reticence on behalf of the disabled victim to report someone that they rely on to the police (Sherry, 2004b).

Ultimately, though, as Quarmby (2008: 13) suggests, the 'great reluctance to believe that disabled people can be, and indeed are, victims of hate crime' may be one of the most important factors in damaging disabled people's trust and confidence in the criminal justice system. Some of these problems may be evidenced by the lack of priority afforded to the collation of disability hate crime statistics since the implementation of the Criminal Justice Act 2003 in April 2005. For instance, the CPS did not collect disability hate crime data separately until April 2007 (Cook, 2007), while throughout 2007/08 only 141 incidents classified as having a disability element were successfully prosecuted, a very small number in comparison to their racial (6,689) and homophobic (778) equivalents (Quarmby, 2008: 11).

Age-related crime

According to Wolhuter, Olley and Denham (2009: 115), there are approximately 9 million people over the age of 65 in the UK (equal to around 15 per cent of the population) and this figure is set to rise to around 14.5 million, or a quarter of the population, by 2066. This rise in the numbers of elderly people is being accompanied by more vociferous demands from lobby groups for laws that will make age discrimination, in all its forms, illegal (Hensher, 2008).[2]

Interestingly, and despite the clear guidance issued by ACPO (2005), there is a good deal of inconsistency regarding how police forces in England, Wales and Scotland view the status of crimes motivated by prejudice against age. A brief review of the hate crime advice available on constabulary websites, undertaken for this book, revealed that, of the 51 force websites examined, over one-third (19) included age-related offences in their list of crimes that could be viewed as hate crimes.[3] A number of these constabularies appeared to use the seven strands of diversity listed by the Home Office (2008a) – race, religion, gender, gender identity, sexual orientation, disability and age – as a guide to defining which groups can be victims of a hate crime. Others seemingly took the stance that any crime motivated by prejudice or hate against any identifiable group is a hate crime. This section of this chapter will review whether such a prognosis is helpful when studying age-related victimisation.

Like disablist crimes (and indeed other types of 'recognised' hate crimes), there are difficulties in gaining accurate data about the extent of elder abuse as it tends to take place in 'hidden' environments such as the home or institutional settings. It is also the least researched of all the bias-related issues relating to minority groupings (Ray, Sharp and Abrams, 2006). Nevertheless, there is evidence that the scale of elder victimisation is increasing rapidly and that ageism – defined by Ray et al. (2006: 60) as 'stereotypes and prejudices held about older people on grounds of their age' – is a social norm (Spalek, 2008; Wolhuter et al., 2009).

Key to this debate is the nature and extent of elder abuse, defined as 'a single or repeated act or lack of appropriate action occurring within any relationship where there is an expectation of trust, which causes harm or distress to an older person' (O'Keeffe et al., 2007: 13) and which can include physical, sexual, psychological or financial abuse, neglect, and discriminatory treatment (Wolhuter et al., 2009: 108). Help the Aged (2008a) state that, at any one time, over half a million older people are subject to such abuse, with two-thirds of these acts of abuse committed at home by someone in a position of trust. O'Keeffe et al.'s

(2007) research estimates that around 227,000 people aged 66 and over in the UK were neglected or abused in the year leading up to their study. There is also some evidence that the prevalence of abuse varies by socio-economic position, with those at the lower end of the scale being more at risk. Overall, three-quarters of victims of abuse reported that the effect on them was serious to some degree (ibid: 79), with victims stating that the abuse was most commonly perpetrated by partners and other family members, and to a lesser extent also by care workers or close friends (ibid: 59).

Ray et al.'s (2006) survey of nearly 2,000 adults of all ages found that although ageism was the most common form of discrimination experienced by respondents, it was also perceived as being the least serious. This failure to take older people's concerns seriously, and to hold condescending views about them, indicates some commonalities between ageist and disablist attitudes. The fact that elder abuse is a hidden crime, and is often perpetrated by those in a position of trust, may also reveal some similarities between this form of offence and disablist hate crime. A reluctance to report such incidents because they are perpetrated by carers, spouses or offspring, and the suggestion that older people may be viewed as 'easy' targets by offenders, may also link these two crimes (Carlton et al., 2003). Similarly, older people, like disabled people, may be less likely to be believed when they do report victimisation (Wolhuter et al., 2009). There may also be some overlap between the two types of victimisation, as around four out of ten older people have a disability and thus may be subject to disablist *and* ageist harassment (Burnett, 2006).

However, despite these similarities, it may not be helpful, within the broader context of developing an understanding of hate crime, to think of elder victimisation as a form of hate crime *per se*. As Lister and Wall (2006) observe, the elderly are not a homogeneous minority group but instead form a very diverse section of society, varying greatly in wealth and social status. For example, while 2.5 million pensioners were living below the official poverty line in 2008 (Bennett, 2008), the elderly also own a 'disproportionately large share of the country's wealth' (Wolhuter et al., 2009: 115). If hate crime victims are from already stigmatised and marginalised groups, as Perry suggests they are (2001: 10), then it could be argued that a significant proportion of the elderly who are comparatively prosperous and of high social status, could not fit into this category. Although they may be subject to ageist attitudes and victimisation, it may be stretching the hate crime 'umbrella' too far to categorise these particular victims as victims of hate crimes, particularly if we are to acknowledge the historical roots of hate crime as evolving from the civil rights struggles of minority groups in the USA. This is not to deny that elderly people can come from deprived backgrounds, nor to ignore the seriousness of ageism as a form of discrimination or the impact of elder abuse. What is being suggested here is that such attitudes and actions against elderly populations should not be thought of as 'hate crimes' as such, as this would distort the concept by including categories of victims from privileged sections of society who may, in reality, have little or nothing in common with victims of other hate crimes who are from historically marginalised and persecuted communities.

Attacks upon members of youth subcultures

Central to this book's themes is fear of 'difference', especially when such fear can manifest itself in hate crimes, such as attacks upon members of youth subcultures. Such attacks are not new – Savage (1991), for example, refers to the frequency with which punks were assaulted by 'ordinary' members of the public in the mid-1970s – but have come to public prominence in recent times due to the horrific murder of goth Sophie Lancaster in 2007 by a gang of youths (see Case Study 6.2). The manner of her death precipitated a campaign to widen the definition of hate crime to include those perpetrated due to the victim's appearance or membership of a youth subculture (Purdy, 2008).

Case Study 6.2: The murder of Sophie Lancaster

Late on the night of August 10 2007 Sophie Lancaster (aged 20) and her boyfriend Robert Maltby (aged 21), both dedicated goths, decided to cut across Stubbylee Park in Bacup, Lancashire, on their way home after a night at a friend's house. They bumped into a gang of youths and initially chatted with them amicably. Suddenly, and without provocation, one of the youths struck Maltby, precipitating a violent and savage assault upon the 21-year-old by the assailant and four other youths.

The attackers kicked and stamped upon Maltby until he lay unconscious. As she cradled her boyfriend's head, Lancaster pleaded with them to stop, only to become the subject of a vicious assault herself. A witness later told police: 'It looked like they were running over and just kicking her in the head, jumping up and down on her head' (Jenkins, 2008a: 24). When paramedics arrived they found the victims lying side by side, unconscious and covered in blood. Both were in a coma and, while Robert recovered enough to be able to leave hospital about two weeks later, Sophie died as a result of the brain injuries she suffered (Wainwright, 2008).

After the assault the killers boasted to their friends that they had 'done summat good' and that: 'There's two moshers [goths] nearly dead up Bacup park – you wanna see them – they're a right mess' (ibid: 15). The BBC reported that, 'The attackers did not know the couple, who were both goths, and the only motive was they simply looked different' (*BBC News*, 2008d).

At the subsequent trial at Preston Crown Court the prosecution alleged that Maltby and Lancaster had been 'singled out not for anything they had said or done but because they dressed differently' (Jenkins, 2008b: 25). Interestingly, Judge

---

Anthony Russell QC commented to the youths that 'This was a hate crime against these completely harmless people targeted because their appearance was different to yours' (*BBC News*, 2008d). The ringleader, 15-year-old Brendan Harris, was found guilty of murder and given an 18-year prison sentence and Ryan Herbert, who was also found guilty of murder, was sentenced to 16 years.

Sophie was a goth: a youth subculture which emerged in the late 1970s and which is based around music with a 'doomy ambience [and] darkness' coupled with a physical appearance characterised by a 'deathly pallor, backcombed or ratted black hair, ruffled Regency shirts, stovepipe hats, leather garments, spiked dog collars, the ensemble accessorised with religious, magical or macabre jewellery' (Reynolds, 2005: 420, 423). In other words, goths look strikingly different, something which often precipitates harassment and victimisation for no other reason than their appearance (Purdy, 2008). In a town like Bacup, economically deprived, geographically isolated and almost mono-ethnic, those who look radically different stand out starkly, whether they be goths or the few from visible minority ethnic backgrounds. Hodgkinson's investigation into the nature of the town found that minority ethnic families 'get firebombed out of their houses and given a whack with a baseball bat to make sure they get the message' (Hodgkinson, 2008: 31), and suggested that this hostility towards difference was what also motivated Sophie's killers into attacking her. This fear and resentment of the 'other' characterises many such monocultural communities and can manifest itself in acts of harassment and violence (Garland and Chakraborti, 2006a).

That Sophie's gothic appearance precipitated her death is beyond doubt, as is the fact that it was an unprovoked and horrific crime. Whether it should be categorised as a 'hate crime', though, is a moot point, for while it was undoubtedly motivated by the hatred of the difference of a marginalised group, including it as a 'hate crime' may again be stretching the parameters of the concept too far. If hate crimes are understood to be committed against groups who have been historically marginalised and discriminated against, then perhaps violent crimes like that committed against Sophie should be kept separate. To include goths alongside disabled or transgendered victims of hate crime (for example) may, in the eyes of those groups, belittle their own history of marginalisation and their own experiences as victims of hate. This is not to downplay the impact of Sophie's death upon her friends and family and the wider goth 'community'; indeed, the fact that her killing shares a number of characteristics with other hate-related murders (such as those of Jody Dobrowski and Stephen Lawrence, for instance) highlights just how problematic and contentious a process framing boundaries of hate crime can be.

Sectarianism

Another significant issue within the context of this discussion – and one which can be covered only briefly here – is sectarianism. Unlike their counterparts in England and Wales, the Police Service of Northern Ireland's (PSNI) collation of hate crimes statistics includes a 'sectarian' category which underlines the historical and contemporary significance of sectarianism in Northern Ireland. Jarman (2005: 2) sees sectarian acts as including:

> ... violence, harassment and intimidation perpetrated by members of the Protestant/ Unionist/Loyalist communities on members of the Catholic/Nationalist/Republican communities and vice versa. The primary interest is in acts of non-militarised violence, including attacks on both persons and property, rather than on acts committed by members of paramilitary organisations. However, sectarian violence does include acts of extreme violence and may involve paramilitary activity.

Interestingly, therefore, sectarian hate crimes are different from the hate crimes featured elsewhere in this book in that the victim does not necessarily have to be from a disadvantaged minority group, but instead can be from either the majority (Protestant) or minority (Catholic) communities. However, it is important to note the complexities of the situation, with many divisions other than just religious ones evident, including, for instance, Nationalist and Unionist, or Gaelic Irish and Ulster Scot (Cramphorn, 2002: 12), and this makes sectarian hate crimes very difficult to characterise as either religious or indeed racist hate crimes (and hence their discussion within this chapter).

Sectarian harassment can have a considerable impact upon the victim's sense of identity and self-worth (Morrissey and Smyth, 2002). Jarman's (2005) analysis of data relating to sectarian hate crime suggests that it is a serious problem in some urban areas and can manifest itself in the street, on public transport, at home or at the workplace, in the form of criminal damage, assault, verbal harassment or public disorder. For example, police figures indicate that there have been an average of five attacks a month on churches, chapels, community centres or sports and social clubs every year since 1994 (Jarman, 2005: 3) and that sectarianism is the most common form of hate crime in Northern Ireland, with 1,584 incidents recorded in 2007/08 (PSNI, 2008).

Worryingly, although Jarman argues that the worst of the Troubles may be behind Northern Ireland, not only are sectarian hate crimes still common, but incidents of a racist or homophobic nature have risen significantly in frequency in recent years. The House of Commons Northern Ireland Affairs Committee (2005) observed a dramatic rise in the number of homophobic incidents reported to police during the mid-2000s, and suggested that a decline in overt sectarianism had been replaced by a rise in the visibility and frequency of attacks perpetuated against LGBT and disabled communities (ibid: 3). Thus, as one form of hate crime may be declining, other forms are increasing, indicating that prejudice and intolerance towards 'othered' groups are still significant problems in Northern Ireland, but just may be taking different forms than before.

Acts of terrorism and hooliganism

Of course, within the confines of this chapter it has not been possible to examine every conceivable 'borderline' form of hate and readers may well be able to think of other offences which could fit within the framework of what might be classified as a hate crime. For instance, to refer to one such example, acts of terrorism such as the London bombings of July 7 2005, which resulted in the deaths of 52 members of public, might be conceived by some, quite understandably, to be a relatively clear-cut illustration of a hate crime, particularly when earlier in the book we have seen the authors argue that certain types of 'low-level' offending, such as name-calling, should be classified as hate crime.

However, despite the horrific nature of the events of 7/7, it is contended here that the 7/7 bombings, and similar atrocities, should not be defined as hate crimes, and this is for two main reasons, both relating to the most complete definition of hate crime – that offered by Perry (2001). First, it should be stressed that the victims of this terrorist attack were ordinary civilians from a variety of ethnic, religious, national and cultural backgrounds who were not killed because of their membership of a historically marginalised or disadvantaged group. We are therefore again left with the conundrum of whether anyone, no matter what their status, can be the victim of something termed a 'hate crime' or whether such a concept as hate crime, if it is to have any meaning, can only be experienced by disadvantaged minority groups. If this is the case then the 7/7 bombings, for all the hurt and pain caused, cannot be included under this definition. Secondly, Perry's (2001: 10) instructive definition of hate crime states that it is a 'mechanism of power and oppression' perpetrated by dominant groups in order to 'reaffirm the precarious hierarchies that characterise a given social order'. The 7/7 bombings were neither perpetrated by dominant groups nor aimed at keeping subordinate ones 'in their place'. They may well have been message crimes, but they were not consistent with ideas of preserving social hierarchies in order to keep privileged sections of society at the top.

Another issue worthy of brief consideration is football hooliganism. Arguably, some incidents of football hooliganism do have some elements in common with hate crime acts, in that they may involve a genuine hatred of opposition supporters due to their group affiliations. Attacks on rival fans are therefore 'stranger danger' acts of violence as the individual identity of the supporters is (by and large) irrelevant. Such acts may also be influenced by intense regionalism and community identification that some supporters may use to rationalise their actions, in a similar fashion to the way that hate crime perpetrators' actions are 'bolstered by belief systems which (attempt to) legitimate such violence' (Sheffield, 1995: 438). Hooliganism may therefore act as a vehicle for confirming the '"appropriate" subordinate identity of the victim's group' (Perry, 2001: 10) while reconfirming the dominant position of the perpetrators.

Yet despite these commonalities, it is contended here that football hooliganism has too many dissimilarities with hate crimes for it to be treated as such. Although some football-related violence may well take the form of 'stranger danger' acts that are intended to convey a message to other members of the victim's group, and involve a degree of 'belief' in the action that justifies the subordination of that group, it is still difficult to see how victims of hooliganism are from 'stigmatised' or 'disadvantaged' groups, as Perry (ibid) suggests victims of hate crimes should be. It is also difficult to justify that acts of hooliganism are motivated by prejudice towards, or hatred of, other fans. As Garland and Rowe (2002: 19) suggest, more often than not, hooliganism may be motivated by fierce territorial loyalty and a propensity among young men to become involved in violence. In any case, these explanations do suggest one thing: a lack of prejudice, or hatred, on the part of perpetrators of hooliganism, at least in the way that we understand those concepts within the context of hate crime. Football hooliganism, for all the violence that it involves and fear that it induces, simply does not share many of the characteristics of the other hate crimes we have already discussed in this book.

Conclusion

This chapter has assessed forms of crime that have historically been located on the margins of the broader hate crime debate. It began by examining disablist victimisation, a type of hate crime that often finds itself lower down the hate crime 'hierarchy' than its racist, religious, homophobic or transphobic equivalents (Sherry, 2004b: 52). It is accorded less analysis by academics and lower priority from practitioners, despite disabled people being at a higher risk of hate-related victimisation than non-disabled sections of the population. This has meant that the opportunity to tackle it, through social interventions, police action or through the courts, has, to a large extent, been missed.

The chapter then turned to ageist crimes. It noted the prevalence of ageist attitudes within society and also the worrying levels of elder abuse that occur in institutions or the home, making it a hidden form of crime that has not received the attention from criminal justice agencies that it deserves. Even when they do report such abuse to the authorities, older people, like disabled people, are often not viewed as credible witnesses by the police or CPS. While the chapter noted the disturbing nature and harmful consequences of elder abuse, it was nevertheless suggested that it should not be defined as a hate crime, as the older population is so heterogeneous, and in parts so well off financially that it does not constitute the type of stigmatised and marginalised group that Perry (2001) envisages that victims of hate crime should come from.

The chapter then assessed the targeting of members of alternative youth sub-cultures, to see if they could fit under the hate crime 'umbrella'. The targeting of those from subcultures that look strikingly different from accepted 'norms' was then examined within the context of the killing of goth Sophie Lancaster. It was suggested that this murder was mainly motivated by the perpetrators' hostility to difference itself, and that Sophie's alternative appearance was enough to pre-cipitate the horrific violence that killed her. It was also noted that, in some ways, acts like this did resemble hate crimes, in that they were motivated by hostility towards an othered, outsider group. Ultimately, it was concluded that the sig-nificant historical context of the plight of victims of hate crime would be lost if acts like Sophie's murder were considered hate crimes, but it was acknowledged that these forms of 'othering', perhaps more than any other form of 'borderline' hate, highlight just how difficult and subjective a process it is to settle upon an acceptable threshold for what falls under the hate crime label. Equally, within the discussion of sectarianism it was argued that, while this is correctly thought of as a form of hate crime, it finds itself also rather marginalised from mainstream hate debates as it is (mainly) confined to Northern Ireland and is itself difficult to cat-egorise as either a religious or a racist hate crime. Similar arguments can be made for acts of terrorism and hooliganism. Neither terrorist acts, which tend to be indiscriminate in their nature and are rarely targeted at specific minorities, nor hooliganism, despite often being driven by hatred of opposing supporters' group affiliations, demonstrate all the criteria required to be labelled as hate crimes.

It would seem, therefore, that of all the offences discussed within this chapter it is only crimes motivated by disablism that can be regarded as 'clear-cut' (if indeed such a term can legitimately be used in this context) hate crimes. This then raises an important question: if disablist crimes are so obviously hate crimes, why then are they at the margins of the hate debate? For some the answer may be, as Shakespeare (2007) suggests, that disablism is simply not as serious as other forms of hate crime:

> Non-disabled people are ignorant about disability, they are patronising to disabled people, and they consistently think that disability means that we can't do anything. We often face curiosity and mockery, and sometimes disabled people also suffer vio-lence and abuse. But this does not make disablism equivalent to racism.

However, while not doubting the sincerity of Shakespeare's opinions, or his experiences as a disabled person, it is argued here that disablist victimisation *is* as serious as other forms of hate-motivated victimisation. Instead, it is suggested that it is people's aversion to the disabled – those feelings of 'horror, fear, anxiety, hostility [and] distrust' mentioned earlier (Barton, 1996: 8) – that may fuel feelings of contempt towards disabled victims. Certainly this is an area that demands much more criminological attention, and with this may come an increased standing for disablist hate crime and, perhaps more importantly, an improved criminal justice response to potential and actual victims.

Guide to further reading

There is a wealth of literature on disability although comparatively little on the topic of disablist hate crime itself. An overview of relevant issues is provided by Sobsey in *Violence and Abuse in the Lives of People with Disabilities* (1994). There are also a number of research reports into discrimination and disablism, not least Miller et al., *Disablism: How to Tackle the Last Prejudice* (2004) and Quarmby, *Getting Away with Murder* (2008). The journal *Disability and Society* provides an in-depth analysis of relevant issues and *Disability Now* is also an excellent source of articles on a number of key themes, including disablist hate crime. Spalek, *Communities, Identity and Crime* (2008) summarises a number of key themes regarding age, prejudice and discrimination.

Notes

1 Quarmby (2008) reports that the Home Office has pledged in future to incorporate questions about respondents' experience of hate crime into its annual British Crime Survey, possibly from 2009/10.
2 The Employment Equality (Age) Regulations 2006 applies in England, Scotland and Wales, and provides protection against age discrimination in employment, training and adult education, for people of all ages. Harassment, or bullying, based on someone's age is also unlawful under this legislation. Similar regulations were also introduced in Northern Ireland in the form of the Employment Equality (Age) Regulations (Northern Ireland) 2006.
3 This chapter will use the threshold of 60 and over, as employed by the British Crime Survey and Chivite-Matthews and Maggs (2002).

7

POLICING HATE CRIME

──────────────── Chapter summary ────────────────

In the years following the Stephen Lawrence Inquiry, the police service has been
required to address hate crime issues with more transparency and greater priority
than ever before. Criminological research has consistently shown that the troubled relationship between the police and minority communities has had a profound impact upon police responses to hate crime and upon levels of confidence
in the police among those groups most at risk of hate-related victimisation, and
addressing these problems has formed a central feature of the post-Macpherson
policing agenda.

  This chapter outlines the implications of ACPO's hate crime guidance for
police forces across England, Wales and Northern Ireland before moving on to
examine some of the conceptual, cultural and operational difficulties that have
plagued the policing of hate crime. Through its analysis of these difficulties,
together with its assessment of the positive developments that have taken place
in recent times, the chapter highlights the need for caution when drawing definitive conclusions about the level of progress made post-Macpherson. While significant improvements have been made during this time, it is suggested that
some of the more problematic aspects of policing hate crime still present major
challenges for the police service. As such, it is difficult to say whether the strategic prioritisation of hate crime has transformed the way in which hate crime victimisation is conceived by officers on the ground.

──────────────── Introduction ────────────────

The policing of hate crime is an inherently complex task. The police service is
responsible for recording hate offences and for implementing related legislation, and through its policies and procedures it can influence the way in which

hate crime issues are thought of by the state and by the general public (Gerstenfeld, 2004). In addition, the police service will often be the initial source of contact for victims of hate crime and therefore police responses will need to be sufficiently sensitive to their requirements. However, this is by no means straightforward. Earlier chapters have provided insights into the profound physical and emotional impact of victimisation on individuals, families and wider communities, and have touched upon the importance of recognising this impact within the police response. At the same time, minority groups such as ethnic and sexual minorities and faith communities, who more often than not constitute the core victims of hate crime, are not renowned for having especially high levels of confidence in the police service, and in some respects this makes the policing of hate crime especially difficult. For reasons that shall be explored later in this chapter, these minority groups and the police have experienced an uneasy and, at times, fractious relationship that has impacted upon the way in which hate crime is reported and prioritised.

At a strategic level, hate crime has been afforded considerable attention since events such as the murder of Stephen Lawrence and the actions of David Copeland pushed hate crime to the forefront of policing agendas towards the end of the 1990s. This was especially evident within the Metropolitan Police Service (MPS) in the wake of the Macpherson Inquiry into the flawed investigation of the Lawrence murder. Illustrative of the elevated status of hate crime during this period was the establishment of the Racial and Violent Crime Task Force (known now as the Diversity Directorate), the Independent Advisory Group for visible minority ethnic communities and a similar body representing London's LGBT communities (Matassa and Newburn, 2002). These developments at a corporate level have helped to prioritise the detection and prevention of hate crime within the MPS while improving accountability and transparency through the external scrutiny provided by Independent Advisory Groups. Meanwhile, supplementing these post-Macpherson strategic advancements was the creation of specialist Community Safety Units (CSUs) within every London borough. Supported by the Diversity Directorate, CSUs have a specific responsibility for policing hate crimes, together with related offences such as domestic violence, and their establishment throughout London and indeed within other police services across the UK is indicative of the way in which hate crime has come to be mainstreamed by the police (McLaughlin, 2002).

The ACPO guidance

Arguably the most significant form of acknowledgement of hate crime in policing terms has come through the guidance issued by the Association of Chief Police Officers (ACPO). One of the three main police representative bodies (together with the Police Federation and the Superintendents' Association),[1] ACPO is seen as the most senior, and to all intents and purposes the most effective, police lobbying group in terms of its capacity to influence governmental thinking (Newburn, 2007). Consequently, the guidance document *Hate Crime: Delivering a Quality Service* (ACPO, 2005) commissioned jointly by ACPO's Race and Diversity Working Group and the Home Office Police Standards Unit, serves as a key reference document for police officers and support staff in England, Wales and Northern Ireland. As such, it is worth reiterating and expanding upon some of the points made in Chapter 1 about the ACPO guidance in order to clarify how police forces are expected to interpret and address hate crime.

As mentioned in Chapter 1, ACPO's initial piece of strategic guidance on hate crime was published in 2000 at a time of heightened sensitivity over the victimisation of minority groups. This guidance defined hate crime as 'a crime where the perpetrator's prejudice against *any identifiable group of people* [emphasis added] is a factor in determining who is victimised' (ACPO, 2000: 13), and in so doing earmarked this category of crime as one which encompassed offences motivated by a range of prejudices and not simply racist prejudice. The more recent set of ACPO guidelines (ACPO, 2005) are broadly similar to those laid out in the 2000 strategy but nevertheless contain several distinct features which have important implications for the policing of hate crime. One of these relates to the distinction made between hate incidents and hate crimes (see Case Study 7.1). According to ACPO's guidance (2005: 9), all hate crimes are hate incidents, whereas some hate incidents may not actually constitute a criminal offence, and therefore will not be recorded as a crime. This requirement for all incidents to be recorded by the police, even if they lack the requisite elements to be classified as a crime, widens considerably the scope of the hate umbrella: any hate incident, whether a prima-facie 'crime' or not, must be recorded if it meets the threshold originally laid down by the Macpherson definition of a racist incident – namely, if it is perceived by the victim or any other person as being motivated by prejudice or hate. Quite simply then, perception by anyone that a hate incident has occurred is all that is required for the police to record a hate incident, and they are obliged to do so 'regardless of whether [that person is] the victim or not, whether a crime has been committed or not and irrespective of whether there is any evidence to identify the hate element' (ACPO, 2005: 22).

Case Study 7.1: The ACPO distinction between hate incidents and hate crimes

A physically disabled schoolteacher is supervising a class of teenagers. There are a number of unruly pupils within the group. At various times during the class, the teacher is required to exercise discipline to control misbehaviour. This culminates

(Continued)

(Continued)

in a pupil being sent from the class during which the teacher is told, 'Why don't you **** off cripple!'

The pupil is reacting to the requirement to leave the room and the remark is simply a challenge to the authority of the teacher. The teacher perceives this offensive comment to be motivated by prejudice relating to his/her disability. However, there is insufficient evidence to substantiate a criminal offence and therefore no hate crime has been committed. If reported to the police at this stage, the event must be recorded as a hate incident.

The father of the teenager is a member of a right-wing extremist group, which believes that disabled people are a drain on society and should be eradicated. Having heard of the incident involving the teenager, he waits outside the school the following day with a fellow sympathiser.

They set upon the teacher on leaving the school, causing injuries amounting to actual bodily harm. During the incident they continually use abusive language. 'You **** ing cripple. You're not fit to breathe air. You lot should all be sent to concentration camps like in the war.'

These additional circumstances show that an opportunity arose for this perpetrator to plan and execute a motivated attack on the teacher, based on prejudice towards an identifiable group, in this case disabled people. This event should be recorded and investigated as a hate crime. The same principles would apply if this example was based on sexual orientation, race or faith.

Source: ACPO (2005: 10)

By recommending that the deciding factor lies in the perception of the victim or any other person, ACPO's guidance enables the police to interpret hate incidents in a manner consistent with the post-Macpherson interpretation of a racist incident, thereby prioritising victims' experiences at the expense of police officer discretion and encouraging consideration of a broader range of incidents beyond what would typically be classed as crimes. At the same time, though, ACPO's guidance offers some restriction on the types of incident that should be categorised under the hate umbrella by specifying particular grounds for prejudice or hatred. This is another distinct feature of the 2005 guidance which clarifies the ambiguity inherent within ACPO's (2000) reference to 'prejudice against any identifiable group of people'. As things stand, under the more recent set of guidance it is not just any form of prejudice or hate that could constitute a hate incident or crime; rather, the police are obliged to record hate incidents where the motivation for the prejudice or hate is based upon on 'race', sexual orientation, faith or disability (ACPO, 2005: 10).

As a guidance document for police forces in England, Wales and Northern Ireland, ACPO's (2005) *Hate Crime* manual is not without its flaws. For example, the definitions of a hate incident and hate crime make reference to prejudice and not just hate, thereby indicating that the presence of hate is not necessarily central to the commission of a hate incident or crime. However, the ACPO guidance fails to offer a definition of prejudice and consequently gives police officers little indication of how to interpret the more expansive notion of prejudice. Equally, in the illustration presented by ACPO to distinguish between incidents and crimes (see Case Study 7.1) the perpetrators of the hate crime are described as being far-right extremists: while this may help in one sense to convey the deep-rooted resentment that accompanies some hate crimes, it is not a particularly constructive way of showing that hate crimes are commonly perpetrated by 'ordinary' members of the public. Furthermore, limiting the protection afforded by the hate umbrella to certain groups and not others is in itself contentious as this, in essence, creates a hierarchy of victims, with certain groups seen perhaps as being more important or deserving than others.

A fresh ACPO manual is due to be published in 2009 and it will be interesting to see which, if any, of these points are addressed within the updated set of guidelines. Nevertheless, and as acknowledged in Chapter 1, these problematic issues are by no means relevant only to the ACPO manual, but rather are central to debates over the conceptual basis of hate crime. Taken on its merits as an exemplar of good practice, the ACPO manual gives a clear indication of the strategic prioritisation of hate crime within the police service and presents explicit operational guidance to forces across the country with regards to their understanding and investigation of hate crime.

Policing minority communities

The pronounced emphasis given to the policing of hate crime over the past decade is symptomatic in some ways of the sensitivity that surrounds relations between the police and minority communities. While the police service have had problematic encounters with a variety of groups since the introduction of the professional police in the mid-nineteenth century (Reiner, 2000; Rowe, 2004), the recognition that certain sections of society have distinctive policing needs has been a relatively recent development and one that has presented significant challenges to the police service. Concerns over the discriminatory policing of minorities, and in particular ethnic minorities, have been raised by criminologists throughout the past 30 years or so, and this body of criminological research, together with the momentum for reform that has arisen through high-profile cases, changes in public attitudes and the Stephen Lawrence Inquiry, has unquestionably helped to shape a policing agenda that is more equipped to address the needs of a diverse society.

Nevertheless, any notion that the problems inherent to the policing of diversity would simply disappear as a result of post-Macpherson changes was quickly dispelled following the revelations from two undercover documentaries broadcast during the past decade. The first, and arguably more infamous of these, a 2003 BBC TV programme entitled *The Secret Policeman*, was centred around footage recorded at a police training centre in Warrington by an undercover journalist posing as a fresh recruit to the service. The documentary exposed extreme racist attitudes among a small number of trainees, showing graphic illustrations of racist discrimination, stereotyping and support for far-right political organisations (see McLaughlin, 2007 for a more detailed account).

More recently, the 2006 documentary *Undercover Copper*, filmed as part of Channel Four's *Dispatches* series, again featured an undercover reporter (who this time was an actual police officer) seeking to draw attention to problems of institutionalised sexism at Leicestershire Constabulary. Though not as shocking or extreme as the footage from *The Secret Policeman*, the *Dispatches* documentary uncovered examples of gender bias and poor practice which highlighted the existence of prejudicial attitudes and a lack of professionalism among officers.[2] Documentaries such as these, which broadcast behaviour usually hidden from public gaze, have become a staple component of contemporary media (Rowe, 2007b), and some caution must be adopted when drawing generalisations from broadcasts which present only a limited snapshot of police practice and which inevitably have their own agenda. At the same time, such documentaries can have a damaging impact upon public perceptions of the police and are illustrative of the enduring difficulties confronting a police service keen to shed its image of institutional prejudice.

A variety of cultural explanations have been put forward over the years in order to account for the prejudice expressed towards minority groups by police officers. In general terms the notion of police culture, as noted by Waddington (1999: 287), has been used 'to explain and condemn a broad spectrum of policing practice' and is commonly presented as one of the most significant barriers to police reform. In so doing, however, writers have, often unwittingly, conveyed the misleading assumption that police practice is informed by a culture that is singular, monolithic and unchanging, rather than the more contemporary criminological standpoint that recognises cultural variation within and between police forces (Chan, 1997; Foster, 2002; Newburn, 2007). By acknowledging the existence of police *cultures*, or *culture and subcultures*, we can develop a more nuanced understanding of cultural bias and its influence upon police–minority relations. Moreover, recognising that there is more than just one set of cultural values – or a singular belief system – that informs police behaviour can help us to appreciate why the prioritisation of hate crime at a managerial or corporate level may not always be matched by a similar standard of commitment at a 'street cop' level.

In perhaps the most authoritative analysis of police culture, Reiner (2000: 87–101) refers to a collection of values, norms and perspectives which influence police officers' conduct and which constitute the core characteristics of street cop culture, including a sense of mission, suspicion, solidarity, conservatism, machismo, racial prejudice and pragmatism. While there are positive elements to some of these characteristics – including, for instance, a desire to catch 'the bad guys', collective responsibility, dedication, bravery – they also have more sinister implications in terms of their capacity to foster an inward-looking, cynical and prejudiced police service. These are also characteristics which appear consistently in police research, suggesting that even if the degree to which they are exhibited by individual officers will inevitably vary, the very nature of police work generates a typical cultural pattern (Foster, 2002: 200). The identification of common cultural characteristics has encouraged researchers to question whether these traits are learnt and directly related to the nature of policing or whether they are instead reflective of the types of people who choose to pursue a career in the police service. Related issues that have been the source of criminological enquiry include the extent to which these cultural characteristics are unique to the police and not other organisational cultures, and the capacity or otherwise for police culture to change (McLaughlin, 1996; Chan, 1997). This latter point is especially pertinent in the context of policing an increasingly diverse society, where the negative elements of police culture can undermine the development of more responsive approaches to policing diversity.

Of particular relevance to the present discussion is the cultural trait of racial prejudice and stereotyping within the police. For Reiner (2000: 100), this prejudice derives to a large degree from societal racism which places ethnic minorities in the lower strata of society together with other marginal groups – the unemployed, alcoholics, deviant youth, prostitutes – and which therefore legitimates their treatment as 'police property' (see also Graef, 1989; Holdaway, 1993). Although the majority of studies have tended to single out junior personnel as the perpetrators and African Caribbean and Asian communities as the prime targets of abuse, there is evidence to suggest that cultural prejudice within the police runs wider than this. Reiner's (1991) study of chief constables, for example, has highlighted the existence of racist stereotyping among senior police professionals; the work of Bucke and James (1998) and James (2007) has illustrated the way in which other minority groups such as Gypsies and New Age Travellers can fall victim to similar processes of police discrimination; while Burke (1993) and Waddington (1994) have observed cultures of homophobia within police ranks.

The capacity for cultural bias to tarnish relations between the police and minority communities has of course received official acknowledgement through the Scarman Inquiry of 1981 and the Macpherson Inquiry of 1999. Both of these major reports have been described as watershed moments in the context of policing and race relations and both have highlighted similar themes in calling for improvements to be made in the policing of minority ethnic communities (Foster, 2002). However, perhaps the most significant difference between the two reports lies in their respective explanations of police prejudice. Lord Scarman's 'bad apple' approach, so called because it attributes police racism to individual officers or 'bad apples' who have sneaked into the barrel and need to be removed in order to prevent the entire barrel from rotting, is clearly an approach based more upon individual behaviour rather than collective responsibility. Macpherson's emphasis on institutional racism, on the other hand, gives much greater weight to the processes and structural context through which individual prejudices are shared within police organisational culture. As Macpherson makes clear in his definition of institutional racism (1999: para. 6.34), the problem is not simply one of individual culpability but relates instead to 'the collective failure of an organisation'; equally, it does not just include direct or deliberate acts of prejudice, but rather 'discrimination through unwitting prejudice, ignorance, thoughtlessness, and racist stereotyping'.

However, despite this formal acknowledgement of cultural bias within the police service and the extensive programme of reform that has followed, opinions are divided over the extent to which institutional prejudice has been addressed in the years since the Macpherson report. Crucially, and as graphically illustrated through the undercover documentaries referred to above, concerns persist over the police's understanding of diversity issues and their capacity to engage with minority communities. While much of the discussion thus far has focused upon the expression of cultural prejudice towards ethnic minorities, it is important to recognise that the lingering concerns surrounding the policing of diversity apply equally to other minority groups, as will be outlined in more detail shortly. Notwithstanding post-Macpherson drives to improve relations between the police and all minority groups, the legacy established through a history of discrimination and mutual mistrust has meant that question marks still remain over the policing of homophobia (Williams and Robinson, 2004; Moran, 2007), faith-hate (McGhee, 2005; Chakraborti, 2007) and disablism (Deal, 2007; Holt, 2008). This has important implications for the policing of hate crime in all its recognised forms, and the chapter now proceeds to consider these implications in more depth.

Problems associated with the policing of hate crime

Somewhat invariably, the well-documented forms of stereotyping and discrimination that have historically influenced the policing of hate crimes have served to erode confidence in the police among minority groups (Clancy et al., 2001; Jones and Newburn, 2001). Eliciting the support and trust of the public plays an important part in the policing of crime generically, but this has proved to be especially problematic in the context of hate crime where negative attitudes towards the police may have become entrenched through media reports, indirect knowledge and personal experience of discriminatory practice. Such attitudes are often rooted in the historical tensions and oppressive policing that have blighted police–minority relations over the past 50 years or so.

The issue of over-policing and under-protection has been documented extensively, particularly with regards to the policing of black communities (Hunte, 1966; Hall et al., 1978; Bowling, 1999), although there is evidence to suggest that such feelings have also featured strongly in the experience of gay communities (Williams and Robinson, 2004). Rather than dissipating over time, this sense of resentment towards the police has been reinforced, most notably within sections of some British Muslim communities as a result of concerns over the policing of the 2001 disturbances in northern towns between Pakistani and white youths as well as through concerns over the disproportionate use of stop and search and other perceived discriminatory policing practices introduced in successive pieces of counter-terrorism legislation (Burnett, 2004; Ansari, 2005; Chakraborti, 2007).

In practical terms, this lack of confidence in the police has resulted in the well-documented under-reporting of hate crime by minority groups. We have seen in earlier chapters the sizable difference between official police records of hate crime and the consistently higher numbers identified through victim surveys, and this variation is reflective of victims' reluctance to report incidents to the police. The reluctance of minority ethnic groups to share their experiences with the police is well documented (see, for example, Fitzgerald and Hale, 1996; Clancy et al., 2001), and may of course be attributable to wider factors than simply disaffection towards the police. As Spalek (2006: 110) suggests, the more 'traditional' minority ethnic communities may sometimes be more reticent with regards to speaking out about traumatic events such as victimisation for fear of exacerbating or drawing attention to the situation. This was certainly the case for some of the older interviewees in Garland and Chakraborti's (2006b, 2007) studies of rural racism who explained that they had grown accustomed to sharing problems within their own ethnic or faith community, and not with mainstream organisations. Nevertheless, the overriding impression conveyed by respondents in those studies was an enduring and widespread sense of reluctance among all minority ethnic communities to report racist incidents to the police, and this tended to derive from the misgivings many people continue to hold about the police's institutional response to racism. Despite changes that may have occurred within the police service in the aftermath of the Macpherson report, many minority ethnic interviewees still appeared to share a profound mistrust of the police's commitment to tackling racism, and this will inevitably impact upon levels of reporting (see also Bowling and Phillips, 2002; McLaughlin, 2007).

Crucially, the problem of under- or non-reporting is not confined exclusively to minority ethnic communities. In their focus groups with vulnerable communities, Wong and Christmann (2008) found that their LGBT group of research participants were especially reluctant to report incidents of verbal abuse because they felt that agencies would be unable to act. Equally, Herek, Cogan and Roy Gillis's (2003)

Californian-based research illustrated that victims of homophobic hate crime were considerably less likely to report incidents to the police than victims of 'ordinary' crimes, and Williams and Robinson (2004) have suggested that up to three-quarters of such victims fail to report to the police primarily because they perceive the police to be 'anti-gay' and are fearful of secondary victimisation from officers. Similar concerns have been expressed over the policing of transphobic hate crime (Dittman, 2003), while the under-reporting of disablist hate crime has been recognised as a serious issue within the criminal justice system (CPS, 2007d) and has exacerbated the invisibility of disability-based victimisation to front-line law enforcers and criminal justice practitioners (Grattet and Jenness, 2003a; Holt, 2008).

The practical problem of under-reporting may be related to the more conceptual problem of the process-incident contradiction. Earlier chapters have underlined the importance of viewing hate crime victimisation as an ongoing social process which, to be fully understood and appreciated, needs to be considered in the context of a broader range of factors, including historical patterns of prejudice; the lived experiences of the individuals, families and communities targeted; the dynamics of the local population; the attitudes and behaviour of offenders, their families and communities; and wider local, national and global discourses (Bowling, 1999: 285). Conceiving of hate crime victimisation in this manner encourages recognition of the broader dimensions of such victimisation, and gives emphasis to 'low-level' or everyday experiences of prejudice which in themselves may not appear especially serious but which cumulatively, and when considered in their proper context, can have a deep and lasting impact upon the victim, their family and wider community.

However, the police, together with other criminal justice agencies, tend to recognise and respond to incidents and not this ongoing social process. For Bowling (1999: 285–286) it is this contradiction that explains why hate crime victims may feel dissatisfied with police responses while officers, on the other hand, may believe that they have responded effectively:

> ... the process of law enforcement – policing and the administration of criminal justice – is constituted in the response to tightly-defined *incidents*. An incident is a one-dimensional, narrowly restricted time-slice, within which only the actions of the immediate protagonists are of any relevance. ... Incidents are describable and measurable but appear random and inexplicable. When context is drained from lived experience, it becomes impossible to understand the significance of the event to the individual or community targeted, or how and why the event occurred. As the incident is transformed from the world of the victims' experience into an object for policing it is placed in the new context of the police organisational and cultural milieu. [emphasis in original]

Clearly, the process of victimisation can create difficulties for police officers more accustomed to dealing with detached incidents. Reducing the process to a series of disconnected, 'one-off' events may allow the policing of hate crime to become more quantifiable, but at the same time this events-oriented outlook can result in the police failing to treat experiences of victimisation with the gravity that they deserve, regardless of any procedural changes introduced at a strategic level. Moreover, while police officers have often sought to adopt relatively informal methods, such as verbal warnings or mediation, as a way of resolving what they see as low-level expressions of prejudice, pursuing such methods (and not resorting to legal sanction) may simply maintain the ongoing process of victimisation and leave the victim feeling more vulnerable that they did prior to the intervention (Goodey, 2005; Garland and Chakraborti, 2006b).

A related idea developed by Bowling, following the earlier work of Grimshaw and Jefferson (1987), offers further insights into the problems that arise in the policing of hate crime. The 'hierarchy of police relevance' refers to a hypothetical set of values that police officers use, sometimes subconsciously, other times knowingly, to inform their response to different types of incident. Depending on the nature of the incident and requirements of the law, officers may be required to exercise discretion in determining the relevance of the incident to the police, and this process of categorisation will invariably be informed by that officer's understanding of the 'natural agenda' of police work. At the summit of this imaginary hierarchy is what Bowling refers to as 'good crime': unambiguous criminal offences with a 'good' victim (credible, high status, willing to testify), a 'good' perpetrator (an experienced or ideally a professional criminal), and ones which offer the prospect of a 'good' arrest being made (a high likelihood of securing a conviction). Lower down the hierarchy is 'rubbish' crime, so called because of the low social status of the victim, the low likelihood of detection and arrest and the possibility that the victim might withdraw their allegation at a later date. At the bottom end of the hierarchy are incidents described as 'disputes' or 'disturbances', which include those events regarded as highly irrelevant or legally ambiguous (Bowling, 1999: 246–251).

In his analysis of police officers' categorisation of racist incidents, Bowling (1999: 256) found that patterns of harassment were rarely recognised by officers, who instead tended to view racist incidents as spontaneous or random acts of yobbishness which by and large fell under the banner of 'rubbish crime'. Only the most serious racist incidents were regarded as 'crimes' and in only the most serious of these was prosecution initiated.[3] In all other cases, incidents were mostly seen as having little or no practical relevance to the police. Even in the incidents typically classified as 'good crime' – robberies, assaults and thefts – Bowling observed that evidence of racial motivation was irrelevant to how officers went about their work aside from requiring the completion of an additional item of paperwork.

Clearly, in the years since Bowling's research there has been considerable change to the policing agenda as a result of the political and legal prioritisation of racist and indeed other forms of hate crime. One could argue, therefore, that hate crime has now been afforded an elevated status within the hierarchy of police relevance as a result of these developments. Indeed, the ACPO guidance itself is testimony to the significance of hate crime in the eyes of the police. At the same time, though, one of Bowling's key findings – namely, that the 'top-down' view of racist incidents as a force priority conflicted with the operational 'common-sense' attitude held by rank-and-file officers – is highly significant to our present-day understanding of hate crime as it suggests that some of the more negative aspects of police occupational culture can retain a stubborn influence on police practice irrespective of changes to police policy.

It has been well documented that many officers have felt resentment towards the term 'institutional racism' and have regarded the post-Macpherson agenda for change as little more than a politically correct distraction from core policing tasks (Rowe, 2004, 2007b). Indeed, the relatively limited impact of police diversity training upon the delivery of policing and the behaviour of junior officers (Rowe and Garland, 2007) is in many ways illustrative of the difficulties associated with translating policy to practice in a post-Macpherson environment. With this in mind, we must be wary of assuming that the various problems in policing hate crime outlined above will simply disappear as a result of its prioritisation at a managerial level. While elements of police discretion have in theory been removed through the ACPO hate crime guidance, and in particular through the instruction to record incidents in line with the Macpherson definition of a racist incident, the attitudes and decision-making processes of individual officers still have the capacity to influence responses to hate crime and relationships between the police and hate crime victims.

Policing hate crime post-Macpherson

The complex relationship between the police and minority communities has been – and will no doubt continue to be – one which requires considerable sensitivity and careful monitoring. This clearly has implications for the policing of hate crime, and the preceding discussion has highlighted some key areas of concern. However, in seeking to understand the more problematic aspects of policing, we should not lose sight of the progress that has been made in the years since the Stephen Lawrence Inquiry. In the immediate aftermath of the report's publication in 1999 an unprecedented raft of measures was introduced to improve responses to hate crime, including a Home Office Code of Practice on Reporting and Recording Racist Incidents for all statutory, voluntary and community groups; the establishment of what was then the Racial and Violent Crimes Task Force and the creation of CSUs, as discussed above; and of course the ACPO guidance *Identifying and Combating Hate Crime* (2000) (Bowling and

Phillips, 2002; Hall, 2005a). By 2003 the Home Office had published four annual reports describing the initiatives undertaken to address Macpherson's recommendations, while countless action plans and programmes have been developed within police forces outside London and indeed within other public sector bodies as a result of the Race Relations (Amendment) Act 2000 (Rowe, 2004).

Central to the post-Macpherson reform agenda has been the establishment of a more victim-focused police service and the delivery of an improved response to victims of hate crime. The needs of crime victims more generally have featured increasingly prominently on political and policing agendas over the past 30 years, and the range of initiatives that has since developed, such as victims' charters, the deployment of restorative justice and enhanced legislative protection, are testimony to the way in which victims have reached a place at the heart of criminal justice considerations (Goodey, 2005). ACPO's (2005: 24–25) guidance document makes explicit reference to the prioritisation of hate crime victims, and suggests a number of practical ways in which officers should treat their needs as paramount, including listening to and acting upon the views of victims; undertaking regular risk assessments; providing victims with a consistent point of contact; and appointing, where appropriate, an interviewing officer who shares the same gender, ethnicity or other characteristic as the victim.

Hate crime victims can also benefit from other forms of assistance introduced to improve police responses to victimisation, including victim information packs containing information about specialist support services, other agencies and preventive measures,[4] and the deployment of family liaison officers with specialist skills in supporting victims and their families following an incident (ACPO, 2005: 27). In addition, Victim Personal Statements enable the victim to describe how they have been affected by a crime and the courts to understand not just the crime but the context in which it has occurred, while further protection for victims is available through the Code of Practice for Victims of Crime, which sets out the obligations of the CPS towards victims (CPS, 2007a).

Third-party reporting is another increasingly common strategy used to encourage victims of hate crime to obtain support. Designed to increase both the reporting of hate crime and the flow of intelligence from the community (ACPO, 2005: 21), third-party reporting schemes generally work by allowing victims to complete a self-reporting form online or via the post, or alternatively by enabling victims to share their experiences with a third-party agency should they prefer not to speak directly to the police. As yet there is little evidence that these schemes are being utilised to any great degree by hate crime victims. For example, only 6 per cent of victims of homophobic hate crime in Dick's (2008: 23) study reported their incident to a third party, while an overwhelming majority of participants in Wong and Christmann's (2008: 29) study of hate crime reporting were unaware of the existence of non-police reporting centers within their locality. Nevertheless, third-party reporting mechanisms offer a less intimidating way of reporting incidents than visiting a police station, particularly for groups such as refugees and asylum seekers who are known to be especially reluctant to report directly to the police.[5]

Furthermore, the more inclusive policy agenda developed in response to the Macpherson report has resulted in concerted efforts being made by police forces across England and Wales to engage more effectively and more imaginatively with all minority groups, including those who may before have felt marginalised from policing diversity strategies. James (2007), for instance, has noted the emergence of good practice nationally with regards to the policing of Gypsies and Travellers, while McGhee (2005) and Williams and Robinson (2004) have documented the progress that some forces have made with regards to dismantling barriers between themselves and LGBT communities. Similarly, as a result of the increased diversification of both urban and rural environments, the police have been required to address the hate directed towards a broader range of communities than ever before, including asylum seekers, eastern European migrants and seasonal workers from other parts of the world.

The police have also made significant strides over the past ten years with regards to the deployment of more sophisticated consultation methods with communities. Research has highlighted the particular importance of improving communication with under-represented and vulnerable groups such as asylum seekers, refugees and transgendered people as well as the more established minority groups (Jones and Newburn, 2001; Dittman, 2003; Crawford et al., 2005), and police forces nationwide have taken active steps to adapt existing consultative strategies through the development of a more inclusive approach to engagement. Central to the success of consultative fora, advisory groups, specialist committees and associated forms of consultation strategies has been the work of multi-agency networks in combating hate crime. Evolving from the establishment of Crime and Disorder Reduction Partnerships (CDRPs) under the Crime and Disorder Act 1998, multi-agency approaches have enabled police forces to work in partnership with other statutory, voluntary and community-based organisations in order to address the needs of minority groups more effectively (see, *inter alia*, Jalota, 2004; McGhee, 2005).

While the policing of hate crime has unquestionably benefited from the more inclusive, partnership-based approaches developed over the past decade, it is important to maintain some degree of caution when considering their success. For instance, the effectiveness of community consultation strategies can sometimes be limited through a reliance upon community leaders or opinion formers whose views may not in fact be representative of the wider communities whom they purportedly represent; through a preference for one-way communication as opposed to two-way dialogue (Jones and Newburn, 2001); and through a failure to recognise the complexity of communities in terms of their diverse needs and perceptions (Rowe, 2004). Partnership approaches to hate crime can also commonly suffer from a range of problems, including a lack of information-sharing within and between organisations, poor recording practices, political and personal rivalries or a lack of commitment among some agencies, all of which can result in tokenistic responses (Garland and Chakraborti, 2006b).

Equally, although the post-Macpherson environment has given the police service the impetus for reform, it is difficult to gauge with any precision the extent to which the flurry of activity at policy-making level has been matched by improved responses to hate crime at ground level. An evaluation of post-Macpherson progress is beyond the scope of this text (see Rowe, 2007, for a comprehensive overview), but the impression conveyed by the academic literature would seem to indicate that progress has been mixed in a number of respects, whether in the context of disproportionate stops and searches (Stenson and Waddington, 2007); the effectiveness of police diversity training (Foster, Newburn and Souhami, 2005; Rowe and Garland, 2007); police officers' understanding of institutional racism (Holdaway and O'Neill, 2006); or the recruitment, retention and progression of minority officers (Stone and Tuffin, 2000; Foster, 2002).

The mixed success of post-Macpherson initiatives is perhaps illustrative of differences between reform at the levels of policy and practice. For instance, the allegation of institutional racism directed at the media in January 2006 by no less a figure as the Metropolitan Police Commissioner, Sir Ian Blair, for what he saw as its failure to devote sufficient coverage to the murders of ethnic minorities in many ways symbolises the way in which senior police personnel have come to accept and embrace Macpherson's reform agenda (see Gibson and Dodd, 2006). This, though, stands in marked contrast to the views expressed by police officers in Docking and Tuffin's (2005) study of the policing of racist incidents, where it was found that some officers admitted to using racist language when talking among themselves and could not appreciate why such language might be any different in nature or impact to insults based on other physical attributes such as being overweight or short-sighted. Moreover, the allegations of discriminatory practices in the higher echelons of the Metropolitan Police Service, made by senior minority ethnic officers in 2008, reveal that the perception of racism and unfairness still persists up to the highest level of the police service despite the positive policy developments of the post-Macpherson era (Fresco, 2008). Ultimately, while the Macpherson report has been the catalyst for significant developments in the context of policy development, its impact may not have been as profound or as consistent as hoped with regards to police practice.

Conclusion

The policing of hate crime is without question a complex task that requires a considerable level of commitment and sensitivity. On the basis of what we have learnt in this chapter, there are three key points to take forward when evaluating policing in this area. First, and crucially, we must acknowledge the significant progress that has been made in the years since the Lawrence Inquiry. The political prioritisation of hate crime during the past ten years or so has required the police service to develop a more informed and inclusive stance towards hate crime, and a raft of policies, programmes and initiatives have been established in response to recommendations of the Macpherson report that unquestionably give greater recognition to the needs of hate crime victims. Secondly though, despite the positive developments that have taken place in recent times, some of the more problematic aspects of policing hate crime still present major challenges for the police service, whether in terms of raising levels of trust and confidence in the police or encouraging minorities to report. The strained police–minority relationship has left a legacy of mistrust among minority groups which has yet to be fully overturned despite post-Macpherson improvements.

Thirdly, there is evidence to suggest that the residual mistrust affecting the policing of hate crime has left its mark not just upon minority perceptions of the police but also upon police perceptions of minorities. We have seen that problems still remain at an operational level with regards to the police's response to hate crime and diversity issues, and it is hard to say with any certainty whether the strategic prioritisation of hate crime has fundamentally altered the way in which officers on the ground conceive of the process of victimisation or place hate crime within the hierarchy of police relevance. Without doubt, the establishment of community safety units with a specific hate crime remit has given this category of crime a firmer footing on police agendas across forces in England and Wales. Police personnel within these units will almost invariably be committed to providing as strong a response as possible to victims of hate crime, but at the same time past research has raised concerns over the disparaging way in which officers involved in community-oriented policing are perceived by 'real' police officers (Fielding, 1995). This may have implications for the effectiveness of police hate crime units whose excellent work in the community and knowledge of diversity issues might not be shared, appreciated or valued by colleagues working in other fields of policing.

A final note of caution should be added. Although, due to confines of space, this chapter has focused primarily upon the public police, it should be recognised that modern-day policing involves a range of actors who supplement the work of sworn police officers, whether this be community support officers, special constables, neighbourhood wardens, other forms of municipal policing or private security guards. The policing of hate is therefore not just the responsibility of the police service *per se*, but that of the wider police family, and it is imperative that any strategic commitment to challenging hate crime and promoting diversity is extended to all plural policing personnel. Consequently, when seeking to assess the quality and thoroughness of police responses, hate crime scholars should be mindful of accounting for variations between the responses of different forms of policing in addition to variations between and within forces.

Guide to further reading

There are a number of useful texts that explore issues relating to the policing of hate crime, although these centre predominantly upon 'race' and racist crime. Among them, Bowling and Phillips, *Racism, Crime and Justice* (2002) and Rowe, *Policing, Race and Racism* (2004) offer the most comprehensive accounts of the historical and contemporary relationship between the police and minority ethnic communities, while the progress made following the Lawrence inquiry is assessed in Rowe (ed.), *Policing beyond Macpherson* (2007a). Bowling, *Violent Racism* (1999) offers theoretical insights into the police perspective on hate crime, and Foster neatly summarises cultural explanations for the police's antagonism towards minority communities in her book chapter 'Police Cultures' (2002). Readers should also refer to ACPO's *Hate Crime: Delivering a Quality Service* (2005) and to their updated 2009 guidelines.

Notes

1 By far the largest police representative body, the Police Federation represents rank-and-file police officers, and is generally the most 'union-like' of the three bodies. The Superintendents' Association is a much smaller body representing the middle tier of the police service, which in some respects makes it less effective than the larger Police Federation and the more senior Association of Chief Police Officers (Newburn, 2007: 600).

2 The 'eponymous hero' of the *Secret Policeman*, BBC reporter Mark Daly, covertly recorded conversations with fellow recruits who conveyed a particular hatred of Asians and demonstrated a willingness to racially discriminate while on operational duties. Nina Hobson, the *Undercover Copper* in the 2006 documentary obtained footage showing male colleagues disbelieving rape allegations, watching pornography during night shifts and making sexist comments.

3 Bowling (1999: 278) notes that out of the 152 incidents recorded by the police in the 18 months between July 1 1987 and December 31 1988, the police conducted interviews with perpetrators in only ten cases and brought charges in two cases. This amounted to a prosecution rate of 1.3 per cent.

4 True Vision is an example of an information pack designed to improve the service provided by the police to victims of hate crime: see http://www.report-it.org.uk/.

5 According to Wong and Christmann's (2008: 27) research, the fear of being charged with an immigration offence acts as an especially strong reason for refugees and asylum seekers not to report hate incidents to the police.

8

PERPETRATORS OF HATE CRIME

──────────────── Chapter summary ────────────────

This chapter assesses the profile, motivations and activities of hate crime perpetrators. Although there has been a significant amount of research into the experience of victims of hate crime, there has been less study of the perpetrators of
such crime. We shall see that, typically, those engaging in hate acts are not neo-
Nazi skinheads or white power extremists, but are instead 'ordinary' members of
the public. Often, those convicted of hate crimes are male, from deprived backgrounds and with a history of criminal or violent behaviour. They frequently act
in groups when carrying out their offending, creating a dynamic that may exac-
erbate the severity of the incident. They may also be familiar with their victim
and thus cannot be classed as 'strangers', and this raises questions over definitions which conceive hate crimes as 'stranger danger' acts. The chapter also suggests that while members of far-right political parties carry out only a small
proportion of hate offences, these incidents may be more severe and premeditated than 'everyday' hate crimes. The influence of some of the far right's ideas
on immigration and multiculturalism, and the potency of their symbolism, may
also be more far-reaching and impactful than many would like to think.

──────────────── Introduction ────────────────

When seeking to understand the motivations behind acts of hate, it is often tempting to conceive of hate crime perpetrators as being somehow distinct from the
perpetrators of ordinary crimes. A good illustration of this process is provided by
the nailbombings of April 1999 perpetuated against London's minority ethnic and
gay communities. These horrific attacks were orchestrated by David Copeland, a
neo-Nazi and loner who fitted the common public perception of a perpetrator of
hate crimes as someone '"out-of-control", psychologically disturbed, distant and

different from the rest of us' (Ray and Smith, 2001: 205). This portrayal may not be inaccurate in extreme cases like Copeland's, but for more 'everyday' hate crime it may be misleading. As Ray and Smith (2001: 221) note, it is 'right to say that the majority of hate crimes are not organized by hate groups but by teenagers, especially white males [on the basis of] underlying prejudices which on occasion spill over into criminal conduct'. As this implies, hate crime is a complex and varied form of offending. At one extreme, Copeland's premeditated attacks, or the violence of Stephen Lawrence's racist murder and Jody Dobrowski's homophobic killing can be shocking, and yet on the other hand the more routine, 'low-level' forms of harassment can be 'virtually unremarkable' (Mason, 2005a: 838), although their effect can still be debilitating for the victim. As Craig (2002: 86) argues though, hate acts are 'a qualitatively distinct form of aggression' and thus may possess motivations different from those behind other forms of crime.

A good place to begin this assessment of offenders' motivations is Sibbitt's (1997) influential study of the perpetrators of racist violence on two deprived south London housing estates. Sibbitt developed a typology of offenders categorised by age (from eldest to youngest), as she felt that the racist attitudes of older members of families can be 'learned' by their offspring, who in turn exhibit racist views that are condoned by their elders. Cultures of racism are thereby created and reinforced in localities that become hostile environments for minority ethnic residents. Many white people living on Sibbitt's estates felt bitterly let down by local authorities who were blamed for the allocation of resources to those who, in their eyes, did not deserve them (minority ethnic groups) at the expense of those who did (white people). This resentment manifested itself in racist abuse which could become violent. In parallel with Dunbar and Crevecoeur's (2005) and Ray and Smith's (2001) work, Sibbitt suggested that those who engaged in this violence often had a history of criminal behaviour and routinely invoked aggressive behaviour to resolve disputes. They were commonly part of families that had poor physical or mental health, coupled with a lack of formal education.

Sibbitt's work helped to develop an understanding of the 'everyday' racism that can be located in deprived urban neighbourhoods. Ray, Smith and Wastell (2004) built upon Sibbitt's work, and found that many of the perpetrators of racist violence in their study came from dysfunctional families, and none had had more than a basic education, with most being unemployed. Like Sibbitt's offenders, many in Ray et al.'s study employed violence as an everyday way of resolving disputes. The researchers also outlined similarities between the profiles of racist offenders and those who had perpetrated non-hate crimes, concluding that, 'in respect of their offending, the sample was not significantly different from the total population of known offenders serving community sentences' (Ray et al., 2004: 351). Ray et al. acknowledged the 'uncomfortable truth' that the perpetrators of hate crime are commonly not 'Nazis' but are instead 'ordinary' members of the public, albeit often ones with criminal histories.

Gadd, Dixon and Jefferson's (2005) study of racist hate crime in North Staffordshire also reflected many of Sibbitt's findings. They too found that local minority ethnic populations (in this case immigrants and asylum seekers) were blamed by many white working-class residents for the problems befalling Stoke-on-Trent. Racist views predominated in many of these deprived neighbourhoods and were held by those who had been convicted of a racist incident, and those who had not. Perpetrators were not 'hardened race haters committed to attacking or harassing people from other ethnic groups' (Gadd et al., 2005: 9), but did have life stories characterised by deprivation, mental health problems, domestic violence, drug and alcohol issues, and patterns of criminal behaviour. As Gadd et al. (2005: 9) explain, the perpetrators in their study were:

> ... a familiar cross-section of those routinely arrested by the police and sentenced before the courts. Living in communities where so many of 'our' misfortunes are blamed on a few of 'them', and where 'their' perceived lack of respect for 'us' is matched by the indifference (or worse) of national and local political elites, it is hardly surprising that some of North Staffordshire's most severely disadvantaged and vulnerable residents feel justified – in some cases compelled – to project their feelings of shame, envy, and disgust on to minority groups.

McDevitt, Levin and Bennett's (2002) analysis of Boston police hate crime cases in the early 1990s mirrored aspects of these findings. It revealed that a quarter of such acts were carried out in order to 'protect' the offenders' neighbourhood from those viewed as outsiders or intruders. Typically, these cases involved white residents who felt that minority ethnic incomers had no right to attain 'their' housing and other resources. Hate crimes were therefore enacted when neighbourhoods were in *transition* from all-white communities to multi-ethnic ones, and were meant to send a stark message to minority ethnic incomers that they were not welcome. For Perry (2001), such offending is designed to maintain society's social hierarchies, which privilege white, heterosexual males and stigmatise those who do not conform to these hegemonic identities. Tension between these identities can erupt into hate-inspired violence if the position of the dominant group is threatened. The boundaries between 'in-' and 'out-groups' – 'essentialist, mutually exclusive categories of belonging' (Perry, 2001: 46) – are thereby reinforced, with victims reminded of their 'lower' place within the hierarchy.

It is interesting to note that Perry's ideas of structure and dominance would appear to be in contradiction with Sibbitt's (1997) and Gadd et al.'s (2005) suggestion that racist hate crime is more likely to occur in deprived neighbourhoods, where perpetrators would not appear to be privileged or at the top of a social hierarchy. However, for Perry, this contradiction is resolved by the *relative* position of the dominant and subordinate groups within a social structure that confers 'dominance, normativity, and privilege' on certain identities – of which whiteness is one – 'and subordination, marginality and disadvantage' on others, such as minority ethnic identities (Perry, 2001: 47). Therefore, even within poor housing estates a 'relative hierarchy' can exist, with white populations higher up than minority ethnic groups.

For Franklin (2000), the presence of dominant ideas of heterosexual masculinity among perpetrators of anti-gay harassment, as well as elements of homophobia, influenced much of this behaviour. As such, this research seems to chime with Perry's suggestion that, by not 'doing gender properly', gay people may be susceptible to homophobic victimisation in a society that privileges heterosexuality. However, for Franklin, a key motivating factor was also 'thrill seeking', meaning that perpetrators undertook homophobic harassment simply because it was *fun*. These findings are reflected in the work of McDevitt et al. (2002), who noted that, in two-thirds of police hate crime cases they examined, youths told police that they had perpetrated the incident because they were bored and looking for some excitement. In most of these examples, the perpetrator(s) left their neighbourhood to search for a target in another location and that this victim (linking in with Perry's ideas) was selected because the offender perceived them to be somehow 'different'. These attacks were mainly carried out by teenagers or young adults acting in groups.

That such a large proportion of incidents was perpetrated for 'thrills' is intriguing, especially as they were carried out in groups, and is indicative of the importance of peer pressure and inter-group dynamics (Franklin, 2000). What is also revealed is how the victim must be 'dehumanised' in the eyes of the perpetrator, whose 'fun' is enacted at the expense of an 'other' whose suffering is of little consequence to the attacker. There is therefore more to these attacks than bored youths simply seeking 'thrills' as they reveal the existence of negative attitudes and stereotypes about marginalised outgroups that somehow render their pain meaningless. The work of Byers, Crider and Biggers (1999) provides some background to this suggestion. They studied the motivations of (mainly) groups of young men whose acts of intimidation targeted members of the nearby Amish community in Fulham County, USA. Like McDevitt et al., Byers et al. (1999: 84) concluded that the key motivation behind this harassment was 'thrill seeking', typically finding that their perpetrators:

...travelled the country back roads looking for victims – often while out drinking – cruising for Amish. Once found, the Amish were often targets. These attacks tend to be random and anonymous ... [and the] offending rests largely with the thrill or excitement experienced.

As Sibbitt (1997) and Gadd et al. (2005) found, the target of this harassment was a minority group subject to widespread negative stereotyping (the Amish were seen as 'stupid, dirty, stinking, backward and hypocritical' (Byers et al., 1999: 83)). Thus, even in cases where hate crimes were committed supposedly just for 'thrills', negative stereotypes exist about certain groups that serve to justify their victimisation. Of particular relevance here is Byers et al.'s suggestion that there was a tendency among perpetrators to rely on neutralisation techniques that can be employed by some offenders to rationalise an offence after it has been committed. Offenders separated the commission of their hate acts from their own responsibility for them by denying that their actions had caused any real harm to the victim, or that the victim 'had it coming' and possessed such low social status that any injury has no real impact anyway. Such arguments again reveal how outgroups can become dehumanised in the eyes of perpetrators.

Byers et al. (1999) also found that the anti-Amish hate crimes were almost always carried out by groups and sometimes this was used as a justification for their behaviour, as the crimes were seen as bonding exercises that brought friends closer together. Research more broadly suggests that 'hate crimes typically involve multiple perpetrators', making them different from 'other aggressive offences' (see also Bowling, 1999; Craig, 2002: 87). The group dynamic may affect the nature of the incident, with evidence suggesting that the larger the group of perpetrators is, the more severe the hate crime can be (Dunbar, 1997). Craig also asserts that individuals within groups may feel 'pressured to behave in unusual ways when encountering or interacting with either victims or members of the victim's social group' (Craig, 2002: 87). There may also be a diffusion of responsibility within groups, coupled with a lack of recognition of normal social constraints, meaning that 'When individuals temporarily act in socially prohibitive ways with diminished capacity for social control, the outcome of their behaviours is especially likely to be extreme' (ibid: 88). Thus individuals, acting in groups, may lose their normal sense of perspective and feel less responsible for their actions, factors which, combined together, can produce more vicious assaults.

McDevitt et al. (2002) have suggested that there are four different levels of culpability for those involved in group-enacted hate crimes, ranging from the 'leader' (who encourages the others to participate), through, at the other end of the 'culpability scale', to the 'hero' (who actively tries to stop the crime from occurring, and will help the victim and notify the police). Perhaps the most interesting levels, though, are those in the middle of this scale: the 'fellow travellers' (who actively or hesitantly participate in the offence) and 'unwilling participants' (who do not actively participate in the perpetration yet do nothing to stop it either). Both of these categories illustrate Craig's idea of the influence of the group, and Byers et al.'s notion of the significance of peer pressure, and show how those who are neither leaders nor sufficiently confident enough to be group 'rebels' will, to a certain extent, just go along with the enactment of the hate crime. As we can see in Case Study 8.1, one of Jody Dobrowski's killers, Thomas Pickford, arguably began the assault through peer pressure as he wanted to impress his companion, Scott Walker, but when Walker assumed the role of 'leader' and began murderously attacking Dobrowski, Pickford became an 'unwilling participant', too scared to stop him.

Case Study 8.1: Profiling perpetrators of hate crime

As was detailed in Chapter 4, in October 2005 Jody Dobrowski, a 24 year-old gay male, died from injuries sustained in a horrific attack on Clapham Common. The unprovoked assault was carried out by Thomas Pickford (who was 26, unemployed and of no fixed address) and Scott Walker (33, a decorator from Clapham). At their subsequent trial Judge Barker sentenced Walker and Pickford to a minimum of 28 years each under the Criminal Justice Act 2003, which facilitates harsher sentences for offences aggravated by homophobia *(BBC News,* 2006).

On the evening of the assault, Pickford and Walker, who had been drinking heavily, chanced upon Dobrowski as they cut across the Common. Pickford became the primary aggressor, shouting insults before striking him. A witness heard the pair screaming 'fucking queer, bastard, faggot, poof' as they undertook their prolonged assault (Kennedy, 2006) before fleeing back to their hostel as the police arrived. Pickford was later heard boasting to a fellow resident: 'I've just kicked the crap out of someone. I feel great.' The same resident noticed that Pickford's jeans were soaked in blood. A while later Walker was also heard bragging about the attack. The pair were arrested a week later (Shoffman, 2006).

Pickford confessed to police that he had started the attack as he wanted to impress Walker. However, it was Walker that was the most aggressive assailant, with Pickford admitting in interview that he was too scared to get Walker to stop. 'I just wanted to look like a hard man', Pickford admitted (Shoffman, 2006). These two fit the typology of perpetrators of hate attacks who do so in order to gain status in the eyes of their immediate peer group (Franklin, 2000: Byers et al., 1999). While filled with prejudice against gay people, Walker and Pickford also seem to have carried out the attack partly for the thrill of it, actively seeking out a target from a despised outgroup in a location close to where they were staying (McDevitt et al., 2002). Their criminal convictions and history of violence – Walker had been out on licence from a 15-month prison sentence given to him for trying to strangle his own mother, while Thomas had previously committed a string of burglaries (Kennedy, 2006) – also closely fit notions that many hate crime offenders have previously committed other offences, some of them violent (Ray and Smith, 2001).

The victim–perpetrator relationship

Hate crimes are commonly conceived as offences in which the individual identity of the victim is *irrelevant* to the perpetrator, who simply targets the victim because they are an identifiable member of a despised minority group (see Chapter 1). It is their prejudice towards that group that drives their harassment of the victim rather than any personal animosity that may exist between the two parties. As Perry (2001: 29) argues: 'These brutal acts of violence are commonly perpetrated on strangers – people with whom the perpetrator has had little or no personal contact.' Therefore, for a hate crime to be understood as such, there must be scant evidence of any prior relationship between perpetrator and victim. Hate crimes are thus classic 'stranger danger' crimes that, by targeting a minority group, are designed to send an intimidating message to other members of that group.

Jarman and Tennant's (2003) study of homophobic incidents recorded by police in Northern Ireland, for example, revealed that in 8 per cent of the cases where the victim had seen their assailant, the perpetrator was identified as a neighbour of the victim, while in 14 per cent the perpetrator was identified as a 'local person', and in a quarter of the cases the perpetrator 'could be identified by the victim' (Jarman and Tennant, 2003: 29). In their own survey of victims of homophobia, the same authors found that in a third of all cases the victim believed that the incident had been homophobic because the perpetrator actually *knew* of them and their sexuality (ibid: 48). Mason (2005a) posits that police hate crime statistics show that the victim and assailant are strangers in less than 20 per cent of cases of homophobic or racist hate crime in London, a finding supported by Moran's (2007) work. Craig (2002: 98), however, notes that in some studies of hate crime in the USA the victim and perpetrator have been strangers in as many as 90 per cent of cases.

The implications of this somewhat contradictory evidence for our understanding of hate crime are significant, for if hate crime is *not* a 'stranger danger' form of crime in which the victim is targeted solely because of their minority group membership, then does this mean that the very concept itself is undermined? Or do the complexities of such crimes play a part in influencing the nature of the victim–perpetrator relationship? Sibbitt (1997) suggests that it is the *type* of such harassment that may indicate the level of familiarity between perpetrator and victim. She identified three types of harassment: common assaults (involving physical contact between perpetrator and victim), indirect assaults (where there is no direct physical contact between the two parties) and acts of intimidation (including verbal abuse, nuisance behaviour and damage to property). In cases of common and indirect assaults, Sibbitt's research showed that they were often carried out by groups of white youths or adult males against people they did not know, thus conforming to the model of 'stranger danger' hate crime. For acts of intimidation, however, there was evidence of white children and adults routinely abusing those who lived near them and whom they therefore must have known, at least to some degree. There was also evidence, though, of 'low-level' harassment taking place against any identifiable 'outgroups', as Sibbitt found gangs of children harassing 'anyone in the area who looked different, including people with disabilities' (Sibbitt, 1997: 48).

Kielinger and Paterson's (2007) analysis of faith hate incidents recorded by the Metropolitan Police Service also found that the extreme cases, such as GBH or murder, were more likely to have been committed by strangers than by someone whom the victim knew. However, in two-thirds of the cases of less extreme types of harassment (where the victim provided information to the police) the perpetrator was someone known to the victim, whether they were neighbours, local schoolchildren or work colleagues. This suggestion, that it may be possible to infer the status of the victim–perpetrator relationship from the type of hate incident experienced (with strangers more likely to be involved in cases of physical assault), is borne out by other research. Bartlett (2007: 577), for example, found that the assailant and deceased were strangers in almost half of the cases of gay sexual homicide that he examined, causing him to suggest that 'stranger violence is much more significant here than in attacks on women, or general attacks on men'. Herek, Cogan and Roy Gillis (2003: 246) also found that in cases of 'bias person crimes' the perpetrator and victim were more likely to be strangers than in more 'low-level' cases, and Morrison and Mackay's (2000: 1) analysis of homophobic harassment in Edinburgh found that violent incidents were 'mostly carried out by strangers'.

Interestingly, though, (and as was mentioned in Chapter 6) there is a suggestion that victims of disablist hate crime may be very familiar with perpetrators, as often they are a carer or 'friend' of the victim. Quarmby (2008) notes that this is especially the case with extreme disablist hate crimes (such as murders) when the perpetrator is commonly someone that the victim knows and trusts very well. She therefore suggests that these types of disablist crime differ markedly from their racist or homophobic equivalents, where the victim and perpetrator *are* very often strangers. Thus in cases where physical attacks are involved, some forms of hate crime (such as homophobic) appear more readily to fit Perry's 'stranger danger' model than others (such as disablist).

However, much of the discussion regarding 'hate' and victim–perpetrator relationships takes place within more traditional understandings of hate crime in which the two parties occupy the same geographical space. Such accounts fail to acknowledge the relatively recent phenomenon of 'cyberbullying', which is now seen as a significant form of bias-related harassment, especially for young people (Hunt and Jensen, 2006), and which occurs remotely. It can take place via internet message boards, or via social networking sites such as Facebook and Bebo, in an environment that offers anonymity to the perpetrator and thus may facilitate even more vicious harassment than may occur in a 'physical' environment where the chances of being caught are greater. Whether such anonymity means that the perpetrator and their target are necessarily strangers is a moot point, though, as it may be the case that such anonymity is embraced as a way of disguising the perpetrator's identity from a victim that would otherwise know exactly who they are.

The location of hate incidents may also be important in developing an understanding of the complexities of the victim–perpetrator relationship. Mason's (2005b) examination of homophobic and racist harassment cases reported to the police revealed that 90 per cent occurred at or near the victim's home and 10 per cent at work, which indicates that there is a strong likelihood of some pre-existing relationship between victim and perpetrator.

Interestingly, however, Mason suggests that those living in close proximity can be known to each other and yet still be strangers. Drawing upon Bauman's (1991) idea of the stranger as 'emotionally distant but physically proximate', Mason argues that although both 'sides' involved in a hate incident are emotionally estranged from one another, their physical proximity means that it is 'virtually impossible for them to be strangers in terms of the interpersonal relations of everyday life' (Mason, 2005b: 587). Indeed, it may be the case that most perpetrators know just enough about their intended victim to realise that they offer a suitably vulnerable target (Stanko, 2001).

Ray, Smith and Wastell's (2004: 351) study of racist offenders would seem to support this premise as they felt that 'virtually all offenders knew their victims, though not well'. This knowledge was usually gained as a result of commercial transactions with shopkeepers, taxi drivers, or those working in restaurants and takeaways, where many of the incidents took place. However, as Mason (2005a: 855) suggests, this kind of knowledge is not equal to the 'depth of intimacy that exists between friends, partners or family members' and does not provide the perpetrator with a level of emotional empathy with their intended target(s). Indeed, it could be argued that there must inherently be some kind of emotional distance between offender and victim for the former to undertake any form of harassment against the latter. The victim *must* therefore be some kind of a stranger to their assailant who, by their act of violence or intimidation, confirms their distance from the victim and hence the latter's 'outsider' status. Having examined hate crimes commonly perpetrated by 'ordinary' members of the public, this chapter now turns to an examination of the minority of such crimes that are carried out by extremists whose prime motivation really is *hate*.

Hate crime extremists

By their name, 'hate crimes' would appear to be types of offence committed by someone consumed with prejudice, a 'committed and politically conscious hater' (Ray and Smith, 2001: 221). Some of the most notorious perpetrators of violent acts targeted at minorities, such as the neo-Nazi David Copeland (see Case Study 8.2), would appear to fit this profile. The reality, though, may be very different from this, as there is evidence that extremists only perpetrate a low percentage of hate crimes. McDevitt et al. (2002: 309), for instance, found that only 1 per cent of the cases in their study (discussed above) were committed by 'mission' offenders 'totally dedicated to bigotry'.

Nevertheless, Sibbitt's (1997) findings suggest that the influence of far-right groups goes further than these statistics may indicate. Sibbitt argues that while the British National Party (BNP) garnered little electoral support from the residents of the housing estates she studied, what the party did achieve was to channel the sense of grievance and anger that some white people felt about their own poor living standards towards local black people:

> In general, the young people were not members of these organisations. However, they were aware that the far-right presence and propaganda were threatening towards ethnic minorities. The young people therefore co-opted the language and insignia of these organisations into their own activities, such as graffiti or writing and posting threatening notes. (Sibbitt, 1997: 38)

Gadd et al.'s (2005) assessment of the influence of the far right upon white residents in deprived parts of Stoke-on-Trent revealed that the BNP appealed to those who felt that the main political parties had prioritised service provision towards minority ethnic residents, migrants and asylum seekers. This had created a strong sense of injustice among some white communities, who felt that their own needs had been unfairly overlooked by a 'politically correct' liberal elite. In such a climate, the BNP's vocal opposition to immigration and multiculturalism, together with its determination to stand up for 'British culture', gained the party a significant amount of support among some white households as 'according to the binary logic of racial politics, a vote for the BNP was most clearly intelligible as a vote for "us", and against "them"' (ibid: 7). It is difficult to discern whether in this racialised and tense climate the BNP's popularity directly led to an increase in racist harassment, but of those 15 perpetrators of such incidents in Gadd et al.'s study, two were BNP activists, two had far-right associations and another had sympathies with extremist groups (ibid: 2).

This profile suggests that although far-right activists may only be responsible for a minority of hate crimes, their ideas can influence the wider perpetration of hate offences. There is also some evidence that membership of extremist groups may be related to a more predatory form of hate crime offending, with hate group members going to greater lengths to seek out their targets and that such offenders commit more severe and more impactful hate crimes than perpetrators who are not members of bias-oriented groups (Dunbar and Crevecoeur, 2005). Therefore, although the numbers of such incidents are comparatively small, they may be characterised by an extreme violence that causes more harm than those hate acts carried out by 'ordinary' members of the public. Interestingly, the same research found that members of extremist groups who commit hate crimes had more extensive criminal and violent histories than other hate crime offenders and posed a greater risk for perpetrating ongoing aggressive acts, thereby reflecting 'the popular image of the violent hate crime offender as a highly dissocial and aggressive individual' (ibid: 13).

Case Study 8.2: The London nailbomber

During April 1999 London witnessed a series of bombings that deliberately targeted the capital's minority ethnic and gay communities. The blasts claimed three lives, wounded 129 people and were perpetrated by a lone white male, 22 year-old David Copeland, who had a history of involvement with far-right groups. He first struck on Saturday April 17 when he left a bag packed with explosives and nails outside a supermarket in Brixton, south-east London. The bomb detonated as the police arrived, injuring 50 people, a number of them seriously. Shocked security services and the police initially had no idea who was behind the nailbomb, and began a frantic search for those responsible before they struck again.

A week later Copeland's second nailbomb exploded in Brick Lane in London's East End, where the capital's Bengali community is concentrated, injuring 13 people. While some neo-Nazi groups, such as the White Wolves and Combat 18, tried to claim responsibility for the explosions, the police's first breakthrough came after they released CCTV images of their main suspect – a clearly identifiable Copeland. The footage panicked Copeland into bringing his next bombing forward a day to Friday April 30. This time targeting London's gay communities, he planted a nailbomb in the Admiral Duncan, a well-known gay-friendly venue in Soho. It exploded in the early evening, killing three people and injuring 79 (Hopkins and Hall, 2000). By this time the police had identified the person featured in the CCTV footage, and hours later apprehended Copeland at his flat, who calmly admitted his guilt to arresting officers (McLagan and Lowles, 2000).

Under police interrogation Copeland confessed to being racist, homophobic and a committed national socialist. 'My main intent was to spread fear, resentment and hatred throughout this country, it was to cause a racial war,' he told detectives. 'There'd be a backlash from the ethnic minorities, I'd just be the spark that would set fire to this country' (*BBC News*, 2000). Copeland had been heavily influenced by *The Turner Diaries*, a fictional work by American neo-Nazi William Pierce that depicts a 'race war' triggered by the activities of white supremacists (Lowles, 2001). Some of the psychiatrists who interviewed Copeland thought he was suffering from paranoid schizophrenia, although others felt his bombing campaign revealed a more rational mind (Hopkins and Hall, 2000). At his trial, a prosecution expert testified that Copeland 'had overwhelming anxiety over his sexual orientation and intense rage and hatred of others that led to extreme views and a desire to destroy' (Hopkins, 2000). He was found guilty of murder and sentenced to six life terms.

Copeland suffered from cripplingly low self-esteem (he was deeply self-conscious about his lack of height and was terrified that people thought he was gay) and his fascination with violence and bombing 'provided him with a calling, something to aim for, a direction in what had until then had been an unhappy, unstable life' (McLagan and Lowles, 2000: 14). He had briefly been in the BNP but left to join the National Socialist Movement, a small neo-Nazi grouping that believed in white racial supremacy and virulent antisemitism – a 'poisonous cocktail which eventually led him to his terrible acts' (Lowles, 2001: 298).

Before the chapter turns to an assessment of two of the most significant far-right extremist organisations in Britain (the BNP and Combat 18), it is worth reflecting upon the definitions of such organisations. Fascism, according to Copsey (2007: 64), is 'a revolutionary ultra-nationalist ideology, an attempt to create a new type of post-liberal national community – an alternative modernity – by a movement or regime that *aspires* to the total or "totalitarian" transformation of culture and society', and Copsey (ibid: 80) sees the BNP as being a 'recalibration and modernisation' of this fascist tradition. Interestingly, though, it is the BNP's prioritisation of British cultural and economic interests that is scorned by white supremacist groups like Combat 18 (or C18 for short), who see such an ideology as obstructing the global unity of the white Aryan race. For such groups, the BNP's focus on Britain is far too narrow and restrictive, even if they may have sympathies with the racism and fervent anti-communism of some of the BNP's members. Instead, groups like C18 are unashamedly neo-Nazi, a 'label pinned on post-war movements of the ultra-right that aim specifically to resurrect the ideology and style of the German Nazi Party' (Davies and Lynch, 2002: 320). It is to a discussion of these two groups, beginning with the BNP, that this chapter now turns.

Organised hatred: the British far-right

The British National Party has been the most successful far-right political party in Britain in the last 20 years, gaining dozens of council seats and a significant presence in several local council chambers. Formed in 1982, the BNP initially adopted many of the National Front's fascist and racist policies, opposing all immigration and supporting the repatriation of minority ethnic people (Copsey, 2007). These types of policy tended to attract young, disillusioned males with a disposition for violence, and while the party would never have openly advocated the attacking of minority ethnic populations, there is little doubt that some of its more volatile 'footsoldiers' did so (Wainwright, 2004).

However, the BNP's electoral success in the 1990s was minimal (Copsey, 2000), precipitating a change in its leadership in 1999. Its new figurehead, Nick Griffin (a Cambridge-educated farmer), was a 'moderniser' determined to rid the party of its old fascist image (Copsey, 2007). The 'new' BNP's stance therefore focused on being tough on law and order, opposing the European Union, preserving sterling and promoting British farming and countryside 'traditions'. However, the beliefs of the old BNP were never far from the surface. In 1997 Griffin himself was caught on camera saying that '[i]t is more important to control the streets of a city than its council chambers' (Roxburgh, 2002: 233), seemingly drawing on the party's streetfighting past, and indeed his own history includes a conviction for inciting racial hatred (Williams, 2008a). In 2001 the BNP appeared to inflame tension between local white and Asian communities in Oldham that culminated in several days of rioting in May of that year (see below).

Since then the party has had some success in local elections, gaining around 50 council seats, with strongholds in Barking and Dagenham, Stoke and Burnley (Williams, 2008b). Notably, the BNP also won over 800,000 votes in the 2004 European elections (*BBC News*, 2004). However, perhaps the party's biggest achievement has been the 'mainstreaming' of some of its ideas and values. In 2002, for example, the then Home Secretary David Blunkett voiced concerns over schools being 'swamped' by the children of asylum seekers (Travis, 2002), while in 2007 Prime Minister Gordon Brown was accused of 'using the rhetoric of the BNP' when speaking of his desire to create 'British jobs for British workers' (Moore, 2007). That such 'strong' sentiments could come from prominent and moderate politicians is in itself a sign that the BNP's influence may be greater than many would like.

However, the BNP's attempts at presenting itself as a 'respectable' party that represents a clean break from its fascist forerunners have not always been popular with certain sections of the party's rank-and-file membership, whose racist ideals had attracted them to the far-right in the first place. This disillusionment was evidenced in the early 1990s when some members began to formulate their own separate faction based around the vicious 'street politics' that the BNP was trying to leave behind. Thus Combat 18 was born, an openly neo-Nazi grouping that took the '1' in its name from the 'A' in Adolf (the first letter in the alphabet) and the '8' from the 'H' in Hitler (the eighth). Its belief, that the Aryan 'race' was being corrupted by immigration and multiculturalism, was complemented by a potent antisemitism exemplified by their conviction that the global economy was in the grips of a Jewish conspiratorial elite that must be overthrown through revolution.

Far more akin to white supremacist groups in the USA than the homegrown BNP, C18 was an underground 'movement' made up of loosely affiliated cells united under the concept of 'leaderless resistance' (Ryan, 2003). It attracted a mixture of football hooligans, racist skinheads and disaffected Nazis, swelling its numbers to around 200 nationally but with many more occasionally becoming involved in its activities (ibid: 17). Within months of its inception it had gained a fearsome reputation for violence through its attacks upon minority ethnic people, immigrants, left-wing radicals and anti-racist campaigners at a time of an increase in racist incidents and the racist murders of four young black men. Its battering of members of a Chelsea anti-racist supporters group in 1994 is but one example of C18's attempts to terrorise those whose politics they despised (Lowles, 2001). The evolution of the Redwatch website, where personal details of anti-racist activists are publicised, is another. Equally, though their role in the riot at the abandoned Republic of Ireland versus England football match in 1995 has often been exaggerated, not least by C18 themselves, their links to Ulster Loyalist paramilitaries are well documented and have formed an important part of their activities.

The significance of the racist skinhead music scene to the group's prestige and finances should also not be overlooked. In the last decade or so the scene has flourished, with the popularity of British bands growing rapidly via the white power internet network (Williams, 2007a). The ISD Records website, the self-styled 'hate factory of white power music', sells a 'vast array' of CDs, MP3 music files and has a link to Blood and Honour radio, an extremist online station (Williams, 2007b: 3). Therefore, in contrast to its relatively humble beginnings in the 1990s ISD Records now has a truly global reach, and has provided hundreds of thousands of pounds for C18 to fund its campaigns of terror and hatred (Lowles, 2001).

The use of the internet by extremist groups such as C18 has been a key development in their recent activities (Hall, 2005a). As well as providing a means by which to raise finances, the internet has also provided a multimedia environment that has given hate groups a more visible public presence, and a much more accessible platform, than they have enjoyed before. The Simon Wiesenthal Centre and the Anti-Defamation League have estimated that there are about 2,800 hate-related websites worldwide, with the Ku Klux Klan, Nazis and neo-Nazis, racist skinheads and the Christian Identity Movement having the most visible presence (Moritz, 2007). It is not surprising that C18, and indeed the BNP, have been quick to see the power and potential of the internet to spread their message.

C18's links to football hooliganism are also significant, as it has been alleged that these links played a pivotal role in the outbreak of the racialised disorders in Oldham in May 2001. As noted above, for a while the north-west town had been experiencing heightened tension between its local Asian and white communities. In an attempt to inflame this situation, Combat 18 attracted sympathisers from its national hooligan network to Oldham for the last match of the 2000/01 football season, ostensibly to engage in disorder in Westwood, a part of the town with a large Asian presence. Three weeks later, they recongregated in the town and engaged in violent confrontation with local Asians, precipitating widespread rioting. As Lowles (2001: xiv) argues, whatever the underlying social causes were for the disturbances, they had undoubtedly been triggered 'by the actions of C18 thugs and their football hooligan allies who … had finally got what [they] wanted. Race war.'

However, in the first decade of the twenty-first century C18 has lost some of its potency. A number of factors have contributed to this, including the imprisonment of several of its figureheads, the suspicion that C18 may have been infiltrated by the security services, and the negative publicity surrounding David Copeland's murderous campaign (Ryan, 2003). Nevertheless, it is still being associated with the commission of racist and religiously motivated hate crime, including the recent rise in antisemitic attacks in Britain and the increase in racist activity in Northern Ireland (Vasager, 2007). Even if its powers and size are somewhat diminished, C18 is nevertheless an influential grouping on the neo-Nazi right and remains a vehicle for intimidation and violence.

Conclusion

This chapter set out to explore typologies of hate crime offenders, as well as their motivations and their relationships with their victims. Drawing initially upon the work of Sibbitt (1997), Ray et al. (2004) and Gadd et al. (2005), it discussed the profile of those who commit hate crime on working-class housing estates in England. It was suggested that the majority of this crime was perpetrated by groups of young men, many of whom had criminal records and often used violence as a routine method of settling disputes. Their resentment against identified outgroup targets was fuelled by the (unsubstantiated) suspicion that these groups were 'stealing' their jobs, housing and other resources, and were also responsible for the deterioration of the living conditions in the locality. It was also noted that there has been a widespread perception that the main political parties had neglected the needs of white British communities while prioritising those of minority ethnic populations. Generally, though, far-right political parties had failed to capitalise on these sentiments in all but a handful of areas, although there was evidence that their ideas held sway in certain communities. Importantly for the context of this book, a significant amount of research indicates that far-right extremists are only responsible for the perpetration of a small proportion of hate crime, although when they do commit hate offences, the incident may be more premeditated and extreme than those perpetrated by 'ordinary' members of the public.

Perhaps the most debated facet of the nature of hate crime perpetration is whether they can be categorised as 'stranger danger' crimes, where the victim is chosen by the offender because of their membership of a despised minority group, rather than any specifically individual characteristics that they may possess. Thinking of hate crime as solely a 'stranger danger' form of crime may mean that the conception of the perpetrator itself becomes 'othered' and distorted into a 'devilish image for symbolic sacrifice' (Bowling, 1999: 305) that creates a false impression of those who actually commit such acts. As Ray and Smith (2001), Mason (2005a) and Moran (2007) posit, large proportions of hate crimes are committed either in or near the victim's home, neighbourhood, or workplace, and as Stanko (2001: 329) suggests: 'I would, however urge all of us to think carefully about sitting too comfortably with terms such as "hate" crime. Such a term continues to privilege the danger of the stranger above that of the neighbour.'

Moran (2007: 433) points out that minority communities sometimes embrace the notion of hate crimes as 'stranger danger' offences as this can be comforting for victims, who may not want to admit to themselves that risks of further assault may lie 'closer to home' than they would like to realise. Instead, simplified constructions of a stranger as 'evil' and 'distant' reinforce the comforting thought that the stranger is 'distinct, separate and distant from the friend; geographically, socially, culturally'. However, as Bauman (1991, cited in Moran, 2007: 434) points out, the stranger is a much more complex proposition than this, and, rather than being an embodiment of evil, is in fact 'neither friend nor enemy; because he may be both'.

Therefore, within the context of the hate crime debate perhaps the concept of the 'stranger' needs to be reconfigured into a more complicated figure whom the victim can simultaneously *know* and yet be emotionally *distant* from; familiar with and yet still remote. This may help us understand hate crime as a 'stranger danger' crime even if they are, in fact, commonly perpetrated by people who are familiar with their target. As Stanko (2001: 323) suggests, it is how 'assailants turn *those known* to them into *strangers*' that is of crucial importance here, rather than simply whether the two parties know, or know of, each other. After all, if someone is capable of committing a hate crime against another, then it indicates that they cannot feel much empathy for the victim, and thus must inherently be *apart* from them – in other words, a stranger.

Guide to further reading

Sibbitt's influential report *The Perpetrators of Racial Harassment and Racial Violence* (1997) offers a detailed explanation of racist hatred in a deprived urban area, as does Ray, Smith and Wastell, 'Shame, Rage and Racist Violence' (2004). McDevitt, Levin and Bennett, 'Hate Crime Offenders' (2002) and Chapter 2 of Perry, *In the Name of Hate* (2001) provide an overview of perspectives on hate crime perpetration. Mason, 'Hate Crime and the Image of the Stranger' (2005a) critiques 'stranger danger' theories of hate crime. Those interested in further study of neo-Nazis should read Lowles, *White Riot* (2001), Ryan, *Homeland* (2003) or McLagan and Lowles, *Mr. Bad* (2000). An excellent resource on the contemporary far-right is *Searchlight* magazine.

9

REASSESSING HATE CRIME

──────────────── Chapter summary ────────────────

This final chapter reassesses the concept of hate crime in light of the debates that have been examined in previous chapters, and begins by reviewing their key points. By taking stock of the various complexities that have been outlined thus far – whether this be the similarities and differences between the more recognised and more marginalised forms of hate crime, the nature of hate crime victimisation and perpetration, or the legitimacy of legislative responses – we can begin to recognise just how problematic a concept this can be.

   Drawing these ideas together, the chapter then goes on to discuss the implications of three especially contentious aspects of hate crime: its conceptual, legal and procedural ambiguity. In each of these respects hate crime has the capacity to divide opinion and, as we shall see, there are no straightforward solutions to any of these difficulties. Indeed, by way of exploring alternatives to hate crime, the chapter seeks to identify other, potentially less problematic ways in which we might choose to conceive of hate crime were we to reconfigure the concept. However, while there are persuasive reasons for wanting to inject greater clarity to this subject area, it is suggested that despite its flaws, the concept of hate crime has considerable value to criminologists, to criminal justice practitioners and perhaps most importantly to potential and actual victims.

──────────────── Introduction ────────────────

This book has sought to present an overview of hate crime by identifying the various forms that hate crime can take, the nature and impact of hate crime victimisation, factors that motivate hate crime perpetrators and the appropriateness of criminal justice responses. In so doing, previous chapters have highlighted the complexity that surrounds this subject area: there is little that is straightforward or unproblematic about hate crime, whether one is approaching the subject through a theoretical or empirical lens, or from a scholarly, political or policy-making perspective. Similarly, we have seen that there are a number of highly contentious issues relevant to contemporary debates about hate crime which have served to divide opinion over its conceptual and legal basis. All of this means that making sense of the topic can be a difficult, and at times bewildering, process unless and until one accepts that hate crime is not a fixed entity but rather a more fluid social construct that can mean different things to different people. We shall return to this point in due course, but first it is worth briefly recapping some of the main themes covered thus far.

We began in Chapter 1 by establishing the origins of hate crime and by examining a variety of academic and official definitions in order to develop our understanding. This process confirmed that there might be more to the concept than meets the eye: rather than referring simply to crimes motivated by hatred, the hate crime label has been associated with a complex range of characteristics, including notions of group identity, bigotry and prejudice and frameworks of power, hierarchy and oppression, all of which feature prominently in various academic interpretations. While hate crime scholars have engaged with some of the perceived intricacies associated with the term, official classifications used by criminal justice practitioners and legislators in the UK have tended to be simpler, though not without their own ambiguities. Consequently – and despite the relatively late emergence of hate crime discourse in this country compared with the USA, where the concept is more firmly enshrined – various pieces of legislation have been introduced in the UK which adhere to the principle that crimes motivated by hatred or prejudice towards particular features of the victim's identity, such as their ethnicity, faith, sexual orientation or disability, should be treated differently from 'ordinary' crimes.

Subsequent chapters then went on to explore specific types of group identity which are recognised as forming the basis of hate crime motivation. The most widely recognised category of hate crime – racist hate crime – was the focus of Chapter 2, and this chapter began by charting the development of the UK's 'race' agenda and the post-Lawrence surge of interest in the victimisation of ethnic minorities before then discussing the scale of racist hate crime. As well as accounting for the experiences of groups often overlooked by researchers and policy-makers and assessing the effectiveness of the legislative framework in place to tackle racist harassment and discrimination, Chapter 2 also supported Bowling's (1993, 1999) recognition of the process of racism, where the broader and often prolonged impact of victimisation is acknowledged within the wider historical, political and social context in which it prevails. Viewing racist, and indeed all forms of hate crime, as a process and not merely a singular, isolated event allows us to recognise the cumulative effects of the more mundane, so-called 'low-level' forms of prejudice upon victims' freedom and quality of life.

The next two chapters examined two further strands of the subject: religiously motivated and homophobic hate crime. Religiously motivated hate, or faith-hate, is an issue of growing significance to academics and policy-makers, and Chapter 3 explored various factors that have resulted in increased levels of political and legal intervention, not to mention media interest, in issues of religious identity and intolerance. Homophobic hate crime is equally harrowing, and Chapter 4 outlined its nature, extent and impact as well as criminal justice responses to victims of homophobia. In recent years, controversial legislation has been introduced to protect people against the incitement of hatred, on the grounds of both religious identity and sexual orientation, and the rationale behind and implications of these provisions were examined in Chapters 3 and 4.

The complex range of ideas that fall under the hate crime umbrella became even more apparent during the analysis of more marginalised forms of hate that followed in subsequent chapters. Gender and transgender issues were the subject of Chapter 5, where the complexities of definitional issues surrounding sexuality, sex and gender were outlined. The nature and extent of harassment aimed at transgendered people was discussed, and it was suggested that, while there are a number of commonalities between transphobic and homophobic hate crimes, there are also enough differences between the experiences of victims to cast doubt over the utility of the oft-used and all-embracing 'LGBT' term.

A key issue in the gender and hate debate is masculinity, and especially the role of dominant notions of heterosexual masculinity within society. Some theorists suggest that males can utilise violence to maintain their powerful position at the top of the gender hierarchy, whether this is in the context of homophobic or domestic violence. Chapter 5 also noted that domestic violence has on occasion been defined as a hate crime by practitioners, although it argued that it was difficult to include domestic violence under the hate crime umbrella as it was neither a 'stranger danger' form of crime, nor were the victims from a 'marginalised minority group', as they could be either male or female.

Chapter 6 began by outlining the forms, frequency and impact of a crime that has often been marginalised from the hate debate: disablist hate crime. The chapter noted the disturbing nature of these crimes and observed that, unlike other forms of violent hate crime where the perpetrator and victim are often strangers to each other, in the case of disablist murders the perpetrator is commonly a 'friend' or 'carer' of the victim. It was argued that the continued absence of disablist harassment from mainstream hate crime discourse might be due to the widespread prevalence of disablist attitudes within society. Consideration was also given to other expressions of prejudice, such as elder abuse and attacks upon members of youth subcultures, and it was concluded that, despite the seriousness of such offences, it is only crimes motivated by disablism that have the requisite characteristics associated with other types of 'clear-cut' hate crimes.

In addition to examining various forms of victimisation and the scope of the hate crime umbrella, the book has also analysed police responses to hate crime and their relationship with those groups most at risk of being the victims. Chapter 7 looked at some of the conceptual, cultural and operational difficulties that have affected the policing of hate crime before moving on to assess the more positive post-Macpherson developments that have given hate crime a much more prominent position upon policing agendas, at least in strategic terms. The policing of hate crime is a far from straightforward task, not least because, as we learnt in Chapter 8, the perpetrators of hate crime tend more often than not to be 'ordinary' members of the public and not the neo-Nazi skinheads or white supremacists we might automatically associate with the commission of hate offences. Through its analysis of everyday and more extreme acts of hate crime, together with the relationship between victims and perpetrators, this chapter cast doubt over the oft-assumed profile of perpetrators as far-right extremists and the tendency to conceive of these crimes as being exclusively 'stranger danger' in nature. Rather, it would appear that much of what is referred to as hate crime includes relatively 'ordinary' types of offence committed by relatively 'ordinary' types of people who might not necessarily be a stranger to their victim but instead might simultaneously be familiar with but still remote from them. While this does not mean that hate crime is any less painful (emotionally or physically) for the victim, it does suggest that the term is much more intricate than may at first be imagined.

Contested issues

It should be fairly apparent by this stage that hate crime has the capacity to divide opinion in an academic, political and criminal justice context. In general terms, and without wishing to downplay some of the other problematic aspects of hate crime covered previously, we would argue that there are three main areas of inconsistency which create particular difficulty for scholarship.

Conceptual ambiguity

As has been alluded to previously in this text and by other scholars, hate crime is a conceptually ambiguous term and this can be problematic in several respects. Crucially, and rather perversely, the concept of hate crime extends not just to crimes but to incidents too. As ACPO's (2005) guidance makes clear, any hate incident must be recorded by the police even if it lacks the requisite elements to be classed as a notifiable offence later in the criminal justice process. While one might ordinarily assume there to be a marked difference between an incident and a recordable crime, in this context there is little distinction in practical policing terms between the recording of a hate incident and a hate crime, meaning that the number of hate 'occurrences' that come to official attention is significantly higher than would be the case were only legally defined crimes to be covered (Hall, 2005a: 13). Therefore, much of what falls under the remit of hate crime may not be crime as such, but (in line with the Macpherson threshold) incidents perceived by the victim or any other person to be motivated by hate or prejudice.

This last proviso – incidents motivated by hate or *prejudice* – takes the point about conceptual ambiguity a step further: namely, hate crimes may not necessarily be crimes as such, nor may they be motivated exclusively by hate. Despite the variations that exist between different scholarly and official interpretations, definitions are generally consistent in recognising hate crime as conduct motivated by prejudice on particular grounds or directed against particular groups of people. However, by extending our conceptual understanding of hate to include the more expansive notion of prejudice, we could, in theory at least, be criminalising all manner of commonly held rational and irrational prejudices unless we choose to create a hierarchy of acceptable and unacceptable prejudices. Indeed, and as we have seen in earlier chapters, ACPO have done just this by making explicit reference to particular grounds for prejudice and hatred in their guidance to police officers, thereby indicating that it is not just any form of prejudice that could form the basis of a hate crime but particular types of prejudice. But while limiting the scope of hate crime makes the concept more manageable and in some ways more meaningful, it does require difficult moral decisions to be made about the types of prejudice that we should wish to outlaw and those that we should tolerate; and equally the groups of people we should wish to protect through hate crime laws and those whom we deem undeserving of such protection.

Moreover, it is not just the decision over which forms of prejudice to punish that causes concern to hate crime scholars, but also the strength of the causal relationship between the prejudice and the offence. This point has been lucidly illustrated by Jacobs and Potter (1998: 22–28) through the use of the theoretical model displayed in Figure 9.1 (see Hall, 2005a: 15–18 for further explanation). The horizontal axis denotes the level of the offender's prejudice (high prejudice or low prejudice) while the vertical axis marks the strength of the causal relationship between prejudice and the offending behaviour (high causation or low causation).

By looking at each cell individually one can begin to appreciate the strength of Jacobs and Potter's argument. In Cell I we can include offences which are carried out by highly prejudiced perpetrators and whose prejudice has a strong causal bearing on their offending behaviour. These are what Jacobs and Potter (1998: 22) describe as 'clear-cut, unambiguous hate crimes', crimes which one might immediately think of when conceiving of 'hate' in its literal sense, including organised extremist hatred (the activities of the Ku Klux Klan, for example) or acts of violence clearly motivated by hatred of a particular group identity (the murder of Stephen Lawrence or the actions of David Copeland). As Jacobs and

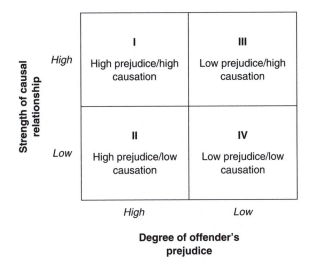

Figure 9.1   A model of hate crime causation and prejudice (Jacobs and Potter, 1998: 23)

Potter observe (1998: 23), there would be nothing ambiguous or controversial about hate crime were its scope restricted to cases like these, but equally the label would cover relatively few cases and would have little practical utility since such extreme crimes will already be punishable under the highest possible sentencing structure.

It is the other three cells which are more contentious. Cell II contains offences which again are committed by highly prejudiced offenders but whose offending behaviour is not strongly or exclusively linked to their prejudice. This cell, there-fore, would contain offenders whose prejudice bears little or no relation to the offence in question; as such, for Jacobs and Potter, it would be wrong to assume that all offences committed by prejudiced offenders against minority groups are hate offences for their offences might well be motivated by other factors and not their prejudice. Conversely, Cell III includes offenders who are not especially prejudiced individuals but whose prejudice, perhaps subconsciously, bears a strong link to the offence. Within this cell one could expect to find offenders who, according to Jacobs and Potter (1998: 25) 'are not ideologues or obsessive haters' but who might be 'professional or at least active criminals with short fuses and confused psyches … hostile and alienated juvenile delinquents … [or] ignorant, but relatively law-abiding'. Those authors argue that it is offences from this cell that constitute the majority of officially designated hate crimes in the USA because it is often assumed that a hate crime has taken place when a crime is committed by a member of one group against a member of another, irrespec-tive of the strength of the prejudicial motivation. Cell IV, meanwhile, includes what they refer to as situational offences. These are offences which are neither the product of highly prejudiced beliefs nor strongly linked to the offender's prejudice, but which instead arise from *'ad hoc* disputes and flashing tempers' (ibid: 26). Such offences are sometimes classed as hate crimes and sometimes not, depending on differing interpretations.

Ultimately, Jacobs and Potter's typology helps to confirm what we know already: namely, that hate crime is a social construct open to different interpretations. Arguably, it is this malleability – and the implications this has in terms of creating hierarchies of acceptable and unacceptable prejudices and potentially criminalising behaviour motivated only in part by prejudice – that leaves it so susceptible to criticism. While concerns over the criminalisation of prejudice are understandable, it is equally important not to become unduly alarmist about the implications of this conceptual ambiguity. As Hall (2005a: 36) rightly asserts, it is not a crime to harbour prejudiced attitudes, nor is it a crime to hate – that prejudice or hate needs to be manifested through some form of behaviour or action before the police, the CPS and ultimately the courts can decide whether it constitutes a hate crime and deserves to be dealt with in accordance with the available set of laws in place to punish perpetrators of such crimes. With this in mind, we shall now turn to consider a second 'grey area' that has been contested by academics, lawyers, politicians and the public at large: namely, legislation.

Legal ambiguity

The notion of hate crime has been afforded explicit recognition by legislators in the UK through the introduction of both penalty enhancement and incitement legislation. This legislation has by no means been universally welcomed; indeed, as we have seen in earlier chapters, the effectiveness, legitimacy, scope and interpretation of these laws have all been questioned at one stage or another. Nonetheless, their introduction has given weight to the principle behind hate crime by encouraging criminal justice agencies and sentencers to regard hate crimes as qualitatively different from the same crimes motivated by different reasons, and by conveying a message to the public at large, and perhaps more specifically to the far-right and the bigoted, that denounces hatred as not just unacceptable but criminal (see Lawrence, 2002; McGhee, 2005).

A review of the existing literature would indicate that message-sending is one of the key justifications for hate crime laws, but as Jacobs and Potter (1998: 67–68) suggest in their critique of North American provisions, such legislation may in fact be designed to transmit messages to several different audiences of whom perpetrators are arguably the least important. For Jacobs and Potter, the introduction of hate crime laws sends a clear message of solidarity to lobbyists and supporters of such laws to show that the government is on their side and can be relied upon. Equally appealing in a political sense is the message that hate crime legislation conveys to the general voting population – that it shows that the government condemns prejudice and intolerance – and the moral claim to popular support that comes therewith. The third and final audience referred to by Jacobs and Potter consists of potential and actual hate crime offenders who, in theory at least, may be deterred from engaging in such activity because of the declaratory message of condemnation conveyed through the introduction of specific laws.

This third type of message, argue Jacobs and Potter, is the weakest of the three as it would be difficult to think of offenders being any more responsive to this message than they are to the threats and condemnations contained in other laws which they might regularly contravene. The mixed messages conveyed by hate crime laws have been noted by other authors too. For instance, as we saw in Chapter 2, Bowling and Phillips (2002) have referred to the unintended backlash that the introduction of such laws can create among those who believe that minority groups receive preferential treatment, while in a similar vein Dixon and Gadd (2006) have noted that those prosecuted under hate crime legislation might conclude that they are less the perpetrators of a heinous offence and more the victim of a legal system biased in favour of minorities.

Furthermore, it is not just the ambiguity of the message conveyed by hate crime legislation that has been questioned, but also the ambiguity within the wording of the legislation. In the context of aggravated offences where hostility based on ethnicity, religious identity, sexual orientation or disability is central, concerns have been raised over the level of evidence required to justify the imposition of enhanced punishment. Hostility is not defined by legislation, and, as the CPS (2008) acknowledge in their response to an all-party enquiry into antisemitism, proving that offences are motivated by prejudice is often difficult in practice and requires either a clear statement of intent by the accused or background evidence of motive that is often not forthcoming. They go on to observe that many hate crime cases result in No Further Action (NFA) and do not progress to the prosecution stage because of insufficient evidence or because the victim is unwilling to support a prosecution (CPS, 2008), a point which in itself is worthy of more extensive investigation.[1]

Certainly, the disparity in the number of prosecutions brought under the respective aggravated provisions raises some element of doubt over the effectiveness of the provisions. According to CPS figures for 2006/07 (CPS, 2007e), 822 cases identified as having a homophobic or transphobic element were brought forward for prosecution, as compared with 27 religiously aggravated cases and 9,145 racially aggravated cases. The difference between the number of prosecutions brought under the racial and religiously aggravated legislation is particularly eye-catching, and may be largely attributable to the way in which the CPS decides how an offence should be charged. This is indicated in their response to the all-party enquiry into antisemitism (CPS, 2008: point 23):

> The CPS determines whether an offence should be charged as racially or religiously aggravated. This will depend upon the circumstances of the case. If the evidence proves hostility towards the Jewish people, the charge will be racially aggravated.

If the hostility is directed more specifically towards the Jewish faith, the charge will be religiously aggravated.

According to this tenuous distinction, the CPS would class hostility directed towards the Jewish people as evidence of racial aggravation whereas hostility directed towards their faith is regarded as religiously aggravated. Notwithstanding the fact that distinguishing between ethnicity and faith is more complicated in the case of Jews (and Sikhs) because they are recognised ethnic groups (see Chapter 3), these grounds for determining whether offences should be charged as racially or religiously aggravated are barely distinguishable and will invariably result in 'race' and faith being conflated, which in itself runs contrary to the original intention behind the introduction of separate provisions on religious aggravation. Arguably, therefore, the lack of prosecutions brought under the religiously aggravated provisions is illustrative of how the laws have been interpreted, and should not *per se* be seen to suggest that the provisions are difficult to enforce or are unnecessary additions to the statute book.

Prosecutions for disablist aggravation have been equally scarce: according to the CPS, only 141 incidents classified as having a disability element were successfully prosecuted in 2007/08 (Quarmby, 2008: 11). Again, though, this may in part be attributable to the way in which disablist hate crimes have been prosecuted. For instance, in the case of Brent Martin (see Case Study 6.1 in Chapter 6) – one in a series of recent cases where people with physical or mental disabilities have been fatally attacked – the perpetrators were not prosecuted under the existing legislation on disablist aggravation, despite this case offering prosecutors and sentencers a clear opportunity to use the available laws for the purpose for which they were intended and to raise the profile of disablist hate crime. Indeed, rather than raising Brent Martin's attackers' sentences in line with the penalty enhancement provisions introduced by the Criminal Justice Act 2003, their minimum prison sentences were instead reduced on appeal, prompting despair among disability campaigners with regards to the criminal justice system's treatment of disabled people (Quarmby, 2008; Scope, 2008b).

There is also some degree of inconsistency with regard to the way in which legal provisions relating to the incitement of hatred have developed in recent years. Incitement to racial hatred provisions criminalise words, behaviour or material that are threatening, abusive or insulting and which are either intended to stir up hatred or where hatred is likely to be stirred up. The corresponding incitement to religious hatred provisions, however, tighten this threshold by criminalising only threatening words, behaviour or material and requiring evidence of subjective intention to incite hatred. A similarly tight threshold has been laid down for incitement to hatred on the grounds of sexual orientation, meaning that there is a clear legal distinction between the broader framework of protection guarding against the incitement of racial hatred and the somewhat narrower framework governing the incitement to hatred on the grounds of faith and sexual orientation. This is confirmed by the inclusion of explicit defence clauses for freedom of expression inserted into the Public Order Act by the Racial and Religious Hatred Act 2006 and the Criminal Justice and Immigration Act 2008 in sections 29J and 29JA respectively.

29J Protection of freedom of expression (religious identity)

Nothing in this Part shall be read or given effect in a way which prohibits or restricts discussion, criticism or expressions of antipathy, dislike, ridicule, insult or abuse of particular religions or the beliefs or practices of their adherents, or of any other belief system or the beliefs or practices of its adherents, or proselytising or urging adherents of a different religion or belief system to cease practising their religion or belief system.

29JA Protection of freedom of expression (sexual orientation)

In this Part, for the avoidance of doubt, the discussion or criticism of sexual conduct or practices or the urging of persons to refrain from or modify such conduct or practices shall not be taken of itself to be threatening or intended to stir up hatred.

The inclusion of these clauses is reflective of the delicate balance legislators have sought to strike between the criminalisation of incitement to hatred and adhering to the right to freedom of expression enshrined within Article 10 of the European Convention on Human Rights. The fact that this balance has been struck at different levels for certain forms of incitement may at face value appear inconsistent, although as we have seen in earlier chapters there is a credible line of reasoning behind the imposition of varying evidential thresholds for different types of hate speech. Without question, this area of hate crime has proved to be especially contentious and has split the opinions of academics, campaign groups, commentators and politicians (see, for instance, Cumper, 2006; Hari, 2007; Meer, 2008; Stonewall, 2008). However, at this relatively early stage in the implementation of the legislation it is difficult to conclude with any certainty whether the heated debates associated with the faith and sexual orientation incitement laws have resulted in an effective set of laws or an ineffective watered-down set of compromises, and hate crime scholars should keep a keen eye on the practical application of these provisions.

Procedural ambiguity

The practical application of hate crime is a third area of ambiguity surrounding this concept. It has been argued in this volume that hate crime can mean different things to different people, and this sense of ambiguity is reinforced when one considers how it is conceived and dealt with by criminal justice practitioners. Scholars of the subject may have sought to develop and refine various definitions of hate crime, but in many respects these definitions and those that shape practitioners' understanding of the concept are worlds apart, to the extent where newcomers to this field of study might quite legitimately conclude that entirely different concepts are being discussed.

One can begin to appreciate the stark differences between theory-driven and more practically-oriented notions when considering some of the key themes underpinning definitions referred to in Chapter 1. Scholars are generally in agreement that hate crime is a social construct with no self-evident or universal definition and have put forward a variety of significant characteristics which they feel are central to our recognition of hate crime, be they the group affiliation of the victim, the imbalance of power between the perpetrator and the victim, the relevance of context, structure and agency to the dynamic social process of hate crime, or the notion of hate acts being 'message' crimes designed to create fear within the wider community to whom the victim' belongs. Some of these scholarly definitions are more complex and convincing than others, but all convey the idea that there is more to hate crime than those less familiar with the topic might assume.

However, what is and what is not a hate crime, in practical terms, is shaped by the broad, victim-oriented definition presented by ACPO (2005), which requires no evidential test for the recording and investigation of a hate crime. Taken at face value, this is a much less complicated take and requires few of the machinations inherent to academic interpretations. Equally, what ultimately becomes prosecuted as a hate crime may bear little resemblance to what might be envisaged as one, according to these academic interpretations, as the decision rests on whether or not the CPS chooses to prosecute and if so whether the offence is prosecuted under the available hate crime legislation. In some respects, then, we could conceivably produce as many academic definitions as we like, but ultimately official classifications of hate crime are shaped by the interpretation of the victim and the criminal justice system, and not academia.

There is also a certain degree of ambiguity relating to the appropriateness of criminal justice responses to hate crime. For instance, while prosecuting an offence as a hate crime might in one sense symbolise the importance of confronting expressions or manifestations of hate, as Burney (2002: 108) notes there may be alternative and more effective ways of marking disapproval, including informal warnings and more restorative modes of justice. Using restorative justice in the context of hate crime has been broadly encouraged for its capacity to educate perpetrators and repair relationships with victims (Gerstenfeld, 2004; Northern Ireland Affairs Committee, 2005), and restorative interventions have been deployed with increasing regularity in recent years to assist in the development of more constructive strategies to address hate incidents.

The promotion of alternative modes of punishment is illustrative of the limitations of adopting an exclusively punitive response to hate crime. Although imprisonment and the use of enhanced sentences may be entirely appropriate in certain contexts, there are equally many forms and perpetrators of hate crime for which and for whom such punishment might not be especially effective. Hall (2005b: 203) highlights this point by offering three criticisms of the use of imprisonment for hate crime offenders. First, he suggests, prison has limited deterrent value to these offenders; secondly, prisons are often divided along the lines of 'race' and ethnicity and may therefore simply reinforce intolerant attitudes and inadvertently encourage hate-related activity and recruitment; and thirdly, the overcrowded prison environment offers little opportunity for the kind of rehabilitation that is necessary to truly address prejudicial beliefs. Invariably, the type of punishment meted out to perpetrators will vary according to the nature of the offence committed and in this sense there is little difference between hate crime and other forms of offences. The limitations of traditional custodial and community-based sentences have been dissected extensively within the context of criminology more broadly (see, for example, Raynor, 2007; Sparks, 2007) and there is no reason to disagree with Hall's (2005b) assertion that while the more innovative community-based sentences may have the greatest potential in the context of hate crime, the development of successful programmes can be hampered by our inability to fully understand the complex nature of hate and prejudice.

Future directions for hate crime thinking

The search for alternatives

Where, then, does this leave hate crime? Is it a flawed concept whose limitations outweigh any positive developments that may be associated with the introduction of related laws? For some, the answer would appear to be a resounding 'yes'. Jacobs and Potter's work has been credited for injecting a necessary note of scepticism into the debate (Perry, 2002: 485), and for these writers the concept of hate crime raises too many problems for it to be of any real value in terms of law enforcement and criminal justice. In support of their critique, they offer a series of arguments which cast doubt over the efficacy of hate crime laws. For example, they suggest that hate crimes are by no means the only crimes to have an impact beyond the immediate victim or to have a profound psychological or emotional impact upon the victim, while the introduction of American hate crime laws has, they argue, done little to stem the frequency or severity of those crimes in that country (Jacobs and Potter, 1998; Jacobs, 2003).

The case presented by Jacobs and Potter is certainly a compelling one. However, the implications of their critique do not necessarily lend themselves to a straightforward or viable alternative, and it is perhaps easier to point out flaws in the conceptual interpretation and practical application of hate crime than it is to suggest constructive alternatives. For instance, were we to simply abandon the concept of hate crime, would this involve repealing existing sets of laws on aggravation and incitement and, if so, would this unjustly reduce the level of protection available to those communities who are typically targeted through hate acts and hate speech? Would abandoning hate crime send out an appropriate message to the more vulnerable groups in society or to those who feel it is legitimate to perpetuate hatred against such groups? And would it lead to a regression in police policy and attitudes following the progress that has been made since the Macpherson report and through ACPO's guidance?

Alternatively, if we were to keep the hate crime tag, as it were, but restrict its application solely to crimes (not incidents) motivated by hate (not prejudice) towards a particular group identity, then this in some ways would help to address the ambiguity inherent to the concept as we presently know it. Under this interpretation – where the label would be applied to perpetrators who truly hated their victim on the basis of their membership of a particular group or community and where this hatred was the sole or predominant cause of the offending behaviour – hate crime would refer to the more violent or extreme acts of bigotry that one might ordinarily associate with crimes of hate (see also Hall, 2005a: 235). However, while this might make hate crime easier to recognise, conceiving it in this restrictive manner would result in us overlooking many of the more subtle, but equally damaging expressions of prejudice which constitute much of what is currently, and quite rightly, classified as hate crime victimisation.

If, then, we feel that this more literal take on hate crime is too constrained, a logical solution might be to reconfigure the label in terms of what it might more accurately represent. If, as most concerned scholars tend to agree, hate crime is not really about hate but more about prejudice, bias, bigotry or -isms, then perhaps re-branding it as 'prejudice crime', 'bias crime' or something along these lines might help to capture the essence of what these crimes are really about. Indeed, the term 'bias crime' is often used interchangeably with hate crime by some scholars and seems to be an established alternative within much of the North American literature (see, for instance, Perry, 2001; Lawrence, 2002; Bell, 2003). From a legal perspective, Goodall (2007: 103–104) refers to the seemingly peculiar situation we have in this country where the term 'hate crime' has become the preferred label for describing statutorily aggravated offences despite being unsuitable for this role:

...commentators regularly use 'hatred' as a synonym when discussing the provisions of statutes dealing with prejudice. This is useful shorthand for a complex topic, used to make the law clearer to the passing reader, but its results are unfortunate. … There are serious implications … if the public and employers do not understand what it is that the legislation punishes. If many think that a conviction for an aggravated crime is proof of an act of 'hatred', they will attach a tag of premeditated bigotry to convictions for something else. If the offenders are characterised as purveyors of extreme forms of racism, the message is lost. Those convicted should be stigmatised for their express acts of abuse, not for imagined acts of hatred.

Hall (2005a and 2005b) also makes explicit reference to the problems in employing the word 'hate' as a catch-all term to describe behaviour motivated by other factors and emotions, and certainly there is something rather curious about our continued use of the catchy misnomer that is hate crime. At the same time, reclassifying these offences in accordance with a more realistic descriptor of the motivation that underpins them does not get around a related and equally thorny conceptual concern: namely, how one should decide which forms of prejudices should count as warranting enhanced punishment. Presently, ACPO guidance stipulates that *anyone* can be a victim of a hate crime if they perceive the offence to be motivated by hate or prejudice, while simultaneously earmarking hate crime as hate or prejudice motivated on particular grounds – race, sexual orientation, faith and disability. Although, and as discussed in earlier chapters, there are entirely understandable reasons for framing the guidance in this way, there is also scope for confusion under this broad, all-inclusive framework.

Therefore, might hate crime be more meaningful if its applicability were restricted to those intended to be the primary beneficiaries of its conception, namely minority groups? Conceiving of these offences as 'targeted crimes' or as forms of 'minority group victimisation' would arguably make the rationale behind hate crime laws more explicit and would divert attention towards the bridging factor that links different types of victim, and away from the ambiguities associated with offender motivation. Indeed, by grouping offences in accordance with what actually unites them (their minority victim status) rather than in accordance with motivation (which is often difficult to gauge) could result in scholars and prosecutors giving less thought to what constitutes 'hate' and more attention to the needs of victims and marginalised communities.

Such a switch in focus could also conceivably encourage greater synergy between public, practitioner and academic understandings of the nuances of minority group victimisation, including the way in which such victimisation can be understood as a process or continuum and can be affected by (perceived or actual) socially subordinate status. Under this framework, the question of *which* minority groups are worthy of extra protection and which are not is still open to debate. However, this simpler recognition of 'minority victim crime' would allow us to move away from asking why certain crimes, which at face value might involve an element of hate – terrorism, domestic violence or football hooliganism, for instance – are not included while others that are not necessarily 'hate-motivated' are.

Taking hate crime on its merits

Ultimately, it may well be that the concept of hate crime is here to stay despite its flaws, and if this is the case, then the search for alternative and more appropriate terms of reference is probably a futile one. This does not mean that effective strategies could not be employed within the existing conceptual and policy framework. For instance, within the field of anti-discrimination law the government have taken action to replace the numerous and complex statutory provisions with a single equality act, thereby bringing 'race', gender, disability and other grounds of discrimination within one piece of legislation. Following on from the introduction in 2007 of a single equalities body – the Equality and Human Rights Commission – the Single Equality Bill is expected to come into force during the current Parliament and has the potential to give equality issues a more coherent legal framework, not to mention a higher public profile, through its package of measures designed primarily to address discrimination in the workplace (Ministry of Justice, 2007; Wintour, 2008). Were concerns over the inconsistency and inaccessibility of existing hate crime laws to grow, it is not beyond the realms of practicality to think of similar moves being made to replace the existing strands of hate crime legislation with a single Hate Crime Act. While this would, in itself, fail to address some of the conceptual and practical problems that have been discussed in this book, giving hate crime a more explicit statutory footing might make the concept less ambiguous while providing consistency with the new anti-discrimination framework.

However, even taking hate crime as it is, without any changes to the present terminology or legal framework, we should perhaps accept that it has value in spite of its flaws. Hall (2005a: 238) suggests that we should not abandon the concept just yet, citing its worth to victims and potential victims as one of the central justifications for keeping faith with it; similarly, Iganski (2008: 5) makes reference to its utility within policy and scholarly domains as 'an emotive banner under which is now rallied a once disparate field of concerns with oppression and bigotry in various guises'. These are important points and there are other related reasons to suggest that we should not lose sight of the value of hate crime. One of these is its capacity to draw attention to the shared vulnerability of particular groups in society. Simply by glancing at the contents page of this book, one can begin to appreciate the significance of various forms of 'othering', and it is not by accident that the emergence of hate crime has coincided with real change in political, cultural and policing attitudes towards prejudice perpetuated against a range of minority groups. Traditionally there may have been something of a hierarchy of recognition among minority groups, with 'race' and minority ethnic concerns arguably receiving the most attention, but it would seem that this hierarchy is levelling out to the point where other identities are rightly attracting increased attention from academics and policy-makers. Importantly, this wider recognition has also facilitated an under-standing of the way in which people can belong simultaneously to different communities, and can therefore have multiple identities and be prone to mul-tiple forms of victimisation.

Equally, and to underline a point made previously, the symbolic value of hate crime as a way of reaffirming society's condemnation of offences perpetuated on the basis of these identities should not be underestimated. While, as we have seen, there are limits to the deterrent capacity of hate crime laws, this in itself does not negate the declaratory role that such laws can have in a society where the values, identities and cultures of particular communities are under increased scrutiny. There is much made in the literature of hate crime being a message crime, whereby perpetrators can convey a sinister message to the victim and to their wider community. Similarly, by criminalising forms of behaviour or expres-sion which violate the core values of a diverse society, governments too can con-vey a message of solidarity to stigmatised communities.

There is, however, a more sceptical way of viewing this message. For McGhee (2005, 2008), offering protection from hate crime may simply be part of a gov-ernmental 'Third Way' strategy, whereby such protection is conditional on the expected beneficiaries becoming less insular and more receptive to the govern-ment's policies on citizenship and national identity. Others, too, have alluded to the tokenism endemic in the government's hate crime agenda as it seeks to soften the blow of its policies on counter-terrorism, immigration and asylum upon communities and voters who might otherwise reject the government alto-gether (see Bridges, 2001; Dixon and Gadd, 2006). Seen in this light, hate crime laws represent little more than a shallow attempt at appeasing alienated or dis-enfranchised communities, a mechanism through which the state can pay lip service to the diversity agenda while pursuing its own repressive agenda.

Although there may well be some truth in the claim that certain laws might have been introduced with one eye on inducing a sense of community cohe-sion, there are also grounds for adopting a less cynical standpoint on the government's support for hate crime. Quite aside from anything else, the gov-ernment has shown commendable determination to push through legislation protecting the gay, trans and disabled communities, and not just minority eth-nic and faith communities, and there is no reason to believe that these steps were taken for any reason other than out of a genuine respect for diversity (a point reinforced through the introduction of the Single Equality Bill). As such, when assessing the value of hate crime and how far the concept has taken us, a sensible stance, and one which conforms with the victim-oriented approaches advocated by writers such as Perry, Iganski, Bowling and others, might be to weigh up its limitations against the not inconsiderable advances that have been made under the banner of hate crime on behalf of potential and actual victims.

Ultimately, this is a subjective process, and in many respects the arguments of sceptics such as Jacobs and Potter are no less or more credible than those of scholars such as Perry, whose work has done much to champion the hate crime agenda. For the authors of this book, wading through hate crime's conceptual minefield has been a challenging yet fruitful journey, and we would suggest that it is easy to become preoccupied by these conceptual debates which, while important, should not overshadow the practical utility of hate crime policies. As noted throughout this book, hate crime means different things to different people, but perhaps the truest test of its value is whether it is has meaning for its intended beneficiaries.

Guide to further reading

Many of the texts recommended in Chapter 1's guide to further reading are relevant to the nature of this chapter's discussion. In particular, Perry (ed.) *Hate and Bias Crime: A Reader* (2003a), Hall, *Hate Crime* (2005a) and Iganski, *'Hate Crime' and the City* (2008) make significant contributions to the hate crime debate, while Jacobs and Potter's *Hate Crimes: Criminal Law and Identity Politics* (1998) presents arguably the most authoritative critique of hate crime laws. There are a number of journal articles which offer different ways of thinking about contemporary hate crime scholarship and policy, most notably Meer (2008), Goodall (2007), Cumper (2006) and Dixon and Gadd (2006).

Note

1 In the context of antisemitic offences recorded by the Metropolitan Police Service and Greater Manchester Police, the CPS (2008) note that 34 per cent of cases (31 out of 90) resulted in NFA, and in 58 per cent (18) of those cases the reason for NFA was the victim was unwilling to support a prosecution.

GLOSSARY

Ageism – prejudiced attitudes or discriminatory behaviour towards older people.

Aggravated offences – criminal acts which can attract longer sentences if it is proved that they were motivated by, or contained acts of, hostility against the victim's perceived minority status.

Amish – deeply religious Christian communities in the USA and Canada whose way of life rejects modern technologies and modes of living.

Antisemitism – prejudice against, or hatred of, Jewish people, culture and religion.

Association of Chief Police Officers (ACPO) – body representing senior police officers all of, or above the rank of, Assistant Chief Constable or their equivalent in the Metropolitan Police.

Asylum seeker – someone who has normally fled from persecution in their home country and is seeking permanent refugee status in the UK.

Blood and Honour – neo-Nazi music network that mainly promotes white supremacist skinhead groups.

British Crime Survey (BCS) – annual Home Office victim survey that examines experiences of crime and anti-social behaviour within England and Wales.

British National Party (BNP) – the most prominent far-right political party in the UK.

Burkka – outer garment worn by women in some Islamic traditions that covers the entire body.

Combat 18 (C18) – a violent neo-Nazi UK grouping formed in the mid-1990s.

Community cohesion – describes the idea of multi-ethnic and diverse communities living in an integrated, co-operative and mutually beneficial fashion with each other.

Community Safety Unit (CSU) – a division of the police that deals with community crime and cohesion issues, often including hate crimes.

Community Security Trust (CST) – organisation that monitors levels and forms of antisemitic harassment and violence in the UK.

Copeland, David – neo-Nazi who undertook a solo nailbombing campaign in 1999 which deliberately targeted London's minority ethnic and gay communities.

Crown Prosecution Service (CPS) – agency with responsibility for decisions relating to the prosecution (or otherwise) of cases passed on by the police, and the preparation of those cases that proceed.

Cyberbullying – a form of bullying undertaken via communications and information technologies, such as mobile phones or the internet.

Disabled – a physical or mental impairment which has a substantial and long-term adverse effect on someone's ability to carry out normal day-to-day activities.

Disablism – prejudiced attitudes or behaviour directed at disabled people based upon the belief that disabled people are inferior to others.

Dobrowski, Jody – gay male murdered in a homophobic assault in London in October 2005.

Domestic violence – acts of harassment, intimidation or violence perpetrated by someone who may be intimately linked to the victim and undertaken within a household setting.

Economic migrant – an immigrant whose main motive in moving to a new country is the hope of better economic prospects for themselves.

Elder abuse – action or inaction within a relationship based upon trust that causes harm to an older person.

Ethnicity – the shared cultures (often including language, religion, music, dress, food, etc.) of people who identify as coming from the same background. Often used as an alternative to the discredited 'race' term.

'Faith-hate' – prejudice towards, or hatred of, someone because of their perceived religious identity.

Feminism – theories and activities centred around ideas of gender difference and inequality, and the championing of women's rights.

Freedom of expression – the right to express any opinion without threat of sanction.

Gender – often described as socially constructed or expected patterns of behaviour based upon one's biologically determined sex.

Griffin, Nick – took over the leadership of the BNP in 1999 in an attempt to 'modernise' the party.

Hate – extreme dislike or abhorrence.

Heterosexism – attitudes or behaviour that privilege heterosexuality within society.

Holocaust – the acts of genocide committed by Nazis in the Second World War which ultimately resulted in the deaths of an estimated 6 million Jewish people.

Homophobia – irrational fear or hatred of lesbian, gay or bisexual people.

Incitement of hatred – acts or speech that are designed to 'stir up' hatred.

Institutional racism – the deliberate or unwitting enactment of policies or procedures by an organisation that disadvantage minority ethnic people.

Islamophobia – prejudice towards, or hatred of, Islam or those of the Islamic faith.

July 7 attacks (7/7) – the four bombings by Muslim extremists that killed 52 people and injured 770 on London's transport network on July 7 2005.

Ku Klux Klan – US white supremacist organisation notorious for being responsible for the murder of African Americans and Jews, particularly in the 1920s.

Lancaster, Sophie – member of the goth subculture killed by youths in 2007 due to their hostility towards her 'different' appearance.

Lawrence, Stephen – black teenager whose racist murder in south London in April 1993 has not yet resulted in the conviction of his killers.

LGBT – the abbreviation commonly used to collectively represent lesbian, gay, bisexual or transgendered people.

'Low-level' harassment – contested term that is used to differentiate non-violent hostile acts from so-called 'serious' criminal offences.

Macpherson report – 1999 report of the official inquiry into the circumstances surrounding the murder of Stephen Lawrence that accused the Metropolitan Police Service of 'institutional racism'. It was responsible for instigating widespread changes in the way that minority groups are policed.

Martin, Brent – a man with learning disabilities and mental health issues who was murdered in a disablist assault by three youths in 2007.

Masculinity – ideas, values, representations and practices associated with maleness which structure relations among men and between men and women.

Message crime – a hate crime designed to send a hostile or intimidating message to other members of the victim's minority community.

Metropolitan Police Service (MPS) – the largest police service in the UK and responsible for policing Greater London (excluding the City of London).

Mono-ethnic – term used to describe a population whose membership consists almost solely of one ethnic background.

Multiculturalism – idea that encourages different ethnic groups to develop their own traditions and cultures while living alongside those from other ethnic backgrounds.

National Front (NF) – far-right anti-immigration political party especially prominent in the 1970s.

Neo-Nazi – contemporary extremists who adopt and adapt the ideologies of the German Nazi Party of the 1930s.

New and Old Commonwealth migrants – immigrants to Britain from either the newly independent and decolonised developing nations of Asia, Africa and the Caribbean (the 'New' Commonwealth), or the predominantly white Commonwealth countries of Australia, New Zealand, South Africa or Canada (the 'Old' Commonwealth).

Police Service of Northern Ireland (PSNI) – police force that covers Northern Ireland, formed in 2001 in place of the Royal Ulster Constabulary.

Politically correct – derogatory term used to denigrate notions of equal opportunities and their associated initiatives.

Prejudice – biased attitudes or feelings towards others based upon perceptions held about their social grouping.

Process-incident contradiction – the clash between the experience of hate crime victimisation as a series of connected events and the need of the police service to prioritise the investigation and prosecution of individual criminal acts.

Process of victimisation – victimisation experienced as a series of connected acts of harassment.

Queer theory – a radical theory of gender, sexuality and sexual identity that challenges society's accepted ideas of these concepts.

Qur'an – the holy book of Islam.

'Race' – the idea that biologically distinct groups of people exist and that these genetic differences manifest themselves not just in physical appearance but also in intelligence and ability. Now largely discredited as having any scientific basis.

Racism – prejudice towards, or hatred of, people on the basis of their perceived 'race' or ethnic background.

Scarman report – the report written by Lord Scarman that was the result of an official inquiry into the causes of the 1981 'race riots' in Brixton and other inner-city areas.

Sectarianism – prejudice or hatred arising from attaching importance to perceived differences between subdivisions within a group, such as between different denominations within a religion or factions within a political movement.

Secular – an absence of organised religion or religious belief.

September 11 attacks (9/11) – perpetrated by Muslim extremists on September 11 2001 and involving the hijacking of four passenger aircraft which were subsequently crashed into the World Trade Center, the Pentagon and into a field in Somerset County, Pennsylvania. A total of 2,998 people lost their lives.

Stonewall – an organisation that campaigns in the interests of gay people.

'Stranger-danger' – the theory that the perpetrators and victims of hate crimes do not know each other and that the act was therefore solely motivated by the perpetrator's prejudice against the victim's perceived minority group status.

Third-party reporting – the mechanism by which victims of hate incidents can report them to other organisations rather than the police service.

Transgender – someone who has adopted the lifestyle and behaviour of another gender without undergoing surgery. Can also be used as a broad term to cover both transgendered and transsexual people.

Transphobia – irrational fear or hatred of transgendered or transsexual people.

Transsexual – someone who has undergone hormone treatment and gender reassignment surgery in order to become a member of another sex.

Transvestite – someone who adopts the clothing of another gender as a lifestyle choice or for sexual pleasure but who does not view themselves as transgendered.

Troubles, The – name commonly given to the period of civil unrest in Northern Ireland, roughly from the late 1960s to the late 1990s, characterised by republican and loyalist sectarian violence, paramilitary and terrorist activity, and conflict with British troops.

Youth subcultures – groupings of young people demarcated by tastes in clothes and music, often underpinned by loosely formed but shared outlooks and associated patterns of behaviour. Typified by such stylised groups as mods, goths, skinheads, punks and emos.

Xenophobia – an irrational fear or hatred of those from another country.

Zionism – movement and philosophy of Israeli nationalism that offers support for the establishment of a Jewish homeland in Israel.

REFERENCES

Ahmed, K. and Bright, M. (2003) 'New Storm Hits Police over "Racist Culture"', *The Observer*, 2 November, p. 1.

Altschiller, D. (2005) *Hate Crimes* (2nd edition), Santa Barbara, CA: ABC Clio.

Ansari, F. (2005) *British Anti-Terrorism: A Modern Day Witch-Hunt*, Wembley: Islamic Human Rights Commission.

Ashdown, J. (2008) *Trans Staff and Students in Higher Education: Guidance 2008*, London: Equality Standards Unit.

Association of Chief Police Officers (ACPO) (2000) *Guide to Identifying and Combating Hate Crime*, London: ACPO.

Association of Chief Police Officers (ACPO) (2005) *Hate Crime: Delivering a Quality Service – Good Practice and Tactical Guidance*, London: Home Office Police Standards Unit.

Barnes, C. (2006) 'Foreword', in P. Miller, S. Gillinson and J. Huber, *Disablist Britain: Barriers to Independent Living for Disabled People in 2006*, London: Scope, pp. 3–4.

Bartlett, P. (2007) 'Killing Gay Men, 1976–2001', *British Journal of Criminology*, 47 (4): 573–595.

Barton, L. (ed.) (1996) *Disability & Society: Emerging Issues and Insights*, London: Addison Wesley Longman.

Bauman, Z. (1991) *Modernity and Ambivalence*, Cambridge: Polity Press.

BBC News (2000) 'Profile: Copeland the Killer', *BBC News*, at http://news.bbc.co.uk/1/hi/uk/781755.stm, 30 June.

BBC News (2004) 'European Election: United Kingdom Result', *BBC News*, at http://news.bbc.co.uk/1/shared/bsp/hi/vote2004/euro_uk/html/front.stm, 14 June.

BBC News (2005) 'Hate Crimes Soar after Bombings', *BBC News*, at http://news.bbc.co.uk/1/hi/england/london/4740015.stm, 3 August.

BBC News (2006) 'Men Jailed for Gay Barman Murder' *BBC News*, at http://news.bbc.co.uk/go/pr/fr/-/1/hi/england/london/5087286.stm, 16 June.

BBC News (2008a) 'Phillips Warns of Race Cold War', *BBC News*, at http://news.bbc.co.uk/go/pr/fr/-/1/hi/uk/7356993.stm, 20 April.

BBC News (2008b) 'Police Arrest 198 over Hate Crime', *BBC News*, at http://news.bbc.co.uk/go/pr/fr/-/1/hi/england/london/7414052.stm, 22 May.

BBC News (2008c) 'Gang Get Life for "£5 Bet" Murder', *BBC News*, at http://news.bbc.co.uk/go/pr/fr/-/1/hi/england/wear/7270808.stm, 29 February.

BBC News (2008d) 'Boys Sentenced over Goth Murder', *BBC News*, at http://news.bbc.co.uk/go/pr/fr/-/1/hi/england/lancashire/7370637.stm, 28 April.

Beasley, C. (2005) *Gender & Sexuality: Critical Theories, Critical Thinkers*, London: Sage.

Bell, J. (2003) 'Policing Hatred: Police Bias Units and the Construction of Hate Crime', in B. Perry (ed.), *Hate and Bias Crime: A Reader*, London: Routledge, pp. 427–438.

Bennett, R. (2008) '100 Years after Reform, Poverty in Old Age is Rife', *The Times*, 31 July, p. 16.

Bettcher, T.M. (2007) 'Evil Deceivers and Make-believers: On Transphobic Violence and the Politics of Illusion', *Hypatia*, 22 (3): 43–65.

Beyond Boundaries (2003) *First Out ... Report of the Findings of the Beyond Boundaries Survey of Lesbian, Gay, Bisexual and Transgender People in Scotland*, Glasgow: Beyond Boundaries.

Bhavani, R., Mirza, H. and Meetoo, V. (2005) *Tackling the Roots of Racism: Lessons for Success*, Bristol: The Policy Press.

Boeckmann, R.J. and Turpin-Petrosino, C. (2002) 'Understanding the Harm of Hate Crime', *Journal of Social Issues*, 58 (2): 207–225.

Bornstein, K. (2006) 'Gender Terror, Gender Rage', in S. Stryker and S. Whittle (eds), *The Transgender Studies Reader*, New York: Routledge, pp. 236–243.

Bourne, J. (2001) 'The Life and Times of Institutional Racism', *Race and Class*, 43 (2): 7–22.

Bourne, J. (2002) 'Does Legislating against Racial Violence Work?', *Race and Class*, 44 (2): 81–85.

Bowling, B. (1993) 'Racial Harassment and the Process of Victimisation', *British Journal of Criminology*, 33 (2): 231–250.

Bowling, B. (1999) *Violent Racism: Victimisation, Policing and Social Context*, Oxford: Oxford University Press.

Bowling, B. (2003) 'Racial Harassment and the Process of Victimisation: Conceptual and Methodological Implications for the Local Crime Survey', in B. Perry (ed.), *Hate and Bias Crime: A Reader*, London: Routledge, pp. 61–76.

Bowling, B. and Phillips, C. (2002) *Racism, Crime and Justice*, Harlow: Pearson.

Bremner, C. (2004) 'Stoned to Death: Why Europe is Starting to Lose its Faith in Islam', *The Times*, 4 December, p. 25.

Bridges, L. (2001) 'Race, Law and the State', *Race and Class*, 43 (2): 61–76.

Bucke, T. and James, Z. (1998) *Trespass and Protest: Policing under the Criminal Justice and Public Order Act 1994*, London: Home Office.

Buckley, M. (2006) 'Gay Man's Killing "Tip of the Iceberg"', *BBC News*, at http://news.bbc.co.uk/l/hi/uk/5080164.stm, 16 June.

Bunting, M. (2006) 'It Takes More than Tea and Biscuits to Overcome Indifference and Fear', *The Guardian*, 27 February, p. 31.

Bunting, M. (2008) 'A Noble, Reckless Rebellion', *The Guardian*, 9 February, p. 36.

Burke, M. (1993) *Coming out of the Blue*, London: Cassell.

Burnett, A. (2006) 'Reassuring Older People in Relation to Fear of Crime', in A. Wahidin and M. Cain (eds), *Ageing, Crime and Society*, Cullompton: Willan, pp. 124–138.

Burnett, J. (2004) 'Community, Cohesion and the State', *Race and Class*, 45 (3): 1–18.

Burney, E. (2002) 'The Uses and Limits of Prosecuting Racially Aggravated Offences', in P. Iganski (ed.), *The Hate Debate: Should Hate Be Punished as a Crime?*, London: Institute for Jewish Policy Research, pp. 103–113.

Burney, E. and Rose, G. (2002) *Racist Offences: How is the Law Working?*, Home Office Research Study 244. London: Home Office.

Butler, J. (1990) *Gender Trouble: Feminism and the Subversion of Identity*, London: Routledge.

Byers, B., Crider, B.W. and Biggers, G.K. (1999) 'Neutralization Techniques Used against the Amish Bias Crime Motivation: A Study of Hate Crime and Offender', *Journal of Contemporary Criminal Justice*, 15 (1): 78–96.

Cahill, S. and Kin-Butler, B. (2006) *Policy Priorities for the LGBT Community: Pride Survey 2006*, New York: Policy Institute of the National Lesbian and Gay Task Force.

Campbell, D., Dodd, V. and Branigan, T. (2006) 'Guilty: the Cleric Who Preached Murder as a Religious Duty', *The Guardian*, 8 February, p. 1.

Carlton, N., Heywood, F., Izuhara, M., Pannell, J., Fear, T. and Means, R. (2003) *The Harassment and Abuse of Older People in the Private Rented Sector*, Bristol: The Policy Press.

Carrell, S. (2007) 'Teenager Jailed for Life for Brutal Murder of Gay Man', *The Guardian*, at http://www.guardian.co.uk/crime/article/0,,2209984,00.html, 13 November.

Chahal, K. and Julienne, L. (1999) *'We Can't All Be White!' Racist Victimisation in the UK*, York: Joseph Rowntree Foundation.

Chakraborti, N. (2007) 'Policing Muslim Communities', in M. Rowe (ed.), *Policing Beyond Macpherson: Issues in Policing, Race and Society*, Cullompton: Willan, pp. 107–127.

Chakraborti, N. and Garland, J. (2003) 'Under-researched and Overlooked: An Exploration of the Attitudes of Rural Minority Ethnic Communities towards Crime, Community Safety and the Criminal Justice System', *Journal of Ethnic and Migration Studies*, 29 (3): 563–572.

Chan, J. (1997) *Changing Police Culture: Policing in a Multicultural Society*, Cambridge: Cambridge University Press.

Chivite-Matthews, N. and Maggs, P. (2002) *Crime, Policing and Justice: The Experience of Older People – Findings from the British Crime Survey*, London: Home Office.

CJINI (2007) *Hate Crime in Northern Ireland: A Thematic Inspection of the Management of Hate Crime by the Criminal Justice System in Northern Ireland*, Belfast: Criminal Justice Inspection Northern Ireland.

Clancy, A., Hough, M., Aust, R. and Kershaw, C. (2001) *Crime, Policing and Justice: The Experience of Ethnic Minorities – Findings from the 2000 British Crime Survey*, Home Office Research Study 223. London: Home Office.

Collins, E. with McGovern, M. (1997) *Killing Rage*, London: Granta Publications.

Commission for Racial Equality (CRE) (2003) *Towards Racial Equality: An Evaluation of the Public Duty to Promote Race Equality and Good Race Relations in England and Wales*, London: Commission for Racial Equality.

Condron, S. (2007) 'Gang Dragged Victim by Belt to His Death', *The Times*, 27 August, p. 10.

Cook, L. (2007) 'Fears over Disability Hate Crime', *BBC News*, at http://news.bbc.co.uk/1/hi/uk/7123039.stm, 2 December.

Copsey, N. (2000) *Anti-fascism in Britain*, Basingstoke: Palgrave.

Copsey, N. (2007) 'Changing Course or Changing Clothes? Reflections on the Ideological Evolution of the British National Party 1999–2006', *Patterns of Prejudice*, 41 (1): 61–82.

Craig, K. (2002) 'Examining Hate-motivated Aggression: A Review of the Social Psychological Literature on Hate Crime as a Distinct Form of Aggression', *Aggression and Violent Behaviour*, 7 (1): 85–101.

Cramphorn, C. (2002) 'Faith and Prejudice: Sectarianism as Hate Crime', *Criminal Justice Matters*, 48, Summer: 10–11.

Crawford, A., Lister, S., Blackburn, S. and Burnett, J. (2005) *Plural Policing: The Mixed Economy of Visible Patrols in England and Wales*, Bristol: The Policy Press.

CPS (Crown Prosecution Service) (2005) *CPS Publish First Full Set of Homophobic Crime Figures*, at http://www.cps.gov.uk/news/pressreleases/archive/2005/139_05.html.

CPS (2007a) *Racist Incident Annual Monitoring Report 2006–2007*, London: Crown Prosecution Service.

CPS (2007b) *Guidance on Prosecuting Cases of Homophobic and Transphobic Crime*, London: Crown Prosecution Service.

CPS (2007c) *Policy for Prosecuting Cases of Homophobic and Transphobic Crime*, London: Crown Prosecution Service.

CPS (2007d) *Guidance on Prosecuting Cases of Disability Hate Crime*, London: Crown Prosecution Service, Equality & Diversity Unit and the Policy Directorate.

CPS (2007e) *CPS Homophobic Crime Data 2006–2007*, at http://www.cps.gov.uk/news/pressreleases/archive/2007/166_07.html.

CPS (2008) *The Crown Prosecution Service Response to the All-Part Parliamentary Inquiry into Antisemitism*, at http://www.cps.gov.uk/publications/research/antisemitism.html#header.

Cull, M., Platzer, H. and Balloch, S. (2006) *Out on My Own: Understanding the Experiences and Needs of Homeless Lesbian, Gay, Bisexual and Transgender Youth*, Brighton: Health and Social Policy Research Centre, University of Brighton.

Cumper, P. (2006) 'Outlawing Incitement to Religious Hatred – A British Perspective', *Religion and Human Rights*, 1 (3): 249–268.

Davies, P. and Lynch, D. (2002) *The Routledge Companion to Fascism and the Far Right*, London: Routledge.

Deal, M. (2007) 'Aversive Disablism: Subtle Prejudice toward Disabled People', *Disability and Society*, 22 (1): 93–107.

Dick, S. (2008) *Homophobic Hate Crime: The Gay British Crime Survey 2008*, London: Stonewall.

Disability Now (2008) 'Killers Jailed for Life, *Disability Now*, at http://www.disabilitynow.org.uk/latest-news2/killers-jailed-for-life, 29 February.

Disability Rights Commission (2006) *Disability Facts and Stats*, London: Disability Rights Commission.

Disability Rights Commission and Capability Scotland (DRCCS) (2004) *Hate Crime against Disabled People in Scotland: A Survey Report*, Edinburgh: Disability Rights Commission and Capability Scotland.

Dittman, R. (2003) 'Policing Hate Crime from Victim to Challenger: A Transgendered Perspective', *Probation Journal*, 50 (3): 282–288.

Dixon, B. and Gadd, D. (2006) 'Getting the Message? "New" Labour and the Criminalisation of "Hate"', *Criminology and Criminal Justice*, 6 (3): 309–328.

Docking, M. and Tuffin, R. (2005) *Racist Incidents: Progress since the Lawrence Inquiry*, Home Office Online Report 42/05, London: Home Office.

Dodd, T., Nicholas, S., Povey, D. and Walker, A. (2004) *Crime in England and Wales 2003/4*, Home Office Statistical Bulletin 10/04, London: Home Office.

Dodd, V. (2005) 'Two-thirds of Muslims Consider Leaving UK', *The Guardian*, 26 July, p. 5.

Dunbar, E. (1997) 'The Relationship of DSM Diagnostic Criteria and Gough's Prejudice Scale: Exploring the Clinical Manifestations of the Prejudiced Personality', *Cultural Diversity and Mental Health*, 3: 247–257.

Dunbar, E. and Crevecoeur, D. (2005) 'Assessment of Hate Crime Offenders: The Role of Bias Intent in Examining Violence Risk', *Journal of Forensic Psychology Practice*, 5 (1): 1–19.

Ekins, R. and King, D. (2006) *The Transgender Phenomenon*, London: Sage.

Ellison, G. (2002) 'Sending Out a Message: Hate Crime in Northern Ireland' in *Criminal Justice Matters*, No. 48, Summer: 10–11.

English, R. (2003) *Armed Struggle: The History of the IRA*, Oxford: Oxford University Press.

Essed, P. (1991) *Understanding Everyday Racism: An Interdisciplinary Theory*, London: Sage.

Fekete, L. (2004) 'Anti-Muslim Racism and the European Security State', *Race and Class*, 46 (1): 3–29.

Fielding, N. (1995) *Community Policing*, Oxford: Clarendon Press.

Fitzgerald, M. and Hale, C. (1996) *Ethnic Minorities, Victimisation and Racial Harassment*, London: Home Office Research Study 39.

Fletcher, H. (2008) 'Gang Who Punched Disabled Man to Death Get Life in Jail', *The Times*, 1 March, p. 11.

Forum Against Islamophobia and Racism (2002) *The Religious Offences Bill 2002: A Response*, London: Forum Against Islamophobia and Racism.

Foster, J. (2002) 'Police Cultures', in T. Newburn (ed.), *Handbook of Policing*, Cullompton: Willan, pp. 196–227.

Foster, J., Newburn, T. and Souhami, A. (2005) *Assessing the Impact of the Stephen Lawrence Inquiry*, Home Office Research Study 294. London: Home Office.

Franklin, K. (2000) 'Antigay Behaviors among Young Adults: Prevalence, Patterns, and Motivators in a Noncriminal Population', *Journal of Interpersonal Violence*, 15 (4): 339–363.

Fresco, A. (2008) 'A "Golden Circle" of White Senior Officers Held Me Back, Claims Asian Commander', *The Times*, 10 July, p. 15.

Fresco, A. and O'Neill, S. (2008) 'Britain's Top Asian Policeman Accuses Scotland Yard of Racial Discrimination', *The Times*, 26 June, p. 9.

Furbey, R., Dinham, A., Farnell, R., Finneron, D. and Wilkinson, G. (2006) *Faith as Social Capital: Connecting or Dividing?* Bristol: The Policy Press.

Gadd, D., Dixon, B. and Jefferson, T. (2005) *Why Do They Do It? Racial Harassment in North Staffordshire: Key Findings*, Keele, University of Keele, Centre for Criminological Research.

GALOP (London Gay and Lesbian Policing Group) (1998) *Telling It Like It Is: Lesbian, Gay and Bisexual Youth Speak Out on Homophobic Violence*. London: GALOP.

Garland, J. and Chakraborti, N. (2004) 'Racist Victimisation, Community Safety and the Rural: Issues and Challenges', *British Journal of Community Justice*, 2 (3): 21–32.

Garland, J. and Chakraborti, N. (2006a) '"Race", Place and Space: Examining Identity and Cultures of Exclusion in Rural England', *Ethnicities*, 6 (2): 159–177.

Garland, J. and Chakraborti, N. (2006b) 'Recognising and Responding to Victims of Rural Racism', *International Review of Victimology*, 13 (1): 49–69.

Garland, J. and Chakraborti, N. (2007) '"Protean Times?" Exploring the Relationships between Policing, Community and "Race" in Rural England', *Criminology and Criminal Justice*, 7 (4): 347–365.

Garland, J. and Rowe, M. (2002) 'Is Football "Hooliganism" a Hate Crime?', *Criminal Justice Matters*, 48: 18–19.

Garland, J. and Rowe, M. (2007) 'Police Diversity Training; a Silver-Bullet Tarnished?', In M. Rowe (ed.), *Policing Beyond Macpherson*, Cullompton: Willan, pp. 43–65.

Garland, J., Spalek, B. and Chakraborti, N. (2006) 'Hearing Lost Voices: Issues in Researching "Hidden" Minority Ethnic Communities', *British Journal of Criminology*, 46 (3): 423–437.

Gerstenfeld, P. (2004) *Hate Crimes: Causes, Controls and Controversies*, London: Sage.

Gibson, O. and Dodd, V. (2006) 'Met Chief Labels Media Institutionally Racist', *The Guardian*, 27 January, p. 7.

Gilroy, P. (1990) 'One Nation under a Groove: the Politics of "Race" and Racism in Britain', in D. Goldberg (ed.), *Anatomy of Racism*, Minneapolis: University of Minnesota Press, pp. 263–282.

Gledhill, R. (2008) 'Churchgoing on Its Knees as Christianity Falls out of Favour', *The Times*, 8 May, p. 6.

Goodall, K. (2007) 'Incitement to Religious Hatred: All Talk and No Substance?', *Modern Law Review*, 70 (1): 89–113.

Goodey, J. (2005) *Victims and Victimology: Research, Policy and Practice*, Harlow: Pearson.

Goodey, J. (2007) 'Race, Religion and Victimisation: UK and European Responses', in S. Walklate (ed.), *Handbook of Victims and Victimology*, Cullompton: Willan, pp. 423–445.

Graef, R. (1989) *Talking Blues: The Police in their Own Words*, London: Collins Harvill.

Grattet, R. and Jenness, V. (2003a) 'Examining the Boundaries of Hate Crime Law: Disabilities and the "Dilemma of Difference"', in B. Perry (ed.), *Hate and Bias Crime: A Reader*, London: Routledge, pp. 281–293.

Grattet, R. and Jenness, V. (2003b) 'The Birth and Maturation of Hate Crime Policy in the United States', in B. Perry (ed.), *Hate and Bias Crime: A Reader*, London: Routledge, pp. 389–408.

Grew, T. (2007) 'Two People Arrested in Trans Murder Case', PinkNews.co.uk, at http://www.pink news.co.uk/news/view.php?id=6197, 29 November.

Grimshaw, R. and Jefferson, T. (1987) *Interpreting Policework: Policy and Practice in Forms of Beat Policing*, London: Allen and Unwin.

Grove, V. (2005) 'Latest Victim of a Homophobia that London Thought It Had Left Behind', *The Times*, 22 October, pp. 38–39.

Gunaratnam, Y. (2003) *Researching 'Race' and Ethnicity: Methods, Knowledge and Power*, London: Sage.

Halberstam, J. (2005) *In a Queer Place: Transgender Bodies, Subcultural Lives*, New York: New York University Press.

Hall, N. (2005a) *Hate Crime*, Cullompton: Willan.

Hall, N. (2005b) 'Community Responses to Hate Crime', in J. Winstone and F. Pakes (eds), *Community Justice: Issues for Probation and Criminal Justice*, Cullompton: Willan, pp. 198–217.

Hall, S., Critcher, C., Jefferson, T., Clark, J. and Roberts, B. (1978) *Policing the Crisis: Mugging, the State and Law and Order*, London: Macmillan.

Hansen, R. (2006) 'The Danish Cartoon Controversy: A Defence of Liberal Freedom', *International Migration*, 44 (5): 7–16.

Hari, J. (2007) 'Gay-bashing Should Not Be a Hate Crime', *The Independent*, 11 October, p. 42.

Help the Aged (2008a) *Enough is Enough: The Issues*, at http://www.helptheaged.org.uk/engb/Campaigns/ElderAbuse/EnoughIsEnough/default.htm.

Hensher, P. (2008) 'Protection for Older People Comes Not before Time', *The Independent*, 23 June, p. 30.

Herek, G.M. (1992) 'Psychological Heterosexism and Antigay Violence: The Social Psychology of Bigotry and Bashing', in K.T. Berrill and G.M. Herek (eds), *Hate Crimes: Confronting Violence against Lesbian and Gay Men*, London: Sage, pp. 149–169.

Herek, G.M., Cogan, J.C. and Roy Gillis, J. (2003) 'Victim Experiences in Hate Crimes Based on Sexual Orientation', in B. Perry (ed.), *Hate and Bias Crimes: A Reader*, London: Routledge, pp. 243–259.

Hester, R. (1999) 'Policing New Age Travellers: Conflict and Control in the Countryside?', in G. Dingwall and S. Moody (eds), *Crime and Conflict in the Countryside*, Cardiff: University of Wales Press, pp. 130–145.

Hickman, M. (2006) 'A Portrait of Gay Britain', *The Independent*, 8 February, pp. 14–15.

Higgins, K. (2006) 'Some Victims Less Equal than Others', *Scolag Journal*, August: 162–163.

Hill, D.B. and Willoughby, B.L.B. (2005) 'The Development and Validation of the Genderism and Transphobia Scale', in *Sex Roles*, 53 (7/8): 531–544.

Hines, S. (2007) *TransForming Gender: Transgender Practices of Identity, Intimacy and Care*, Bristol: The Policy Press.

Hiro, D. (1992) *Black British, White British: A History of Race Relations in Britain* (3rd edition), London: Paladin.

Hodgkinson, M. (2008) 'The Girl Who Dared to be Different', *Observer Magazine*, 3 August, pp. 28–34.

Holdaway, S. (1993) *The Resignation of Black and Asian Officers from the Police Service*, London: Home Office.

Holdaway, S. and O'Neill, M. (2006) 'Institutional Racism after Macpherson: An Analysis of Police Views', *Policing and Society*, 16 (4): 349–369.

Holt, A. (2008) 'Fears over Disability Hate Crime', *BBC News*, at http://news.bbc.co.uk/go/pr/fr/-/1/hi/uk/7203232.stm, 22 January.

Home Office (2008a) 'Equality and Diversity', Home Office website at http://www.homeoffice.gov.uk/about-us/equality-and-diversity1/.

Home Office (2008b) *What Is Domestic Violence?*, Home Office Crime Reduction Domestic Violence, Mini-site at http://www.crimereduction.homeoffice.gov.uk/dv/dv01.htm.

Home Office (1981) *Racial Attacks: Report of a Home Office Study*, London: Home Office.

Home Office and Scottish Home Department (HOSHD) (1957) *Report of the Committee on Homosexual Offences and Prostitution*, London: HMSO.

Hopkins, N. (2000) 'Bomber Gets Six Life Terms: Copeland Driven by Virulent Hatred and Pitiless Contempt, Says Judge', *The Guardian*, 1 July, p. 1.

Hopkins, N. and Hall, S. (2000) 'The Nail Bomber: Festering Hate that Turned Quiet Son into a Murderer', *The Guardian*, 1 July, p. 2.

House of Commons Northern Ireland Affairs Committee (2005) *The Challenge of Diversity: Hate Crime in Northern Ireland: Governmental Response to the Committee's Ninth Report of Session 2004–05*, London: HMSO.

House of Lords (2008) *Hansard*, http://www.publications.parliament.uk/pa/ld200708/ldhansrd/text/80507-0007.htm, column 600, 8 May.

Hudson, B. (2007) 'Diversity, Crime and Criminal Justice', in M. Maguire, R. Morgan and R. Reiner (eds), *The Oxford Handbook of Criminology* (4th edition), Oxford: Oxford University Press, pp. 158–175.

Hudson, M., Phillips, J., Ray, K. and Barnes, H. (2007) *Social Cohesion in Diverse Communities*, York: Joseph Rowntree Foundation.

Hunt, R. and Jensen, J. (2006) *The Experiences of Young Gay People in Britain's Schools*, London: Stonewall.

Hunt, S. (2005) *Religion and Everyday Life*, London: Routledge.

Hunte, J. (1966) *Nigger Hunting in England?*, London: West Indian Standing Conference.

Iganski, P. (1999) 'Legislating against Hate: Outlawing Racism and Antisemitism in Britain', *Critical Social Policy*, 19 (1): 129–141.

Iganski, P. (ed.) (2002) *The Hate Debate: Should Hate be Punished as a Crime?*, London: Profile Books.

Iganski, P. (2004) 'Legislating against Hate: Outlawing Racism and Antisemitism in Britain', in P. Gerstenfeld and D. Grant (eds), *Crimes of Hate: Selected Readings*, London: Sage, pp. 346–353.

Iganski, P. (2008) *'Hate Crime' and the City*, Bristol: The Policy Press.

Iganski, P., Kielinger, V. and Paterson, S. (2005) *Hate Crimes against London's Jews: An Analysis of Incidents Recorded by the Metropolitan Police Service 2001–2004*, London: Institute for Jewish Policy Research.

Jackson, N.A. (ed.) (2007) *Encyclopedia of Domestic Violence*, London: Routledge.

Jacobs, J. (2003) 'The Emergence and Implications of American Hate Crime Jurisprudence', in B. Perry (ed.), *Hate and Bias Crime: A Reader*, London: Routledge, pp. 409-426.

Jacobs, J. and Potter, K. (1998) *Hate Crimes: Criminal Law and Identity Politics*, Oxford: Oxford University Press.

Jalota, S. (2004) 'Supporting Victims of Rural Racism', in N. Chakraborti and J. Garland (eds), *Rural Racism*, Cullompton: Willan, pp. 143–160.

James, Z. (2007) 'Policing Marginal Spaces: Controlling Gypsies and Travellers', *Criminology and Criminal Justice*, 7 (4): 367–389.

Jarman, N. (2005) *No Longer a Problem? Sectarian Violence in Northern Ireland*, Belfast: Institute for Conflict Research.

Jarman, N. and Tennant, A. (2003) *An Acceptable Prejudice? Homophobic Violence and Harassment in Northern Ireland,* Belfast: Institute for Conflict Research.

Jenkins, R. (2007) 'Domestic Abuse Among Couples is "Hidden Menace"' *The Times*, 9 June, p. 13.

Jenkins, R. (2008a) 'Youth Aged 15 "Kicked Woman to Death Because She was a Goth"', *The Times*, 13 March, p. 24.

Jenkins, R. (2008b) 'Boy of 15 Who Attacked Woman for Being a Goth is Convicted of Murder', *The Times*, 28 March, p. 25.

Jenness, V. (2002) 'Contours of Hate Crime Politics and Law in the United States', in P. Iganski (ed.), *The Hate Debate: Should Hate be Punished as a Crime?*, London: Profile Books, pp. 15–35.

Jenness, V. and Broad, K. (1997) *Hate Crimes: New Social Movements and the Politics of Violence*, Hawthorne, NY: Aldine de Gruyter.

Jeremy, A. (2007) 'Practical Implications of the Enactment of the Racial and Religious Hatred Act 2006', *Ecclesiastical Law Journal*, 9 (2): 187–201.

Jinman, R. (2005) 'Anti-Semitic Attacks Rise to a Record Level', *The Guardian*, 11 February, p. 9.

Johnson, K., Faulkner, P., Jones, H. and Welsh, E. (2007) *Understanding Suicide and Promoting Survival in LGBT Communities*, Brighton: University of Brighton.

Jones, T. and Newburn, T. (2001) *Widening Access: Improving Police Relations with Hard to Reach Groups*, Home Office Police Research Series Paper 138. London: Home Office.

Joseph, S. (2006) 'The Freedom that Hurts Us', *The Guardian*, 3 February, p. 37.

Juang, R.M. (2006) 'Transgendering the Politics of Recognition', in S. Stryker and S. Whittle (eds), *The Transgender Studies Reader*, New York: Routledge, pp. 706–719.

Kelly, L. (1987) 'The Continuum of Sexual Violence', in J. Hanmer and M. Maynard (eds), *Women, Violence and Social Control*, London: Macmillan, pp. 46–60.

Kennedy, D. (2006) 'Killers of Gay Barman Jailed for 28 Years under New Laws', *The Times*, 17 June, p. 4.

Kessler, S.J. and McKenna, W. (1978) *Gender: An Ethnomethodological Approach*, New York: John Wiley.

Kessler, S. and McKenna, W. (2002) 'Who Put the "Trans" in Transgender? Gender Theory and Everyday Life', *International Journal of Transgenderism*, 4 (3), http://www.symposion.com/ijt/gilbert/kessler.htm, 12 May.

Kielinger, V. and Paterson, S. (2007) 'Policing Hate Crime in London', *American Behavioral Scientist*, 51 (2): 196–204.

Kirkey, K. and Forsyth, A. (2001) 'Men in the Valley: Gay Male Life on the Suburban–Rural Fringe', *Journal of Rural Studies*, 17 (4): 421–441.

Kundnani, A. (2001) 'In a Foreign Land: The New Popular Racism', *Race and Class*, 43 (2): 41–60.

Kundnani, A. (2002) 'An Unholy Alliance? Racism, Religion and Communalism', *Race and Class*, 44 (2): 71–80.

Lamb, L. and Redmond, M. (2007) *Learning Disability Hate Crime: Identifying Barriers to Addressing Crime*, Bournemouth: Care Services Improvement Partnership.

Lawrence, F. (1999) *Punishing Hate: Bias Crimes under American Law*, Cambridge, MA: Harvard University Press.

Lawrence, F. (2002) 'Racial Violence on a "Small Island": Bias Crime in a Multicultural Society', in P. Iganski (ed.), *The Hate Debate: Should Hate be Punished as a Crime?*, London: Profile Books, pp. 36–53.

Levin, B. (2002) 'From Slavery to Hate Crime Laws: The Emergence of Race and Status-based Protection in American Criminal Law', *Journal of Social Issues*, 58 (2): 227–245.

Levin, B. (2004) 'History as a Weapon: How Extremists Deny the Holocaust in North America', in P. Gerstenfeld and D. Grant (eds), *Crimes of Hate: Selected Readings*, London: Sage, pp. 186–207.

Levin, J. and McDevitt, J. (2002) *Hate Crime (Revisited): America's War on Those Who Are Different*, Boulder, CO: Westview Press.

Lister, S. and Wall, D. (2006) 'The Realities of Elder Abuse', in A. Wahidin and M. Cain (eds), *Ageing, Crime and Society*, Cullompton: Willan, pp. 107–123.

Lombardi, E., Wilchins, R.A., Priesing, D. and Malouf, D. (2001) 'Gender Violence: Transgender Experiences with Violence and Discrimination', *Journal of Homosexuality*, 42 (1): 89–101.

Lowles, N. (2001) *White Riot: The Violent Story of Combat 18*, Bury: Milo Books.

Macpherson, Sir W. (1999) *The Stephen Lawrence Inquiry: Report of an Inquiry by Sir William Macpherson of Cluny*, London: HMSO.

Mason, A. and Palmer, A. (1996) *Queer Bashing: A National Survey of Hate Crimes against Lesbian and Gay Men*, London: Stonewall.

Mason, G. (1997) 'Sexuality and Violence: Questions of Difference', in C. Cunneen, D. Fraser and S. Tomsen (eds), *Faces of Hate: Hate Crime in Australia*, Annandale: Hawkins Press.

Mason, G. (2005a) 'Hate Crime and the Image of the Stranger', *British Journal of Criminology*, (45) 6: 837–859.

Mason, G. (2005b) 'Being Hated: Stranger or Familiar?', *Social and Legal Studies*, (14) 4: 585–605.

Matassa, M. and Newburn, T. (2002) 'Policing Hate Crime', *Criminal Justice Matters*, 48, Summer: 42–43.

McDevitt, J., Levin, J. and Bennett, S. (2002) 'Hate Crime Offenders: An Expanded Typology', *Journal of Social Issues*, 58 (2): 303–317.

McDonald, E. (2006) 'No Straight Answer: Homophobia as Both an Aggravating and Mitigating Factor in New Zealand Homicide Cases', *Victoria University of Wellington Law Review*, 37 (2): 223–248.

McGhee, D. (2005) *Intolerant Britain?: Hate, Citizenship and Difference*, Maidenhead: Open University Press.

McGhee, D. (2006) 'Getting "Host" Communities on Board: Finding the Balance between "Managed Migration" and "Managed Settlement" in Community Cohesion Strategies', *Journal of Ethnic and Migration Studies*, 32 (1): 111–127.

McGhee, D. (2008) *The End of Multiculturalism? Terrorism, Integration and Human Rights*, Maidenhead: Open University Press.

McLagan, G. and Lowles, N. (2000) *Mr. Bad: The Secret Life of Racist Bomber and Killer David Copeland*, London: John Blake Publishing.

McLaughlin, E. (1996) 'Police, Policing and Paperwork', in E. McLaughlin and J. Muncie (eds), *Controlling Crime*, London: Sage, pp. 51–106.

McLaughlin, E. (2002) 'Rocks and Hard Places: The Politics of Hate Crime', *Theoretical Criminology*, 6 (4): 493–498.

McLaughlin, E. (2007) 'Diversity or Anarchy? The Post-Macpherson Blues', in M. Rowe (ed.), *Policing beyond Macpherson: Issues in Policing, Race and Society*, Cullompton: Willan, pp. 18–42.

McManus, J. and Rivers, D. (2001) *Without Prejudice: A Guide for Community Safety Partnerships on Responding to the Needs of Lesbians, Gays and Bisexuals*, London: Nacro Crime and Social Policy Publications.

McNamee, H. (2006) *Out on Your Own: An Examination of the Mental Health of Young Same-Sex Attracted Men*, Belfast: Rainbow Project.

Meer, N. (2008) 'The Politics of Voluntary and Involuntary Identities: Are Muslims in Britain an Ethnic, Racial or Religious Minority?', *Patterns of Prejudice*, 42 (1): 61–81.

Mencap (2007) *Bullying Wrecks Lives: The Experiences of Children and Young People with a Learning Disability*, London: Mencap.

Metropolitan Police Service (MPS) (2007) *Hate Crime Policy*, at http://www.met.police.uk/foi/pdfs/policies/hate_crime_policy.pdf.

Michael Bell Associates (2006) *Crime and Prejudice: The Support Needs of Victims of Hate Crime – A Research Report*, London: Victim Support.

Miller, P., Gillinson, S. and Huber, J. (2006) *Disablist Britain: Barriers to Independent Living for Disabled People in 2006*, London: Scope.

Miller, P., Parker, S. and Gillinson, S. (2004) *Disablism: How to Tackle the Last Prejudice*, London: Demos.

Mills, G. (2002) 'Combating Institutional Racism in the Public Sector', *Industrial Law Journal*, 31 (1): 96–8.

Mind (2007) *Another Assault*, London: Mind.

Ministry of Justice (2007) *Discrimination Law Review. A Framework for Fairness: Proposals for a Single Equality Bill for Great Britain. A Consultation Paper*, at http://www.communities. gov.uk/documents/corporate/pdf/325332.pdf.

Ministry of Justice (2008) *Statistics on Race and the Criminal Justice System – 2006/7*, London: Ministry of Justice.

Mirrlees-Black, C. and Byron, C. (1999) *Domestic Violence: Findings form the BCS Self-completion Questionnaires*, Research Findings 86, London: Home Office.

Mitchell, M. (2004) *'Out About Town' Survey of the Needs of Lesbian, Gay, Bisexual and Transgendered People in Luton 2003/2004*, Luton: Needs Assessment Subgroup of Luton LGBT Steering Group.

Modood, T. (2003) 'Muslims and European Multiculturalism', in S. Spencer (ed.), *The Politics of Migration: Managing Opportunity, Conflict and Change*, Oxford: Blackwell Publishing, pp. 100–115.

Moore, C. (2007) 'Mass Immigration Has Created a Britain Where No One Feels at Home', *Daily Telegraph*, p. 26.

Moran, L.J. (2007) '"Invisible Minorities": Challenging Community and Neighbourhood Models of Policing', *Criminology and Criminal Justice: An International Journal*, 7 (4): 417–441.

Moran, L.J. and Sharpe, A.N. (2004) 'Violence, Identity and Policing: The Case of Violence against Transgender People', *Criminal Justice*, 4 (4): 395–417.

Moran, L.J., Paterson, S. and Docherty, T. (2004) *'Count Me In!' A Report on the Bexley and Greenwich Homophobic Crime Survey*, London: GALOP.

Moritz, M.J. (2007) 'Hate Speech Made Easy: The Virtual Demonisation of Gays', in M. Prum, B. Deschamps and M.C. Barbier (eds), *Racial, Ethnic and Homophobic Violence: Killing in the Name of Otherness*, Abingdon: Routledge-Cavendish, pp. 123–132.

Morley, R. and Mullender, A. (1994) *Preventing Domestic Violence to Women*, Police Research Group Crime Prevention Series Paper 48, London: Home Office.

Morrison, C. and MacKay, A. (2000) *The Experience of Violence and Harassment of Gay Men of the City of Edinburgh*, Edinburgh: Scottish Executive Central Research Unit.

Morrissey, M. and Smyth, M. (2002) *Northern Ireland after the Good Friday Agreement: Victims, Governance and Blame*, London: Pluto.

Namaste, V.K. (2006) 'Genderbashing: Sexuality, Gender, and the Regulation of Public Space', in S. Stryker and S. Whittle (eds), *The Transgender Studies Reader*, New York: Routledge, pp. 584–598.

Neal, S. (2002) 'Rural Landscapes, Representations and Racism: Examining Multicultural Citizenship and Policy Making in the English Countryside', *Ethnic and Racial Studies*, 25 (3): 442–461.

Newburn, T. (2007) *Criminology*, Cullompton: Willan.

Northern Ireland Affairs Committee (2005) *The Challenge of Diversity. Hate Crime in Northern Ireland: Government Response to the Committee's Ninth Report of Session 2004–05*, London: HMSO.

NSPCC (2006) *Calls to ChildLine About Sexual Orientation, Homophobia and Homophobic Bullying*, London: NSPCC.

O'Keeffe, M., Hills, A., Doyle, M., McCreadie, C., Scholes, S., Constantine, R., Tinker, A., Manthorpe, J., Biggs, S. and Erens, B. (2007) *UK Study of Abuse and Neglect of Older People Prevalence Survey Report*, London: National Centre for Social Research.

O'Neill, S. (2005) 'Barman Dies in Attack at Gay Cruising Haunt', *The Times*, 17 October, p. 5.

Office for National Statistics (2006) *Focus on Ethnicity and Religion* (2006 Edition), Basingstoke: Palgrave Macmillan.

Office of Public Sector Information (1995) *Disability Discrimination Act 1995*, at http://www.opsi. gov.uk/acts/acts1995/ukpga_19950050_en_1.

Office of Public Sector Information (2008) 'Schedule 16 Hatred on the Grounds of Sexual Orientation', at http://www.opsi.gov.uk/acts/acts2008/ukpga_20080004_en_33#sch16.

Office of the Deputy Prime Minister (OPDM) (2003) *Equality and Diversity in Local Government*, London: OPDM (www.local.odpm.gov.uk/research/crosscut/crosscut.htm).

Olumide, J. (2002) *Raiding the Gene Pool: The Social Construction of Mixed Race*, London: Pluto.

Online Reporter (2007) 'Transvestite Murder Appeal' http://www.thesun.couk/so/homepage/news/article515014.ece, 27 November.

Open University (2001) *Policing Hate*, Milton Keynes: Open University.

Perry, B. (2001) *In the Name of Hate: Understanding Hate Crimes*, London: Routledge.

Perry, B. (2002) 'Hate Crime and Identity Politics', *Theoretical Criminology*, 6 (4): 485–491.

Perry, B. (ed.) (2003a) *Hate and Bias Crime: A Reader*, London: Routledge.

Perry, B. (2003b) 'Anti-Muslim Retaliatory Violence Following the 9/11 Terrorist Attacks', in B. Perry (ed.), *Hate and Bias Crime: A Reader*, London: Routledge, pp. 183–202.

Perry, B. (2003c) 'Defenders of the Faith: Hate Groups and Ideologies of Power', in B. Perry (ed.), *Hate and Bias Crime: A Reader*, London: Routledge, pp. 301–318.

Petrosino, C. (2003) 'Connecting the Past to the Future: Hate Crime in America', in B. Perry (ed.), *Hate and Bias Crime: A Reader*, London: Routledge, pp. 9–26.

Phillips, C. and Bowling, B. (2002) 'Racism, Ethnicity, Crime and Criminal Justice', in M. Maguire, R. Morgan and R. Reiner (eds), *The Oxford Handbook of Criminology* (3rd edition), Oxford: Oxford University Press, pp. 579–619.

Pilkington, E. (2008) 'Transgender Man Has His Baby, Naturally', *The Guardian*, 5 July, p. 13.

PinkNews.co.uk (2006) 'Gay Priest's Attacker is Jailed', at http://www.pinknews.co.uk/news/articles/2005-1106.html, 10 April.

Police Service for Northern Ireland (2008) *PSNI Statistics: Annual Statistical Report Statistical Report No. 3: Hate Incidents and Crimes 1st April 2007–31st March 2008*, Belfast: Central Statistics Branch, Operational Support Department.

Popham, P. (2008) 'Three Arrested for Plot to Kill Mohamed Cartoonist', *The Independent*, 13 February, p. 18.

Poynting, S., Noble, G., Tabar, P. and Collins, J. (2004) *Bin Laden in the Suburbs: Criminalising the Arab Other*, Sydney: Sydney Institute of Criminology.

Purdy, C. (2008) 'The Darker Side of Life as a Goth', *BBC News*, at http://news.bbc.co.uk/go/pr/fr/-/1/hi/england/lancashire/7314306.stm, 27 March.

Quarmby, K. (2008) *Getting Away with Murder: Disabled People's Experiences of Hate Crime in the UK*, London: Scope.

Quiery, M. (2002) *A Mighty Silence: A Report on the Needs of Lesbians and Bisexual Women in Northern Ireland*. Belfast, LASI.

Quraishi, M. (2005) *Muslims and Crime: A Comparative Study*, Aldershot: Ashgate.

Rainbow Ripples and Butler, R. (2006) *The Rainbow Ripples Report: Lesbian, Gay and Bisexual Disabled People's Experiences of Service Provision in Leeds*, Leeds: Rainbow Ripples.

Ratcliffe (2004) *'Race', Ethnicity and Difference: Imagining the Inclusive Society*, Maidenhead: Open University Press.

Ray, L. and Smith, D. (2001) 'Racist Offenders and the Politics of "Hate Crime"', *Law and Critique*, 12 (3): 203–221.

Ray, L. and Smith, D. (2002) 'Hate Crime, Violence and Cultures of Racism', in P. Iganski (ed.), *The Hate Debate: Should Hate be Punished as a Crime?*, London: Profile Books, pp. 88–102.

Ray, S., Sharp, E. and Abrams, D. (2006) *Ageism: A Benchmark of Public Attitudes in Britain*, London: Age Concern Reports.

Ray, L., Smith, D. and Wastell, L. (2004) 'Shame, Rage and Racist Violence', *British Journal of Criminology*, 44 (3): 350–368.

Raynor, P. (2007) 'Community Penalties: Probation, "What Works", and Offender Management', in M. Maguire, R. Morgan and R. Reiner (eds), *The Oxford Handbook of Criminology* (4th edition), Oxford: Oxford University Press, pp. 1061–1099.

Reiner, R. (1991) *Chief Constables*, Oxford: Oxford University Press.

Reiner, R. (2000) *The Politics of the Police* (3rd edition), Oxford: Oxford University Press.

Reynolds, S. (2005) *Rip It up and Start Again: Post-punk 1978–84*, London: Faber & Faber.

Rickell, A. (2007) 'Attacks on Disabled People are Hate Crimes, Too', *The Guardian*, at http://www.guardian.co.uk, 31 July.

Rossington, B. (2008) 'Teen Dies after Homophobic Attack', *Liverpool Echo*, website at http://www.liverpoolecho.co.uk/liverpool-news/breaking-news/2008/08/02/teen-dies-after-homophobic-attack-100252-21454861/, 2 August.

Rowe, M. (2004) *Policing, Race and Racism*, Cullompton: Willan.

Rowe, M. (ed.) (2007a) *Policing beyond Macpherson: Issues of Policing, Race and Society*, Cullompton: Willan.

Rowe, M. (2007b) 'Introduction: Policing and Racism in the Limelight – The Politics and Context of the Lawrence Report', in M. Rowe (ed.), *Policing Beyond Macpherson: Issues in Policing, Race and Society*, Cullompton: Willan, pp. xi–xxiv.

Roxburgh, A. (2002) *Preachers of Hate: The Rise of the Far Right*, London: Gibson Square Books.

Runnymede Trust (1997) *Islamophobia: A Challenge for Us All*, London: The Runnymede Trust.

Ruthchild, C. (1997) 'Don't Frighten the Horses! A Systemic on Violence against Lesbians and Gay Men', in G. Mason and S. Tomsen (eds), *Homophobic Violence*, Sydney: Hawkins Press.

Ryan, N. (2003) *Homeland: Into a World of Hate*, Edinburgh: Mainstream Publishing.

Said, E. (1978) *Orientalism*, New York: Pantheon.

Said, E. (1997) *Covering Islam: How the Media and the Experts Determine How We See the Rest of the World* (2nd edition), New York: Vintage Books.

Sales, R. (2007) *Understanding Immigration and Refugee Policy: Contradictions and Continuities*, Bristol: The Policy Press.

Salisbury, H. and Upson, A. (2004) *Ethnicity, Victimisation and Worry about Crime: Findings from the 2001/02 and 2002/03 British Crime Surveys*, London: Home Office Research Study 237.

Sandbrook, D. (2007) *White Heat: A History of Britain in the Swinging Sixties*, London: Abacus.

Savage, J. (1991) *England's Dreaming: Sex Pistols and Punk Rock*, London: Faber & Faber.

Scope (2008a) 'Hard-hitting Advert Campaign to Highlight Discrimination Faced by Disabled People Kick-starts Scope's Time to Get Equal Week', http://www.scope.org.uk/cgi-bin/np/viewnews.cgi?id=1212700771, 5 June.

Scope (2008b) 'Scope Comment on Outcome of Brent Martin Appeal', http://www.scope.org.uk/cgi-bin/np/viewnews.cgi?id=1213781866, 31 May.

Scottish Executive (2003) *Working Group on Hate Crime Consultation Paper*, Edinburgh: Scottish Executive.

Sentencing Guidelines Council (2004) *Overarching Principles: Seriousness*, London: Sentencing Guidelines Secretariat.

Shakespeare, T. (2007) 'Disablism Ain't the Same as Racism', at http://www.bbc.co.uk/ouch/columnists/tom/060904_index.stml, February 9.

Sharp, D. (2002) 'Policing after Macpherson: Some Experiences of Muslim Police Officers', in B. Spalek (ed.), *Islam, Crime and Criminal Justice*, Cullompton: Willan, pp. 76–95.

Sheffield, C. (1995) 'Hate Violence', in P. Rothenberg (ed.), *Race, Class and Gender in the United States*, New York: St Martin's Press, pp. 432–441.

Sherry, M. (2003) *Don't Ask, Tell or Respond: Silent Acceptance of Disability Hate Crimes*, Berkeley, CA: University of California at Berkeley.

Sherry, M. (2004) 'Exploring Disability Hate Crimes', *Review of Disability Studies: An International Journal*, 1 (1): 51–59.

Shoffman, M. (2006) 'Pair Get Life for Gay Barman Murder', *Pink News* http://www.pinknews.co.uk/news/articles/2005-1755.html, 16 June.

Sibbitt, R. (1997) *The Perpetrators of Racial Harassment and Racial Violence*, Home Office Research Study 176. London: Home Office.

Smithers, R. (2006) 'Homophobic Abuse on the Rise in Schools, Says Charity', *The Guardian*, 28 August, p. 9.

Sobsey, D. (1994) *Violence and Abuse in the Lives of People with Disabilities: The End of Silent Acceptance?*, Baltimore, MD: Paul H. Brookes Publishing Co.

Somerville, W. (2007) *Immigration under New Labour*, Bristol: The Policy Press

Spalek, B. (2002) 'Muslim Women's Safety Talk and Their Experiences of Victimisation: A Study Exploring Specificity and Difference', in B. Spalek (ed.), *Islam, Crime and Criminal Justice*, Collumpton: Willan, pp. 50–75

Spalek, B. (2006) *Crime Victims: Theory, Policy and Practice*, Basingstoke: Palgrave Macmillan.

Spalek, B. (2008) *Communities, Identities and Crime*, Bristol: The Policy Press.

Sparks, R. (2007) 'The Politics of Imprisonment', in Y. Jewkes (ed.), *Handbook on Prisons*, Cullompton: Willan, pp. 73–93.

Staff Writer (2007) 'Gang Targeting Gay Men in Brighton', PinkNews.co.uk, at http://www.pink news.co.uk/news/articles/2005-4775.html, 28 June.

Staff Writer (2008) 'Man Arrested on Suspicion of Cruising Murder', PinkNews.co.uk, at http://www.pinknews.co.uk/news/articles/2005-6912.html, 20 February.

Stanko, E.A. (1990) *Everyday Violence*, London: Pandora.

Stanko, E.A. (2001) 'Re-conceptualising the Policing of Hatred: Confessions and Worrying Dilemmas of a Consultant', *Law and Critique*, 12 (3): 309–329.

Stenson, K. and Waddington, P.A.J. (2007) 'Macpherson, Police Stops and Institutionalised Racism', in M. Rowe (ed.), *Policing beyond Macpherson: Issues in Policing, Race and Society*, Cullompton: Willan, pp. 128–147.

Stone, V. and Tuffin, R. (2000) *Attitudes of People from Minority Ethnic Communities towards a Career in the Police Service*, Home Office Police Research Series Paper 136. London: Home Office.

Stonewall (2008) 'Incitement to Hatred: Criminal Justice and Immigration Bill', at http://www.stonewall.org.uk/campaigns/1961.asp.

Stormbreak (2006) *Homophobic Crime in London*, London: Stormbreak.

Stryker, S. (1998) 'The Transgender Issue: An Introduction', *GLQ: A Journal of Lesbian and Gay Studies*, 4 (2): 148.

Stryker, S. (2006) 'My Words to Victor Frankenstein about the Village of Chamounix: Performing Transgender Rage', in S. Stryker and S. Whittle (eds), *The Transgender Studies Reader*, New York: Routledge, pp. 244–255.

Stryker, S. and Whittle S. (eds) (2006) *The Transgender Studies Reader*, New York: Routledge.

The Times (2008) 'Disabled Face Hatred', *The Times*, 7 June, p. 37.

Tizard, B. and Phoenix, A. (2002) *Black, White or Mixed Race? Race and Racism in the Lives of Young People of Mixed Parentage*, London: Routledge.

Tomsen, S. (2002) *Hatred, Murder and Male Honour: Anti-Homosexual Murders in New South Wales, 1980–2000*, Research and Public Policy Series No. 43, Canberra: Australian Institute of Criminology.

Tomsen, S. and Mason, G. (2001) 'Engendering Homophobia: Violence, Sexuality and Gender Conformity', *Journal of Sociology*, 37 (3): 257–273.

Travis, A. (2002) 'Minister Stirs Row Over Plans for 15 New Centres', *The Guardian*, May 15.

Travis, A. (2008) 'Officials Think UK's Muslim Population Has Risen to 2m', *The Guardian*, 8 April, p. 14.

Trotter, J. (2006) 'Violent Crimes? Young People's Experiences of Homophobia and Misogyny in Secondary Schools', *Practice*, 18 (4): 291–302.

Vasagar, J. (2007) 'Anti-semitic Attacks Hit Record High Following Lebanon War', *The Guardian*, 2 February, p. 8.

Vertovec, S. (2002) 'Islamophobia and Muslim Recognition in Britain', in Y. Haddad (ed.), *Muslims in the West: From Sojourners to Citizens*, Oxford: Oxford University Press, pp. 19–35.

Waddington, P.A.J. (1994) *Liberty and Order: Public Order Policing in a Capital City*, London: UCL Press.

Waddington, P.A.J. (1999) 'Police (Canteen) Sub-Culture: An Appreciation', *British Journal of Criminology*, 39 (2): 286–309.

Wainwright, M. (2004) 'Five Arrested for Racist Boasts in Television Expose of BNP', *The Guardian*, 21 July, p. 5.

Wainwright, M. (2008) 'Woman Died after Drunken Gang Attacked Couple Dressed as Goths', *The Guardian*, 13 March, p. 15.

Walby, S. (1990) *Theorizing Patriarchy*, Oxford: Blackwell.

Walby, S. (2004) *The Cost of Domestic Violence*, London: Department of Trade and Industry, Women & Equality Unit.

Walby, S. and Allen, J. (2004) *Domestic Violence, Sexual Assault and Stalking: Findings from the British Crime Survey*, Home Office Research Study 276. London: Home Office.

Walklate, S. (1989) *Victimology*, London: Unwin Hyman.

Walklate, S. (2008) 'What is to be Done about Violence against Women?', *British Journal of Criminology*, 48 (1): 39–54.

Webster, C. (2007) *Understanding Race and Crime*, Maidenhead: Open University Press.

Welch, M. (2006) *Scapegoats of September 11th: Hate Crimes and State Crimes in the War on Terror*, New Brunswick, NJ: Rutgers University Press.

Werbner, P. (2004) 'The Predicament of Diaspora and Millennial Islam: Reflections on September 11 2001, *Ethnicities*, 4 (4): 451–476.

Whittle, S. (1996) 'Gender Fucking or Fucking Gender?', in R. Ekins and D. King (eds), *Blending Genders: Social Aspects of Cross-dressing and Sex Changing*, London: Routledge.

Whittle, S. (2002) *Respect and Equality: Transsexual and Transgender Rights*, London: Cavendish Publishing.

Whittle, S., Turner, L. and Al-Alami, M. (2007) *Engendered Penalties: Transgender and Transsexual People's Experiences of Inequality and Discrimination*, Wetherby: Equalities Review.

Williams, D. (2007a) 'The European White Power Scene', *Hate Music: Searchlight Extra*, February, pp. 1–2.

Williams, D. (2007b) 'ISD Records: A Case of Globalisation in Action', *Hate Music: Searchlight Extra*, February, p. 3.

Williams, D. (2008a) 'Nick Griffin: Political Extremist and Veteran Splitter', *Searchlight*, 392, February, pp. 12–16.

Williams, D. (2008b) '2007 BNP Overview', *Searchlight*, 391, January, pp. 16–22.

Williams, M.L. and Robinson, A.L. (2004) 'Problems and Prospects with Policing the Lesbian, Gay and Bisexual Community in Wales', *Policing & Society*, 14 (3): 213–232.

Wintour, P. (2008) 'Ministers Consider Forcing Private Firms to Reveal Gender Pay Gap', *The Guardian*, 26 June, p. 16.

Wolhuter, L., Olley, N. and Denham, D. (2009) *Victimology: Victimisation and Victims' Rights*, Abingdon: Routledge-Cavendish.

Wonfor, S. (2008) 'Brent Judge Praised for Wanting to be Extra Tough', *The Journal*, at http://www.journallive.co.uk/north-east-news/todays-news/2008/03/01/brent-judge-praised-for-wanting-to-be-extra-tough-61634-20544419/2//, 1 March.

Wong, K. and Christmann, K. (2008) 'The Role of Victim Decision-making in the Reporting of Hate Crimes', *Community Safety Journal*, 7 (2): 19–35.

Working Group on Hate Crime (2004) *Working Group on Hate Crime Report*, Edinburgh: Scottish Executive.

Zedner, L. (2002) 'Victims', in M. Maguire, R. Morgan and R. Reiner (eds), *The Oxford Handbook of Criminology* (3rd edition), Oxford: Oxford University Press, pp. 419–456.

Zukier, H. (1999) 'The Transformation of Hatred: Antisemitism as a Struggle for Group Identity', in R. Wistrich (ed.), *Demonising the Other: Antisemitism, Racism and Xenophobia*, Amsterdam: Harwood, pp. 118–130.

INDEX

Page numbers in *italics* indicate figures and diagrams.